GLOBAL SMARTS

GLOBAL SMARTS

The Art of
Communicating
and Deal Making
Anywhere
in the World

———

SHEIDA HODGE

JOHN WILEY & SONS, INC.

New York • Chichester • Weinham • Brisbane • Singapore • Toronto

Published by John Wiley & Sons, Inc.

Published simultaneously in Canada.

No part of this publication may be reproduced, stored in a retrieval system, or transmitted in any form or by any means, electronic, mechanical, photocopying, recording, scanning, or otherwise, except as permitted under Sections 107 or 108 of the 1976 United States Copyright Act, without either the prior written permission of the Publisher, or authorization through payment of the appropriate per-copy fee to the Copyright Clearance Center, 222 Rosewood Drive, Danvers, MA 01923, (978) 750-8400, fax (978) 750-4744. Requests to the Publisher for permission should be addressed to the Permissions Department, John Wiley & Sons, Inc., 605 Third Avenue, New York, NY 10158-0012, (212) 850-6011, fax (212) 850-6008, E-Mail: PERMREQ@WILEY.COM.

This publication is designed to provide accurate and authoritative information in regard to the subject matter covered. It is sold with the understanding that the publisher is not engaged in rendering professional services. If legal, accounting, medical, psychological, or any other expert assistance is required, the services of a competent professional person should be sought.

Designations used by companies to distinguish their products are often claimed as trademarks. In all instances where John Wiley & Sons, Inc. is aware of a claim, the product names appear in initial capital or all capital letters. Readers, however, should contact the appropriate companies for more complete information regarding trademarks and registration.

Library of Congress Cataloging-in-Publication Data:

Hodge, Sheida.
     Global smarts : the art of communicating and deal making anywhere in the world / Sheida Hodge.
          p.   cm.
     ISBN 0-471-38246-9 (alk. paper)
     Includes bibliographical references and index.
     1. Business etiquette.   2. Intercultural communication.   3. National characteristics.   4. Negotiation in business.   5. Competition, International.   I. Title.
HF5389.H63   2000
395.5'2—dc21
                                                                                         99-059990

Printed in the United States of America
10 9 8 7 6 5 4 3 2 1

To my daughter, Susie,
who is my inspiration and the light of my life

ACKNOWLEDGMENTS

I applied mine heart to know, and to search, and to seek out wisdom, and the reason of things.

—Ecclesiastes 7:25

This book is a collection of the wisdom of businesspeople, consultants, and people from all over the world who have attended my programs. Our work together has brought to light the insights shared in this book.

I am grateful to people who have contributed personal stories about their cross-cultural living and working experiences. These stories mean a lot to me because they are the result of a special chemistry created at our programs. During this process we discovered many things about ourselves and others.

I would like to thank my editors at John Wiley & Sons, Renana Meyers and Karl Weber, for being so supportive and pleasant to work with.

I am grateful to the staff at Cape Cod Compositors for their skill and diligence in editing this book in its final stages.

I'd also like to thank Dan Harwig, Ph.D., who assisted me in compiling this material and whose commitment, patience, and editorial skills have made publication of this book possible.

Finally, I'd like to acknowledge Susie Hodge's help in reading the manuscript at its early stages and suggesting ideas to help me communicate effectively with my readers.

CONTENTS

PREFACE   ix

CHAPTER 1.   Thriving in the New Global Marketplace   1

CHAPTER 2.   Developing a World-Based Perspective   9

CHAPTER 3.   What Is Culture?   27

CHAPTER 4.   An American Abroad: Key Cultural Contrast   35

CHAPTER 5.   The Social Setting of International Business   76

CHAPTER 6.   International Business Etiquette   97

CHAPTER 7.   Who Should Go to Assure Success?   115

CHAPTER 8.   The Importance of Establishing Trust and Credibility   123

CHAPTER 9.   Principles of Successful Cross-Cultural Communication   139

CHAPTER 10.   Communicating across Language and Accent Barriers   152

CHAPTER 11.   Political Ping-Pong   158

CHAPTER 12.   How to Deal with Culture Shock   163

CHAPTER 13.   Understanding the Gender Gap in International Business   177

CHAPTER 14.   Negotiating across Cultural Lines   188

CHAPTER 15.   Avoiding Temptation—Ethics Overseas   218

IN CONCLUSION   230

NOTES   233

INDEX   241

PREFACE

Your program did help me a lot. I recognized things that I have been doing without realizing and other things I should have done long ago.

—Wendell Deng, engineer, Boeing Company,
Rocketdyne Division, California

In business as in war, the success of the most elegant and well-thought-out strategy is at the mercy of skillful execution. This book is written for the executives and managers who are charged with implementing their companies' global strategies. Its goal is to transform the potentially intimidating experience of doing business across cultural lines by helping these front-line foot soldiers feel comfortable and confident working with people from other cultures. Mastering this people dimension is essential for companies and individuals that wish to be truly effective and successful in today's global marketplace.

During the years I have spent teaching global business skills, I have discovered that the main challenge facing businesspeople going abroad is this: They don't know what they don't know. Again and again, participants in my seminars have come to me afterward and said, "If I'd only known! It would have made things so much easier!" This book is designed to introduce readers to some of the most important insights and knowledge they need to have and give them some basic tools for navigating the people dimension of global business.

I have written this book for the busy executive on the run. Complex ideas have been stated in a simple manner so that people can relate them to their own experiences. I have avoided the common practice of giving lists of dos and don'ts for particular cultures. International business is in a constant state of flux, and such lists become obsolete very quickly. I have concentrated instead on conveying cross-cultural concepts and skills as operational tools that can be used in a wide variety of cultural situations. I have started with the assumption that the best way to learn about others is first to understand ourselves. Thus, many discussions of specific cultural differences start with an exploration of American values and practices that seem natural rather than cultural—and use this as a bridge to the values and practices that seem natural in other cultures.

One of my most valuable resources has been the experience of executives and managers—both from the United States and from countries around the world—who have attended my training seminars and university courses. The stories they tell of their struggles and discoveries in other cultures give a special kind of insight into the process of doing business internationally. I have included many of these stories as sidebars throughout the book—some to illustrate specific points, others to help readers get a feel for the attitudes and expectations of businesspeople from other cultures.

In the final analysis, this book is the culmination of many years of business experience. Working for General Electric Company gave me the privilege of working with business executives from Europe, Asia, and Latin America. Many years of conducting training sessions for executives from the United States and around the world have allowed me to test and perfect the ideas presented in this book. Thousands of people who have attended these programs have found them to be useful, helpful, and practical for doing business in any cultural situation. My hope is that presenting these ideas in book form will help readers acquire the poise and confidence they need to be truly effective doing business across cultures—both at home and abroad.

CHAPTER 1

Thriving in the New Global Marketplace

When you lose a customer you lose in two ways; first, you don't get the money; second, your competitor does.

—Bill Gates[1]

Success and survival are the key goals in the fierce competition of today's global marketplace. Companies are in constant competition for customers, who in turn are increasingly demanding and discriminating. Losing customers means more than simply losing revenues; it means losing market share to competitors in a global fight to be a major player. The toughest question facing American business in the complex global playing field is how to secure a competitive advantage.

A good example of just how tough things are out there was the competition in 1995 among Boeing Company, McDonnell Douglas, and Airbus to sell 35 airplanes to Scandinavian Airlines System. Boeing finally got the contract, but in order to do so it had to discount its airplanes by almost 50 percent—from $35 million to about $20 million per plane.[2] One high-placed aerospace executive commented that it was a strategic necessity for Boeing to keep SAS as a customer. But when SAS placed another major order in 1998, the order went to Airbus. Then in 1999 Airbus started pursuing airliner sales in the Japanese market—one of Boeing's major strongholds and one of the largest markets for aircraft in the world.[3]

The companies that thrive in the new international marketplace do so by taking a global view. "The growth markets of the world are clearly overseas," says General Motors chairman and chief executive officer John F. Smith Jr. "I think we have to look at GM as a global enterprise," adds GM's vice chairman.[4] Most of CEO Smith's efforts since taking over at GM have been devoted to opening up new markets in China and Eastern Europe. Smith remains optimistic about the future.

This competitive environment has changed the way business is done overseas. When I worked for General Electric in the 1980s, the only difference between going to Boston and going to Beijing was that you packed a voltage converter and a passport for Beijing. People did business by trial and error. There was much more leeway to learn from one's mistakes. Nowadays, with all the downsizing and rightsizing, there are fewer resources and there is less time. Although there are more foreign deals and more foreign trips, the duration of these trips has gotten steadily shorter. With tight schedules and low budgets, executives don't need the extra pressure of doing business by trial and error. If you want to have a competitive advantage in today's global market, you must be cross-culturally competent so that you can hit the ground running and make the most of the time and resources available to you.

Developing a Global Mind-Set

In a survey of transnational CEOs published in 1997, The Conference Board found that culture and people issues are the biggest roadblocks to success in overseas business ventures.[5] In an article about the merger of Daimler-Benz and Chrysler Corporation, the *Los Angeles Times* noted that "cultural frictions have been identified as the primary pitfalls in unsuccessful cross-border joint ventures, of which there have been many. More than 70% of such mergers are given up as failures within three years, according to Daimler's own extensive premerger research."[6]

According to *Fortune* Magazine, when CEOs and senior executives are asked "about strengthening their organizations' competitiveness, on virtually everyone's wish list is having a much stronger cadre of globally minded leaders."[7] But most companies are still poor at actually cultivating internationally minded leaders. In a study, 1,500 executives from global corporations were asked to rate their performance in 34 areas essential for sustaining competitiveness. "The respondents rated their ability to cultivate a global mind-set in their organizations dead last—34th out of 34 dimensions."[8]

Why do companies rate themselves so low if they realize that thinking globally is such a critical issue? The truth is, when it comes to producing a globally oriented workforce, many managers feel completely lost. The idea of doing business in China is as intimidating as trying to learn Chinese.

At the heart of these fears lies the problem of getting a handle on culture. Managers often feel that " 'cultural factors' is a vague and fuzzy concept that does not easily translate into practical applications."[9] People feel that culture is something one learns by intuition, and therefore it can't be reduced to numbers or a clear program for action. For many executives, this means that the best thing to do is simply dismiss it altogether.

Although it cannot be reduced to a cookbook approach, cross-cultural competence is a skill that can be mastered with an open mind and attention to how others' beliefs and values differ from ours. These differences become visible when we examine our own cultural attitudes and values. Learning these basic skills can greatly enhance the success of cross-border business ventures by assuring smooth lines of communication and facilitating the people-to-people interactions that are at the heart of any business transaction.

The Human Factor

Global markets are inherently dependent on the human element. The judgments people make about the market, the kinds of moves they make, the strategic alliances and the mutual chemistry they create can make or break a deal. Is it strategically wise to discount to get your foot in the door, or is that market a quagmire better given to your competition? What kinds of concessions on financing or supplies might swing the deal in your favor? What long-term considerations are most important to the other side? These are questions that—in the final analysis—can only be answered at the people level.

Until recently, however, Americans working abroad largely ignored the way culture influenced this people factor. American products and managerial methods dominated the world marketplace. For U.S. companies operating abroad, there was only one way to do business: the American way. As far as business was concerned, people from other countries were simply "underdeveloped Americans." They might have their own cultural practices, but when it came to doing business they would naturally use the efficient and successful techniques developed by U.S. business.

A retired vice president from a major U.S. corporation comments:

"We have the technology and we know the business but we are not prepared as a country to deal with cultural differences."[10] If anything, the problem has become more acute as global competition increases and the United States does business on an equal footing with many countries around the world.

Americans, especially students, don't know much about other cultures: They're stuck within the borders of their own country. I was in a restaurant speaking with a friend in Portuguese, the national language of Brazil, when a man came up and asked us where we were from. I told him we were from Brazil, and he asked us to show him on a world map drawn on his bag. When I showed him, he said to us: "You stupid Brazilians are destroying the rain forest." I didn't get mad because I knew he really didn't know anything about my country. He didn't even know where it was. Many Americans, in fact, think that Buenos Aires is the capital of Brazil. In their minds, there are Indians on every street corner doing strange rituals. They have no idea that you have to journey into the heart of the rain forest to see primitive Indian tribes. And they have no idea that São Paolo, the city I live in, is one of the biggest and most expensive cities in the world.

—Denys Martins

Technology Cannot Replace People's Insight

A friend of mine who teaches English recently had a disagreement with one of his students who came in to see him during office hours to go over an essay she was writing for his class. After spending half an hour going over the ideas the student was trying to work out, my friend pointed out that it would be easier to follow the argument if she corrected the paper's numerous grammatical errors. "But I ran the grammar-check on my computer," the student protested with a perfectly straight face. "In her mind," my friend said, "she was responsible for having good ideas. It was the computer's job to write the paper."

Many people have the same attitude toward international business. The modern office is full of fancy gadgets—computers and Internet, uplinks and downlinks, videoconferencing and online databases. Why not let all that fancy technology handle the messy task of interfacing with businesses overseas?

The reality of global competition means that companies need to look for any advantage they can get. A fax can never tell you what is going on in the heads of managers in another country. Logging on to the Internet won't let you understand the way decisions are made on the other side of the world. Only understanding people will help you to do that. And in order to understand people you need to understand the cultural context in which they are operating.

Proximity Doesn't Lead to Understanding

We don't learn about others through osmosis. The enormous number of conflicts in the world shows us that proximity doesn't necessarily lead to better communication or understanding. Nor does a plentiful supply of common sense and goodwill take the place of deliberate education.

I know immigrants who have been in the United States for 30 years and still don't understand American culture. Similarly, Americans living as expatriates in other cultures often spend most of their time with other Americans. When this happens, you'll learn little about the country's culture beyond a few superficial customs.

To develop cultural literacy you need to take deliberate steps to learn about the other country's cultural practices and values. This doesn't mean you have to "go native" and live in another culture for 20 years before you can do business there. But you do have to make an effort to learn about the deep values that motivate people and provide the context for their actions.

We See the World through Culturally Tinted Glasses

People of every culture think their way of doing things makes the most sense. Our own rules and values are the ones we know best; therefore, we judge other people's behavior based on our own understanding. This translates into deeply ingrained habits for dealing with other people. In the business world, these habits often take the form of expectations that the other side will behave in a certain way in a given situation, or that others will see a particular problem in the same way we do. These expectations and understandings of the world are often unconscious, and so we have a hard time trying to identify them in others.

Since business is essentially a social activity, it is influenced by these differing perspectives of the people involved. When your counterparts are motivated by a different set of rules—when they see the situation through differently tinted glasses—you have to pay specific attention to what is going on inside their heads. In order to be successful you need to understand what motivates the decisions they make. The business executive who understands this process is usually the winner in business—whether it's domestic or international.

Koreans like to have time to think about their response and they gain time by nodding or simply saying "yes." In Korea, if someone says "yes," it often means "I hear you" rather than agreement. This can often lead to confusion for Westerners. I remember a business meeting in Seoul with a sales respresentative from a French perfume company. I was a buyer for a Korean department store. At the beginning of the meeting, the French salesman asked me if his company's perfume was selling well and whether it was competitive in the Korean market. I answered "yes" to indicate that I had understood his questions. But he thought I had answered "yes" to his questions and started to make proposals to increase the price and decrease consumer incentives. The fact was, however, that his product was not at all competitive and I needed the time to decide how to present this negative information to him.

—Byoung G. Kim

A Presidential Faux Pas

During a state visit to Mexico in 1977, President Jimmy Carter used a good old American strategy for starting on a positive note. Departing from his prepared speech, he began with an impromptu story:

President López Portillo and I have, in the short time together on this visit, found that we have many things in common. We both represent great nations; we both have found an interest in archaeology . . . we both have beautiful and interesting wives; and we both run several kilometers every day. As a matter of fact, I told President López Portillo that I acquired my habit of running here in Mexico City. My first running course was from the Palace of Fine Arts to the Majestic Hotel, where my family and I were staying. In the midst of the Folklórico performance, I discovered that I was afflicted with Montezuma's revenge.[10]

Carter's attempt at cross-cultural humor ended in disaster. Montezuma is a revered cultural symbol in Mexico. To have the president of the United States apparently making fun of this important symbol of Mexican identity was viewed as an affront to the nation's dignity. Mexican newspapers were ordered to ignore Carter's lame attempt at humor, but the incident certainly did nothing to improve the climate between the leaders of these two countries.

Carter's unfortunate remark illustrates one of the most important issues in this book. We are all willing to overlook minor lapses in etiquette—how one bows or shakes hands. These are surface features of a culture, and everyone recognizes that there are differences and takes them into account. Carter's remarks, however, were not concerned with the surface of Mexican culture but with deep cultural values. These deep-seated values and beliefs are often unconscious, and this is where real misunderstandings usually take place. To be successful in international business (or politics!), we have to understand these deep cultural values and how they motivate people to behave the way they do. Without this basic understanding, international business deals will be plagued with costly mistakes and avoidable inefficiencies.

PASSION VERSUS BUSINESS

In Brazil, the major sport is soccer. Most men play the game, and everyone has a favorite team. Sometimes one's soccer team is more important than religion and the family, especially if the Brazilian team is playing in the World Cup. The country stops, nobody works, and there is only one topic of conversation—soccer.

If you are lucky enough to go to a big Brazilian soccer match, it could be one of the most exciting experiences of your life. Of course there are problems. Schedules change without notice. You'll have to stand in big lines; you'll have to pay somebody to take care of your car (which will certainly be vandalized without paying this protection money); and when you get to the arena there will probably be no place to sit. But that doesn't matter, because the important thing is that you are there. The game is incredible and the audience is also a show: fireworks, big flags, people screaming and singing during the game. Fights are common between fans of different teams. There's no need for cheerleaders in Brazil; people there can cheer on their own!

In the United States, sports are much more organized. There are four seasons with a sport for each. The teams are like companies. You know the calendar in advance, and if you want you can buy tickets by phone or over the Internet. The arenas are very comfortable; there are no problems parking your car; and you can buy all kinds of food—hot dogs, french fries, pizza. Sometimes there is even a waitress! I remember during the World Cup in the United States in 1994, a player from a European team was interviewed after the game and asked if it was difficult to play against the United States on its home turf because of all the cheers. The answer: "The problem was not the cheers but the smell of 70,000 hot dogs."

—Andre Farkas Kok

2

Developing a World-Based Perspective

Toto, I get the feeling we're not in Kansas anymore.
—Dorothy on her arrival in Oz
in the film *The Wizard of Oz*

Crossing Borders

When you move from the domestic to the international marketplace, two additional types of factors are added to the mix (Figure 2.1). First, you must consider "hard factors" such as economic conditions, currency fluctuations, political stability, tariffs, and differences in laws and regulations. Although these factors present a significant challenge to doing business abroad, learning about them is fairly straightforward. Government institutions, universities, and think-tank organizations constantly study these issues and publish their findings. Mastering the laws and regulations of other countries or the intricacies of international finance may be difficult, but learning about them is primarily a technical matter—often one that can be farmed out to specialists.

Second are "soft factors"—the way people relate to each other as individuals, how they communicate, how they build trust and credibility, how they work together and make decisions, what motivates them to act, how they relate to authority, and how they maintain their sense of

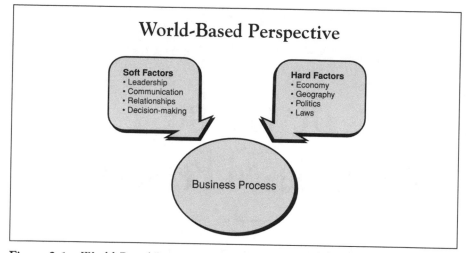

Figure 2.1   World-Based Perspective

identity. It is often difficult to grasp this people-to-people dimension of business. And when you move across cultural borders the process becomes even more challenging.

Many businesses resist addressing cross-cultural issues seriously because they believe that soft factors cannot be easily taught. But companies have discovered that soft skills such as leadership and teamwork are crucial to success and have a big impact on the bottom line. In order for a global enterprise to compete successfully, engineers in India have to communicate effectively with counterparts in the United States. Factory managers in Indonesia must respond to management issues in Los Angeles. Marketing people in New York have to negotiate with distributors in many different countries. Understanding how decisions are made in China can be the factor that clinches the deal. Helping members of multinational teams to harmonize their work styles can mean the difference between efficiency and gridlock.

The Global Stew

The world has become a giant blender where people from all over the globe are being mixed together vigorously. The ingredients of this mix are assembled based on qualifications, brains, and skills instead of nationality. The catalyst that has made this global stew possible is the new communication technology. But unlike computer networks that can "speak the same language" all over the world, people-to-people interactions and communications don't conform to a standard. Human beings come pre-programmed by their environment and bring their own culturally distinct ways of doing things to business interactions.

THE DIFFERENCE BETWEEN HEAVEN AND HELL

In heaven the cooks are French, the policemen are English, the lovers are Italian, the mechanics are Swiss, and the whole thing is organized by Germans. In hell, the cooks are English, the policemen are Germans, the lovers are Swiss, the mechanics are French, and the whole thing is organized by Italians.

—Joke from European folklore

The recent rash of cross-border mergers such as DaimlerChrysler has brought this reality to the forefront of our consciousness. We are being constantly reminded that, technology notwithstanding, people are at the heart of any business deal. And because of the extra challenge of communicating across borders and cultures, interpersonal skills and diplomacy are even more important in the new global marketplace.

Do You See What I See? Learning to See through Others' Eyes

I speak Spanish to God, Italian to women, French to men, and German to my horse.

—Charles V

What do you see when you first look at Figure 2.2? Some people see an old woman, others a beautiful young girl. If you see only one image and not the other, keep looking. The other image will eventually emerge.

I have shown this picture during my seminars hundreds of times. But each time I look at it, I still see the image of the old woman first and then the young woman.

The beauty of this illustration is that it demonstrates how people can

Figure 2.2   Old Woman or Young Woman?

take the same information—the same marks on a page—and assemble it into two completely different pictures. The same principle applies to communication across cultural lines. The two sides may be looking at exactly the same set of facts, but they assemble those facts into two completely different pictures of the situation.

Although people find it relatively easy to see the two versions of this illustration, seeing someone else's perspective is not so easy in real life. Often our own picture of the situation becomes our only reality, and we dismiss the other side's point of view. Remember that the situation may appear completely different when you try to see it from another cultural perspective. Learning to switch back and forth—like learning to see both the old lady and the young lady—makes it possible to frame issues in terms that can be understood by both sides.

Mexicans are warm, gracious, and very hospitable. They like to get to know you and will welcome unexpected visitors into their homes for food and refreshments. You may even get a tour of the house. Americans, on the other hand, are very private and seldom welcome unannounced visitors into their homes. They are very direct and frank, but don't seem that interested in getting to know people on a personal level. It is not surprisiing that Americans are perceived as cold and distant. Especially shocking to Mexicans is the American custom of putting older family members in a retirement home. In Mexico, elders are viewed as national monuments with a lot of wisdom and knowledge to contribute. Americans are also very competitive and materialistic, but this system tends to isolate them. Mexicans, by contrast, are humble and content with the things God has provided for them. Mexicans will not compete openly with each other, though they will defend their territory, their word, and their family honor.

—Miguel Gonzalez

Global Business Is a Contact Sport

Doing business internationally used to be like a tennis match. Multinational companies conducted a one-on-one game with subsidiaries or partners in other countries. These subsidiaries were managed by executives transferred from the United States for extended periods or by managers hired locally. Preparation of expatriates for their new assignments focused on survival skills such as language, etiquette, and social customs. The aim was to develop bicultural competency.

Playing in the new global business environment is more like a football game. It is a team contact sport on a complex, ever-changing playing field. Nowadays executives and managers have shorter tours of duty. They travel to many different countries and work with an increasingly multinational workforce within their own companies. Managers going to Hong Kong to negotiate a deal with another company or work on a project with a Chinese subsidiary may find themselves working with people from anywhere in the world.

The following example illustrates the dangers of using a bicultural approach in a multicultural business world. A multinational oil company sent one of its executives to Kenya to work in the company's small operations in Nairobi. Before he left, he was given a short briefing in Kenya's business environment and culture. The executive was originally from the Middle East, which has many similarities with Kenya in the way it does business, and he felt confident he could handle any minimal culture clashes that might arise. However, his immediate superior in Nairobi was German. Although they both spoke English fluently and shared the same company culture and business goals, the underlying cultural differences created an undertow that unwittingly provoked a series of conflicts. Needless to say, this was a costly undertaking for both the company and the employee, who left the country and his company precipitously.

The multicultural reality of the new global business environment is illustrated by Lucent Technologies, which recently assembled a team of 500 engineers scattered across 13 time zones and three continents to design an extremely complex product. Smooth communication across multiple cultural lines was essential to the success of the venture. Even small misunderstandings could have resulted in huge losses of time and money. Realizing that technology alone could not conquer cultural problems, the two main team leaders put their engineers through special training programs to identify differences and open lines of communication. "Sheer awareness of the differences ('Now I know why you got on my nerves.') began to create common ground."[1]

Preparation for this global environment has moved from bicultural survival skills such as training in the language and etiquette of a single country to developing multicultural "thriving" skills that will allow businesspeople to work comfortably with people from many different cultures.

At a language institute, teaching is the backbone of the business, but it doesn't pay the bills all by itself. Recruitment of new students is the first step for any language school to succeed.

When I arrived in Tokyo, I was trained in the basic cultural dos and don'ts for interacting with prospective Japanese students. My job as an interviewer was to find out what their level of English was, why they wanted to learn English, and, most important, who was going to pay the bill.

I quickly found out that socializing was, in essence, a covert strategy for building up bargaining power for later negotiations with the student. I usually started with the common Japanese custom of offering tea and cookies to my guest. During this time I was able to ask basic questions in a personal, conversational manner. Once I was done with the interview, I would speak with my manager and, using the information I had uncovered, we would agree on a strategy for signing up that student.

—Michelle Hobby

How Can I Learn about All these Cultures?

I do not want my house to be walled in on all sides and my windows to be stuffed. I want the cultures of all the lands to be blown about my house as freely as possible. But I refuse to be blown off my feet by any.

—Mahatma Gandhi[2]

Cultures vary dramatically from one country to the next. Even within the same country, different regions, ethnic groups, companies, and functions have their own unique cultures. This becomes even more complicated in light of the fact that most multinationals do business in over 70 different countries. Some people think that taking culture into account means learning the language and the minute details of every culture they have to interact with—a vast number of tiny nuances, customs, and practices. In practice, of course, this is impossible.

As a practical business tool, knowledge of culture should encompass those areas that facilitate effective business interactions. More in-depth observations and documentation are the domain of anthropologists. In this book we select those values that most impact the process of doing business and explain how they influence crucial people-to-people interactions. The goal is to identify potential trouble spots and to give the reader a feel for dealing with a wide variety of cultures that share certain values and attitudes toward business.

Fortunately, many cultural values are shared among people of different countries (Figure 2.3). Although every country is unique, there are common threads that run through many different cultures. For example, group-oriented cultures share certain similarities in attitudes and beliefs whether you are doing business in Latin America or the Middle East. Whereas Americans, who are generally individualistic in their outlook, feel comfortable getting down to business right away, businesspeople from group-oriented cultures, such as those found in Asia, Africa, Latin America, and the Middle East, usually expect to take a little time at the beginning of a relationship to acknowledge the human element—to "give face" and create a feeling of goodwill and trust. The point is that all these different group-oriented cultures share a similar approach to establishing working relationships. This overlap of cultural traits greatly simplifies the task of doing business overseas.

Learning about cultures is also cumulative. Once you've learned how to operate in one foreign culture, understanding the next one becomes

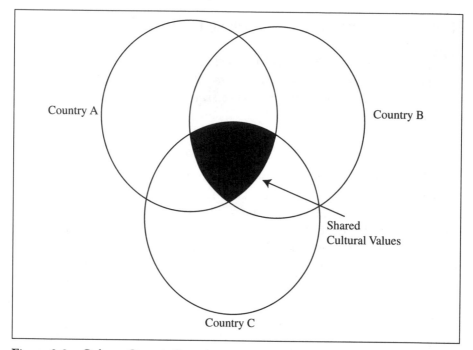

Figure 2.3   Culture Generic Dynamics

much easier. Some of the knowledge gained in one culture can be transferred to another. More importantly, you learn what kinds of things to look for. Experienced international travelers feel comfortable in almost any cultural setting—even if they find themselves in a place where they have little previous experience—because they have learned the general principles for dealing with cultural difference.

Of course it is valuable to know as much as possible about the background and history of each country you are dealing with. But what is most important from a business perspective is learning the core values that affect the way other cultures approach doing business. The surface features of a culture are far less important than these deep values when it comes to being successful abroad. As Jon Thomas, a skilled international negotiator for AT&T, told me: "The niceties, such as how to shake hands or not crossing your legs, are far less important than the deeper cultural beliefs such as saving face and building trust. After all, people understand that you do not necessarily know their customs, just as they do not understand yours, so a great deal of tolerance is present."

Avoiding Stereotypes

When Motorola set up shop in the People's Republic of China, the centerpiece of its operations was its "six-sigma quality program"—which places a lot of emphasis on individual responsibility. This might seem like a poor strategy in a group-oriented culture such as China, which places primary importance on collective identity and responsibility. But Motorola recognized that not everyone would fit the stereotype. There is no average person. Pigeonholing people based on cultural categories is very dangerous. Generalizations about culture can be used as a starting point, as a general map that helps orient us in a complex terrain, but it is not an exact replica of the terrain itself. In this case, Motorola was able to find workers who fit its model of individual initiative and responsibility.[3]

During our visit to Williamsburg, we stayed at a bed-and-breakfast run by a woman in her seventies. We had made the reservations by phone, so she had no idea we were Asians. When we arrived at the door of her house, we were welcomed by her and her little puppy. When she saw us, she immediately picked up the puppy and asked us where we were from. We told her we were from Taiwan, and she asked: "Don't people eat dogs in Taiwan?" We told her that some people did, but not us. We stayed two nights at her house, and we never saw the puppy after that first conversation. I think she hid the puppy out of fear that we would get hungry and eat it.

—*Pam Kuo*

Are We All Becoming Alike?

During my training seminars, there are always a few participants who start by arguing that world cultures are converging into a new global culture and that studying cultures is no longer really necessary. American executives in the group often have the vague impression that other cultures in the world are becoming Americanized. American culture, in their minds, *is* global culture. Foreign executives often fall into the same trap in reverse. For them, the word "culture" conjures up weird customs and images of backwardness. To admit to having a culture means admitting they are not fully modern.

A young Brazilian executive, for instance, argued that cultural differences are not an issue anymore. He pointed out that Brazilians used to be late to meetings, but under the pressure of a global business culture they have now learned to be on time. I asked him how long he had been living in the United States. "Eight months," he said. I then asked him if he had observed any ways his American friends did things differently than people did in Brazil. "Oh, yes," he said. "Americans are very money oriented. They love their money even more than their own kids! As soon as the kids turn 18, the parents kick them out of the house—or, worse yet, charge them rent if they stay at home to live."

The Americans in the group had a completely different view of the situation. They pointed out that Americans throw their kids out *because* they love them. They feel that leaving home is a natural part of becoming independent and learning to make one's own decisions. They don't want to raise a bunch of sissies dependent on their parents.

Now, the point to be made here is that both Brazilians and Americans love their kids—but they have different ways of expressing this. Neither style is good or bad, backward or enlightened. They are simply different ways of doing things. Once this point was established, our group went on to discover dozens of other differences between Brazilian and American cultures—different ways of doing things that had nothing to do with which culture was more modern or advanced.

It may well be true that some aspects of global business culture are converging—hard factors such as the forms of contracts, conflict arbitration, and financing—but the situation is very different when it comes to people. When we do business in foreign countries we are dealing with people rooted in a cultural tradition. These traditions, practices, and behaviors are not likely to converge any time soon.

At the 1998 World Economic Forum at Davos, Switzerland, Bertrand Colomb, the CEO of a large French construction materials company, pointed out that the biggest challenge facing global companies in the next decade will be learning how to communicate and do business effectively in different countries and cultures. He said that some people think that American business values will prevail all over the world and work as a unifying force to bring business practices together. Colomb said he wished world business practices *were* converging—it would make his life a lot easier if they were—but he actually thought things were moving in the opposite direction. The same processes that are making the world smaller and bringing people together, he argued, also generate countervailing forces that compel people to hold tighter to their national traditions and values. The convergence of deeply held values, he concluded, won't happen in our lifetimes.

Nomunication is a popular catch-phrase I often heard during my three-year stay in Japan. *Nomunication* is a combination of the Japanese verb *nomu* (to drink) and the English word "communication." Receptions, dinners, and drinking parties are common occasions for *nomunication*—a chance to build relationships and bonding over drinks. For people on a business trip in Japan, it is easy to see how jet lag, difficult negotiations, and the language barrier can contribute to wanting to skip evening entertainment and *nomunication*. But this socializing is an extremely important part of Japanese business culture, and the opportunity to build relationships should not be missed. *Nomunication* may even be the key to successful business transactions.

—*Nuntica Tanasugarn*

The Global Melting Pot

Public debate may still be held hostage to the outdated vocabulary of borders, but the daily realities facing most people in the developed and developing worlds—both as citizens and as consumers—speak a vastly different idiom. Theirs is the language of an increasingly borderless economy, a true global marketplace.
—Kenichi Ohmae[4]

During the past few years, the argument has often been made that a new global business culture is emerging that overruns the borders of nation-states. Although this is true for business practices such as contracts, financing, and conflict arbitration, it does not apply to people's deeply held cultural values.

The engine driving the emergence of this new global business culture is the fierce competition of international business. As Kenichi Ohmae points out in *The End of the Nation State*, there are four components of this new global competition working to overcome traditional national borders: capital, corporations, consumers, and communication.[5]

CAPITAL

Much of the developed world has huge excesses of investment capital. At the same time many new markets and investment opportunities have emerged—a trend that has accelerated since the end of the cold war. In response to this situation, world capital markets have developed a variety of new mechanisms for transferring capital to areas where the best return on investment can be expected. These mechanisms largely bypass the control of nation-states, which, according to Ohmae, are increasingly irrelevant in international business decisions.

The increasing flow of capital has facilitated the movement of people, business, and information across borders. As capital becomes increasingly international, it is less constrained by local customs and regulations, providing an impetus toward a convergence of business practices in a new world business culture.

CORPORATIONS

As more and more countries open their borders to direct competition, the idea of a "local" or "national" business is rapidly losing its meaning. Even if a company does business only locally, it must still compete within a world business culture. Survival means adopting the most efficient management and production techniques available—wherever they come from.

The lure of the global marketplace and the demand to be globally competitive create a compelling force toward what works in business. Over 10 years ago, American auto executives started dismantling their old system and instituting the Japanese methods of quality control and worker empowerment. Now the Japanese are looking at the American entrepreneurial system as a model for the lean and nimble organizations needed to compete in the information age. South Korea's leading conglomerate, Samsung, is seeking a more prominent position in the world market by eliminating the traditional Confucian hierarchies in its management and adopting Japanese quality control methods. Importing management ideas from the United States, Samsung's president, Lee Kun Hee, advocates "the delegation of more authority to group company heads, encouragement of subordinates to speak more freely with their bosses, and other steps to develop a more individualistic and assertive workforce." Says Lee: "Change everything, except your wife and children."[6]

CONSUMERS

Another factor facilitating the internationalization of business is the emergence of an affluent global middle class, which increasingly demands high-quality goods and services for the lowest price. Until recently, the middle class was limited to the United States and Western Europe. Now there are sizable middle classes in most countries of the world. Countries such as China and Vietnam are developing a middle class. This global middle class shops in a world marketplace of consumer goods and services that is increasingly homogeneous. Their choices determine which business practices succeed and which fail—even in industries that are inherently local.

The global melting pot has made the customer more important—and pickier. When companies can no longer depend on protected markets, they are forced to pay attention to consumer needs. This is true at the level of individual consumers and for business customers as well. When the YTL Corporation from Malaysia solicited bids for $700 million worth of power-generation turbines in 1993, it demanded to meet with the CEOs of the two main bidders: Siemens AG from Germany and General Electric Company from the United States. "I wanted to look them in the eye to see if we can do business," said Datuk Francis Yeoh, manager of the project. The head of Siemens went to Malaysia. The head of GE stayed home. Siemens got the contract.[7]

INFORMATION

The emergence of information and information technologies as the driving force of the new world order also works to create a new global business culture. As information transfer becomes increasingly universal, the importance of physical location becomes correspondingly less important. As Ohmae points out:

> Product designers in Oregon can control the activities of a network of factories throughout Asia-Pacific. Thus, the hurdles for cross-border participation and strategic alliance have come way down. Armies of experts do not have to be transferred; armies of workers do not have to be trained. Capability can reside anywhere in the network and be made available—virtually anywhere—as needed.[8]

Information technology also makes it increasingly difficult for nation-states to maintain control of local economic decisions. Japan, for instance, has imposed low interest rates on savings accounts in an attempt to help banks recover from the real estate collapse at the end of the 1980s. But a Japanese consumer only has to send a fax to Switzerland or log on to an online service in the United States to receive globally competitive rates.

There has been a good deal of resistance to the globalization of culture—often from institutions and nation-states whose existence is threatened by the rapid mixing and "morphing" that characterize the new world culture. For many, the invasion of foreign cultures—especially American—represents corruption and decadence. Jin Kaicheng, who teaches Chinese at Beijing University, complains that the use of English among China's youth is a threat to Chinese identity: "The present pollution of our language is harmful to China's national dignity and image. It's not simply a matter of the language changing; it also reflects people's unhealthy tendency to blindly worship Western culture."[9]

As Ohmae points out, teenagers in Japan have more in common with teenagers in Russia or the United States than they do with their own parents. In this view, it is not Western culture but world culture that is invading China—and this process is inevitable as the new information age technologies progressively annihilate older national boundaries. It is important to note, however, that this convergence of cultures is taking place primarily in the realm of surface features—the way teenagers dress and the music they listen to. It does not address the deeper cultural values and attitudes that structure people's identity.

My first job when I came to the United States from the Philippines was as an account collector for a small consumer electronics firm run by a Persian family. It was a very culturally diverse workplace. There were Persians, of course, but also Hispanics and Filipinos. Our clients were primarily Korean, Chinese, Persian, and Mexican. It was quite a shock to me because Philippine society is very homogeneous. One of the reasons I came to the United States was to work on my English, but I found I spent most of my time working on my Spanish (which I had to take in order to graduate from college in the Philippines).

When I started, I couldn't understand what I was doing wrong. Every morning as my supervisor came into the office, I would greet her with a friendly "Good morning!" But she just ignored me, and I thought there was something wrong with me. I knew I was a good employee, so I couldn't understand why I was treated so rudely. Eventually, I stopped greeting her and learned not to take things personally.

My cultural upbringing conflicted with my job as a collector. When I loaned money to friends in the Philippines, they would always repay me at the time we'd agreed on. I guess it had to do with honor and saving face. On this job, some of our clients would start screaming and cussing at me when I called them. I literally turned red the first time it happened. After awhile, though, I realized that this was just a tactic used by some cultures to get more time to pay their bills. So I started calling them every other day.

One day my boss called me into her office and told me one of their clients had called to complain that I was harassing them. I thought I was going to be fired, but she just smiled and said, "You're doing a good job!" I eventually got quite good at my job and was able to bring down the level of accounts receivable for the company.

—*Erikson Magallona*

The Common-Sense Lure of the American Way of Doing Business

The United States has been the great modern crucible where cultures and customs are blended together to find what works and what doesn't. American culture burns away the inefficient and the irrelevant, leaving the pragmatic, common-sense essence that has great appeal to people all over the world. The American system is a system that *works*. It is the easiest and the closest to human nature. It has searched out the practical way to do things and incorporated them into the "American way of life."

The common-sense lure of American business practices strikes a common chord in the hearts of people in other parts of world. There is a simplicity and directness to American business practices that quickly penetrates the sometimes arcane customs of other countries.

A Russian consultant, for instance, told me that he prefers living and working in the United States because it is more honest and direct. "For example, if I'm extremely busy and an American friend or coworker drops by, I have no trouble saying, 'This isn't a good time; I'm under a deadline on a project.' But in Russia when a friend drops in, you know that saying you're busy would offend your friend, so you put on a fake smile and try to entertain the friend and be pleasant even though it's not what you want to do."

The United States is still the leader in experience-based commodities—movies, video games, tourist trends, and the like. Although American businesses have imported management and production strategies from around the world, they still dominate the emerging world consumer culture. Being hip and modern in most of the world means using American cultural symbols and language. In China, young people say "hi" when they meet and "bye-bye" when they part. *Ku* refers to a "cool" situation and *kao* is a reminder to give each other a call.

When I was in China during the 1980s, the peasants were building houses with pickaxes the same way they did a thousand years ago. But you could hear American music coming from the workers' radios.

Learning about Others: What You Need to Know

Learning about cultural difference and its impact on business is not the same as understanding a culture. It is the job of an anthropologist to understand a culture—if such a thing is really possible. According to Fons Trompenaars, it is impossible to really understand another culture—that is, to "figure them out": "People can't be figured out. We can't even figure out our own children or spouse. It is my belief that you can never understand other cultures."[10]

Fortunately, successful business dealings do not require that we understand everything about a culture or experience it as a native from the inside. We need to understand culture's influence on business in order to prevent cultural differences from getting in the way of good business. Our goal is not to give up our values in the face of other values, nor to make others do business our way.

Splitting the Differences

Success in international business means more than just learning about other cultures. You need to think of the world as your stage of operations. We can't divide the world into foreign and domestic markets anymore. This way of looking at things focuses obsessively on *differences* and tends to see people from other cultures as martians—bizarre aliens that can never be understood. The fact is that we are far more similar than we are different. Of course there are differences, but global executives feel confident in their ability to navigate those differences as successfully as they can navigate the world of business in their own country.

Attaining a global mind-set requires education and training. Learning to do business internationally is an extension of learning to do business here in the United States. This means developing an unconscious competence in dealing with cross-cultural issues and having an internalized map that allows one to deal naturally with differing cultural terrains. A good sign that you are a global manager is when you lose the feeling of foreignness that many people feel when they first travel abroad or negotiate with representatives of a foreign company. It should feel just as natural to drive a hard bargain with a Saudi prince as it does to deal with suppliers in Cleveland.

The trick is to capitalize on similarities without being ambushed by differences. How can you do that? Once we understand the differences, then we move onto the next level where we can focus on similarities. A key caution: The greater the seeming similarity, the deeper the possibility of being caught off guard.

My own prescription for approaching cultural difference involves finding a middle ground. We need to recognize that cultural differences exist but not exaggerate those differences to the point that we turn others into incomprehensible aliens. The proper stance is somewhere between the Ugly American who thoughtlessly tramples on other people's culture and traditions and the Intimidated American who is afraid to act for fear of violating some incomprehensible cultural taboo. It is on this middle ground that we can find our similarities and create a relationship that involves a true empathy with the other.

After I graduated from film school at UCLA, I was commissioned to direct a television documentary for NHK, the biggest TV network in Japan. After completing local photography in Hong Kong, I flew to Japan for postproduction work, which required cooperating with Japanese producers, editors, writers, musicians and technicians. One day, Mr. Masao, the head of the music division, came to the studio to watch a rough cutting of the parts we had just completed. He was very old and solemn.

After the screening was over, he asked: "Where is the director? What are your ideas about music for your documentary film?" Everyone's eyes turned to me. At first I told myself that this was Japan and it was probably better to listen to his opinion first. But then a little voice inside me said: "Come on; be professional. You are the director; it is your job to tell them what kind of music you think will work best on this project." So I gave Mr. Masao a straight answer, speaking my mind directly.

After I presented my ideas, Mr. Masao didn't say anything; nor did anyone else in the room. I felt very embarrassed by this silence and finally suggested: "What I said was just my personal opinion. I hope we can take some time to discuss or exchange our ideas." Unfortunately, the silence continued. Finally, thank God, the executive producer announced the end of the screening session.

At dinner that night, I asked some of the Japanese crew members why no one had spoken up during the meeting. He smiled and replied: "Luke, these crew members are all young people. They don't want to express their opinions in front of influential figures like Mr. Masao."

"If you were me, how would you have answered?" I asked.

"I would probably say, 'I have no particular idea, but I would like to listen to yours, Mr. Masao. You know much more than I do, and it's an honor to work with you.' "

I didn't like this answer, but I realized he was probably right. It was necessary to adjust my Americanized style to fit in with my Japanese coworkers.

—Xiao Kang

What Is Culture?

How Do You Define Culture?

The actions of persons in a foreign culture and social organization are not nonsense; those people are simply driven by an alternative common sense.

—Vern Terpstra and Kenneth David[1]

Have you ever seen a path etched on the land by people taking the same route again and again? The path exists because it solves a problem: It provides a simple, dependable way to get across a certain terrain. Similarly, culture is a mosaic of patterns established by repeated practice. Each of these patterns met a need or solved a problem at a certain point in a people's history. Culture is this accumulation of life experiences spanning generations. For a native, finding a way through this maze of interconnecting paths is second nature, but to an outsider who hasn't learned the paths and doesn't know where the ones that are visible lead, getting across the landscape of another culture is an enigma.

PROBLEMS SOLVED BY CULTURE

- Acquisition of food, clothing, and shelter.
- Provision of protection from enemies and natural disasters.
- Regulation of sexuality.
- Child raising and instruction in socially approved and useful behavior.
- Division of labor among humans.
- Sharing and exchanging the product of human work.
- Providing social controls against deviant behavior.
- Providing incentives to motivate persons to want to do what they do.
- Distributing power and legitimizing the wielding of power to allow setting of priorities, making decisions, and coordinating actions that obtain social goals.
- Providing a sense of priorities (values) and an overall sense of worth (religion) to social life.

SOURCE: Vern Terpstra and Kenneth David, *The Cultural Environment of International Business*, 3d ed., Cincinnati, OH: South-Western Publishing, 1991, 7.

Geert Hofstede, a Dutch sociologist who studies the way different countries do business, describes culture as "the software of our minds"—one of three kinds of "mental programming" that operate in each individual. The pyramid of culture (Figure 3.1) shows how these different levels of mental programming interact to produce the behavior of each person we meet.

At the bottom of the pyramid is human nature. Although we have different kinds of cultural software, we all share the same basic hardware. We all feel fear, love, sadness, and other human emotions. Nothing is in my heart that another human being thousands of miles away hasn't experienced. We share our basic humanity with all other people—no matter how alien or bizarre they might seem. Understanding how to communicate these shared human values makes an instant rapport possible in spite of cultural differences. As Will Rogers once said, "Mothers are the only race of people that speak the same tongue."

At the top level of the pyramid we find personality or "peopleware." Personality is the unique set of traits that define each individ-

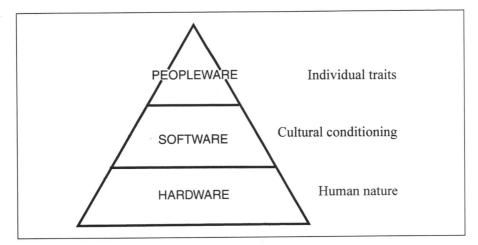

Figure 3.1   Pyramid of Culture

ual as different from everyone else; it is the product of each person's innate disposition. Although personality is affected by both human nature and culture, it is not completely determined by them. Even in relatively closed cultures there is a great deal of variety among individuals. There are people who are shy or outgoing, moody or upbeat, petty or magnanimous no matter where we go.

While human nature is a common inheritance of all people, and individual personalities are the product of each person's particular disposition, *culture is learned from one's social environment.* As anthropologists point out, cultural practices create the reality of a particular culture—the shared symbols, rituals, attitudes, orientations, and values that allow a group of people to work together to interpret the world and their place in it. Culture provides the rules that regulate basic patterns of behavior; it tells us what things we should do and what things we should avoid doing. These rules are based on values and assumptions that are emotionally charged: We make judgments based on these deep values automatically—with little recourse to rational reflection. Our own cultural practices are familiar and reassuring: We generally like our culture better than others because it seems natural to us.

People in a national culture also belong to many different subcultures, such as region, religion, class, ethnicity, and profession. Sometimes these subcultures can be just as important in shaping an individual's behavior as national culture. A doctor and a farmer living in Italy share a common national culture, but they belong to very different professional and class subcultures. Teenagers in Pakistan and Indonesia may both listen to American music and aspire to lifestyles very different from those of their parents. In Japan you might find yourself doing business with a person who has lived most of his or her adult life in the United States and dealt extensively with other cultures. That person's values and cultural reference points might be totally different from an older, more traditional Japanese.

The "circle" is the foundation of the Japanese group system. Circles are like an American club, only people are much closer. I joined a circle when I was at the university. I went on trips with the circle and many of my friends were in the circle. Some couples got married from our circle. Many boys join a circle to look for pretty girls, but once they become members they attend every meeting even if there are no pretty girls available.

Circle members have to pay dues and participate in activities. There are a chairman and vice presidents. Each member receives a booklet of the circle. At the university, our circle opened a shop—actually a kind of bazaar—to sell food and other items to raise money for the circle. We met twice a week to play tennis and have dinner. We shared more time with each other than with our own families, especially if someone was living alone. We talked about our boyfriend and girlfriend problems, dreams for the future, and the worries we had.

After graduation, the members of our circle stayed in touch. We have made a special members list with information about where everyone is working and what they are doing. We get an updated list each year when we meet.

People who are members of a circle get many benefit. One is that they automatically learn how to behave and work in groups. Japanese society is largely based on networks. There is less danger staying in a group than being a single person. I had many benefits when I started working in the office because of my association with a circle. I have many friends in various companies, and if I have questions, I just call one of the members of my circle to get the information I need.

—*Mariko Ishikawa*

For business purposes, culture can be segmented into three spheres: *national culture*, the *business subculture* that exists in that particular culture, and the *corporate subculture* that exists in a specific organization.

Each of these levels of culture is important to the process of doing business abroad.

National cultures establish the basic framework people use for relating to each other—the core values and beliefs, social codes, and rules of etiquette.

Business cultures grow from the larger national culture of which they are a part, and they reflect the values and practices of that culture in a business setting. Management styles, team dynamics, decision-making processes, and negotiating styles are part of learned cultural behavior. The main focus of this book will be on exploring the dynamics of differing business cultures.

Cultural differences can also exist at the level of individual organizations. For instance, even though they are all in computer-related industries, IBM has a different corporate culture from Microsoft, and both are certainly different from a young start-up technology company. Corporations socialize their employees after they are hired much as families socialize their children. Codes of values and priorities are transmitted to employees within a corporation much as they are in the culture at large. Within corporations, there may even exist many smaller subcultures. The marketing, accounting, and engineering departments of a large corporation are certain to look at problems through their own peculiar lenses.

Cultural Symbols and Cultural Values

The only distinguishing characteristic of American character that I've been able to discover is a fondness for ice water.
—Mark Twain

Superficial cultural symbols and practices are easy to recognize: types of food, language, music, gestures, social customs, and etiquette. These outward manifestations of culture are what most people first notice about cultural differences. On the other hand, deep-seated cultural values are etched in the back of one's psyche and aren't nearly as easy to recognize. They are largely unconscious and invisible, both to others and to those who hold them.

When we encounter a new culture, it is much like sighting an iceberg at sea. On the surface are the outward cultural symbols (Figure 3.2). They may seem alien or bizarre, but since we can see them they are easy to deal with. Most training for business executives going

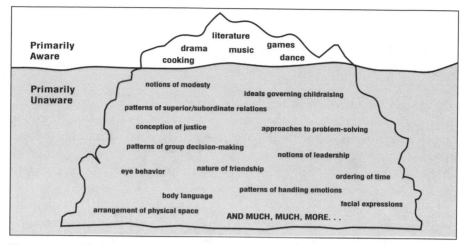

Figure 3.2   The Cultural Iceberg

abroad concentrates on challenges caused by the 10 percent of the iceberg above the surface—how to bow or shake hands, whether to cross your legs, what gestures to use. Much more dangerous, however, is the 90 percent of the iceberg that is under water. Because they are hidden from the casual observer, these deep-seated cultural values can sink the unsuspecting business executive who sails too close. The American executive who—quite naturally from his or her perspective—insists on individual accountability as a way to improve efficiency is likely to encounter incomprehension or hostility in group-oriented cultures, where calling attention to individual success or failure can cause loss of face for some members and severely damage the dynamics of group performance.

Although expressions of love are common among family members in the United States, they are rare in Asia. The father always tries to maintain a certain distance from the children to retain respect. Kissing, hugging, and cuddling are not the way we express love to people close to us. Arguments among family members are allowed, but decisions are always made by the parents—who remain in full control of their children until they are married. Perhaps this is why Asian children are less demonstrative than American children. Their parents love them but the "passion thing" is missing.

—Mona Djaya

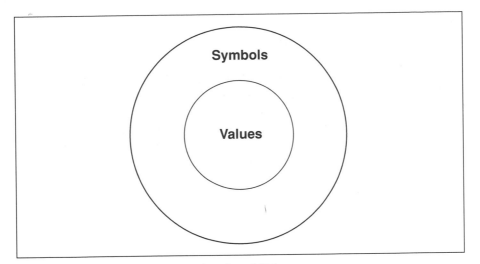

Figure 3.3   Cultural Symbols and Cultural Values

Deep cultural values, which we learn as very young children, are more resistant to change than superficial cultural expressions are. Values seem natural and universal. When we encounter different cultural symbols, people merely seem different, perhaps even colorful. But when they express different values, they seem unnatural, dangerous, or evil.

The relationship between cultural symbols and cultural values can be seen as a series of layers wrapped around a central core—the deep values that motivate people's behavior (Figure 3.3). Cultural symbols are the visible manifestations of culture—the practices and behaviors we can see and catalog. These practices are expressions of deep-seated, invisible core values at the center. It is relatively easy to learn about these surface manifestations of culture, but much harder to get a feel for the significance these practices have.

Deep cultural values have emotions attached to them. Behavior that is in line with our values is persuasive and pleasing. When an action violates our values, we react automatically. We instinctively feel the other side is wrong or being unreasonable, but just as often they feel the same way about us. Since our own values are largely unconscious and emotional, it is often difficult even to recognize what the problem is, let alone deal with it rationally.

It is conflicts in values that most often derail international business dealings. Each party arrives at the table with a different map—that side's own logic and patterns of behavior. These differing maps often cause businesspeople from different cultures to talk past each other. The other side often seems unreasonable, arrogant, or deceitful. Many Asian cultures, for instance, place less importance on the details of a formal contract. Although with globalization all agreements are formalized in contracts, people from these cultures may not have their heart in it. For them, a business relationship is based on trust and should evolve with the circumstances. But for Americans, overlooking the details of a formal contract is a sign of untrustworthiness. The two sides ascribe exactly opposite meanings to the same set of signs!

CHAPTER 4

An American Abroad: Key Cultural Contrasts

Ah me, what are the people whose land I have come to this time,
and are they violent and savage, and without justice . . .
or am I truly in the neighborhood of human people I can converse
with?

—Odysseus arriving on the shores of the Phaiakians[1]

Wandering around the Mediterranean in 1200 B.C., Odysseus faced the same challenge encountered by international businesspeople today: How do you communicate with people who are different from you? For Odysseus, people whose customs were too different from his own Greek culture were violent and savage barbarians. If we don't make a conscious effort to recognize how other people's behavior makes sense within their culture, it is all too easy to make the same mistake today.

I took out my best china and prepared a detailed menu with a variety of food and drinks. I made all kinds of Brazilian appetizers and desserts, and purchased lots of cheese, including a delicious French Brie I'd discovered a few days before. I bought lots of flowers (the gorgeous Dutch flowers) and put them in vases all over the apartment. Before the party I put on a nice dress, makeup, and jewelry.

The invitation was for 8:00 P.M., and everyone arrived at 8:00 P.M. In

Brazil, when you are invited to a party at 8:00 P.M. it means to show up at 9:00. When I started answering the door, I realized I didn't have hangers for everyone's coats. Extra hangers are not an essential part of Brazilian houses—in fact, there are few houses I know that have even one. I put the coats on the bed, but I could hear my guests whispering, "There are no hangers in the house."

I was pleasantly surprised that almost all my guests brought flowers, but at that point I didn't have any vases left to put them in. They noticed that I didn't have any candles. When the Dutch give parties, they adorn the house with colorful candles. In Brazil we use white candles in weddings or formal parties, but we avoid using colorful candles because they have special significance to some African religions that are practiced in Brazil.

My guests were surprised and uncomfortable when they saw the amount of food on the table and the fancy way I'd displayed it. In Brazil we like to have plenty of food when there is a party. In the Netherlands they say: "Eat to live and not live to eat." Dutch cuisine is not varied and does not occupy the prominent place it does in Brazil. Later I learned that Holland's Calvinistic background has had great influence on having fun and expressing emotions. Deep down inside, the Dutch still consider enjoyment a sin—an attitude reflected in their manner of dressing, their sober architecture, and their restrained manner of celebrating. I think Calvinism is the reason they didn't seem to enjoy the Brazilian music I played during the party.

Whenever I offered my guests something to drink, they immediately asked for coffee or tea. I was planning to make coffee at the end of the party as they do in Brazil. I learned later that when the Dutch invite you to their homes they promptly serve you coffee and offer you *one* cookie. Eventually you will be offered another cup of coffee—again with *one* cookie.

As the party went on, I noticed that my guests didn't seem to like the food very much, especially the desserts. I found out later that the Dutch don't have much of a sweet tooth. And the Brie cheese I liked so much was French. The Dutch are very proud of their own cheese, and they gave me lecture on how much better Dutch cheese is, how I should serve cheese, and the kind of cheese slicer I should buy.

They also made comments about how the amount of food I had on the table was enough to feed three times the number of people at the party. When the Dutch invite someone over, they have only enough food for the exact number of people invited. This would be embarrassing to a hostess in Brazil, where there should be plenty of food for everyone, even unexpected guests. In the Netherlands, if you stop to visit someone at dinnertime, you will not be asked to stay. They may even ask you to leave and start eating without you! In order to avoid this, I learned not to visit anyone between 4:00 P.M. and 8:00 P.M.

In addition to comments on the food and the house, my guests made remarks on the way I dressed. By Brazilian standards, I was well dressed but still informal. For the Dutch, I was "overdressed" and looked "too feminine." Displaying expensive clothes or jewelry is considered vulgar in the Netherlands. In Brazil it shows that you care about the occasion.

The conversation at the party was also strange. The Dutch are very good with small talk. You can spend months talking to a Dutch person without learning anything about his or her personal life. Brazilians love to talk about personal issues—what they call "exchanging life experiences." Surprisingly, however, the Dutch will discuss their sex lives quite openly. But never ask them how much money they earn—that is sacred information, and asking is not acceptable!

After the party I called my grandmother in Brazil and told her that everything had gone wrong! She told me that I'd made one mistake. The first rule of a good hostess, she said, was to make the guests feel good about themselves. I'd turned my party into a "Brazilian cultural workshop." But my guests were expecting me to show appreciation for their culture. After all, people all over the world need to feel proud of their roots.

—KL

Like KL, the Brazilian woman washed up on the frozen shores of Holland's reserved, northern European culture in the example above, international businesspeople have to learn to navigate a new set of cultural paths. Some rules are relatively simple—when to serve the coffee or having coat hangers for your closet. But deeply held attitudes and beliefs are harder to address. The Dutch perception that she looked "too feminine," for instance, went straight to the heart of the Brazilian woman's sense of her own identity. Changing the way you express your femininity is a much more difficult task than buying coat hangers.

We can understand something new only if we compare it to something that we already know: namely, our own culture. According to Edward Hall:

> The real job is not to understand foreign culture but to understand our own. I am also convinced that all one ever gets from studying foreign culture is a token understanding. The ultimate reason for such study is to learn more about how one's own system works.[2]

In this chapter we take a look at some American values and attitudes that seem so natural to us that we don't even think of them as "cultural." In each case, learning how these values organize our way of life and the way we look at the world will provide a starting point for understanding the ways people in other cultures do and see things differently.

American Culture Is Individualistic

The nail that sticks up gets hit down.

—Japanese proverb[3]

Individualism is one of the most important elements of American identity and self-image. Americans take a fierce pride in their ability to go it alone. One of the most powerful American myths is the "conquest of the West," in which the solitary hero is portrayed braving the wilderness with only his own resourcefulness and courage to see him through. The modern version of this solitary wilderness hero is the self-made man who creates his identity (and his business empire) from the sheer force of his own ingenuity and willpower. The extraordinarily high compensation rates for American CEOs compared to those in other countries stem from this vision of the corporation as an extension of one individual's vision and will.

The American individual thinks of himself or herself as essentially separate from society. They define their self-worth in terms of individual achievements—the awards or promotions they've received, the books they've published, the deals they've made for the company. For Americans, the pursuit of happiness revolves largely around the idea of self-fulfillment—expressing an interior essence that is unique to each individual. Being a nonconformist, while often frowned upon in reality, is glorified as an ideal in American culture. Americans all like to think they "took the path less traveled."

The ideals of individualism affect the way Americans interact with each other. Relationships to other people are contractual in nature: They are based on the individual's free choice and personal preference. If Americans don't like their friends—or even their families—they simply get new ones. Americans generally respond with hostility to social structures that emphasize group dominance of the individual. The Borg from the popular science fiction show *Star Trek* symbolize this horror of the totalitarian group: Individuals are fitted with cybernetic implants that hook them into a collective consciousness that leaves no space at all for individual will or action.

All this contrasts sharply with group-oriented cultures, where people's identities are inextricably linked to the social network in which they live. Achievement is enjoyed when it attracts recognition from the group, but people from group-oriented cultures are generally not driven, as Americans often are, to think of themselves as the sum total of their achievements. Their identities are guaranteed by their place in the group, not by a series of accomplishments. One could say that people from group-oriented cultures are other-directed while Americans are basically self-directed.

When I arrived in Japan, I was shocked to find the Japanese viewed me as weird for wanting to do things by myself. Having bright-red hair didn't make my assimilation into Japanese culture any easier. But getting used to following someone around all the time was very difficult. For example, my Japanese friends thought I could not ski because I didn't wear brightly colored ski outfits or stay behind the ski leader when going down the hill. The real shock, though, came on the job. Every morning, meetings were held and the manager talked while we listened. The individual opinions of each employee were never taken into consideration.

—*Matthew Reccow*

There is probably no single point that causes more misunderstandings than the contrast in attitude and orientation between individualist and group-oriented cultures. The following passage, from Edward Stewart and Milton Bennett's *American Cultural Patterns*, shows how American children are socialized from early childhood to think of themselves as distinct individuals expected to make their own personal choices:

It is early in the morning and the mother has placed her baby daughter, who is less than one year old, in her high chair and is preparing to give breakfast to the child. The mother selects two different kinds of baby cereal, each kind packaged in a box of distinctive color. The mother holds up a box in each hand before the child and encourages the small girl to select the one she wants. Before the age of one, the child has already learned to express her own preferences and make her own decisions, at least with regard to food.[4]

Japanese companies concentrate on groups when working on projects. Companies train their new employees to be generalists, which means they have to know every detail about their companies. Japanese universities teach how to work in groups and get along with people in addition to traditional studies.

—*Mariko Ishikawa*

The socialization of American children differs markedly from the way children are brought up in group-oriented cultures, where the child learns from his or her earliest years that one's identity is an extension of the group:

In the collectivist family children learn to take their bearings from others when it comes to opinions. "Personal opinions" do not exist: They are predetermined by the group. If a new issue comes up on which there is no established group opinion, some kind of family conference is necessary before an opinion can be given. A child who repeatedly voices opinions deviating from what is collectively felt is considered to have a bad character. In the individualist family, on the contrary, children are encouraged to develop opinions of their own, and a child who only ever reflects the opinions of others is considered to have weak character. The behavior corresponding with a desirable character depends on the cultural environment.[5]

Individualist Cultures	Group-Oriented Cultures
Self-worth is determined by achievement.	Self-worth is determined by group ascription.
The focus is on the task at hand.	The focus is on relationships.
Self-esteem is central.	Face is central.
A person is motivated by guilt.	A person is motivated by shame.
There is direct expression of ambition.	There is indirect expression of ambition.

People from group-oriented cultures act as representatives of an in-group. This in-group can be an extended family or a workplace group. This does not mean that people in these cultures are incapable of independent action. "Notions of machismo, power, and responsibility to family and kin can often drive the Latin [man] to what might be considered extreme, and sometimes inappropriate, assertive behavior."[6] However, unlike the American individualist, who uses assertive behavior to *separate* him- or herself from the group, the Latin's "individualist efforts are undertaken specifically to engender the positive attention of important others."[7]

The concept of professional identity differs markedly between Argentina and Japan. In Argentina, if you ask children what their father does for a living, they will say, "My father drives a truck," or, "My father is an accountant." In Japan, children tell you, "My father works for Sony," or, "My father works for Honda." But you will get no clear idea if their father is president of Sony or merely a chauffeur.

—*Hernan Roel*

THE ROLE OF THE INDIVIDUAL IN DECISION MAKING

Americans think of the individual as the principal actor in social and business transactions. This attitude is especially important in understanding how Americans relate to their jobs. For Western corporations, job description and scope of responsibility are constructed around the individual. Managerial strategies and career advancement are also focused on the individual. Responsibility is delegated to individuals, who are judged by their ability to shoulder the burden alone. Decision making is an individual enterprise—with those able to "make the big decisions" often rising to the top (or losing everything if they fail).

Most of the world's other cultures are more group oriented than is society in the United States. Identification with the group is encouraged throughout life in all social interactions. In many cultures in Asia, Latin America, and the Middle East, children live with their parents until they are married. In some Asian countries, the oldest son will continue living with the parents even after marriage. Consultations with the family or with business associates (to whom family-style loyalties are often transferred) are essential to the decision-making process. Businesses in collectivist cultures thus tend to place tasks, decision making, and even career advancement in a group context:

> With Japanese business organizations, the scope of the job assigned to each individual is not necessarily clearly defined. Work is not designed with the individual's job as the basic unit but is farmed out to each section, department, or other unit of workforce.
>
> As a result, under the Japanese system, priority is put on accomplishing the task assigned to the workforce rather than on the individual employee who is performing the job. This structural mechanism is surprisingly consistent with characteristic features of the Japanese attitude toward responsibility, namely the vagueness of individual responsibility, the idea of joint group responsibility, and the strong sense of responsibility toward the small, close group.[8]

Group orientation has a profound influence on management and negotiation strategies. The individual's actions are still important, but accountability takes place through the group rather than through a direct focus on the individual. According to Hofstede: "Management in an individualist society is management of individuals. . . . Management in collectivist societies is management of groups."[9]

All this does not mean that people in group-oriented cultures are unable to make decisions, or that they lack initiative and competitiveness. But these qualities are expressed *through the group*—which often makes them invisible to Americans, who are conditioned to see overt ambition and decisiveness as signs of individual competence and initiative.

Americans' emphasis on the individual as principal actor and decision maker often leads them into misunderstandings when they do business in group-oriented cultures. American executives, for instance, are conditioned to seek out the "real" decision maker in the other side's organization. In Japan, there may not be someone with final responsibility lurking behind the scenes: Decisions, though ultimately made at the top, are arrived at through consensus rather than made by a single individual. This situation is often confusing to Americans, who tend to think they are simply being deceived and that the real power structure is being hidden from them.

> In the face of unexpected demands, collectivists will wish to confer with those back home. Rarely does a single Japanese representative go to an important negotiation. Yet to Anglo-Saxons, a single representative voting on his or her private conscience on behalf of constituents is the foun-

INTERNATIONAL STYLES OF DECISION MAKING

Authoritative: Decisions are made from the top and passed down. Subordinates have little to say. Negotiators are constrained by the home office. (India, Brazil, France)

Authoritative/consensus: Decisions are made at the top but consensus is sought within the company at all levels. Negotiators confer with each other and with the home office frequently, resulting in a slow decision-making process. (Germany)

Consensus: Decisions are made collaboratively with focus on cooperation between individuals and teams. Negotiators confer frequently with each other and decisions are then communicated to higher-ups. (Japan, Holland, Scandinavia)

Authoritative/individualist: Broad policy decisions are made at the top, but responsibility for particular projects or areas is delegated to individuals who demonstrate willingness and ability to take them on. Individual negotiators are given broad authority to make decisions on their own. This style generally applies to larger corporations. (United States, Australia)

Consensus/individualist: In highly flexible, innovative, generally small companies driven by technology, decisions are made collaboratively but advanced by individual responsibility and innovation. (United States—Silicon Valley high tech)

dation stone of parliamentary democracy. To more collectivist cultures, those at the meetings are delegates, bound by the wishes of those who sent them.[10]

In Korea, decisions move through a series of levels from lower to higher. For instance, a person lower in the company gets a signature and a stamp or *dojang* from the next person in the corporate hierarchy. That person then goes to his superior for approval and so on—often up to the level of president. During the process the decision can be rejected by any level.

—*Yoon Tak Gwak*

Group-oriented approaches to business tend to try the patience of Americans, who think of the "decisiveness" of the individual in charge as one of the strengths of their way of doing business. This is not always the case, however. The decisions reached by consensus in Japan are often much easier to implement than those made by "decisive individuals" in American corporations—where agreements reached by overseas negotiators are sometimes undermined by managers or departments back home who have not been included in the decision-making process.

In recent years, American corporations have moved to incorporate more group-oriented management and decision-making practices. The evolving theory of teams, for instance, was borrowed—at least in its original form—from the Japanese. The results of this experiment are still uncertain, but it seems unlikely that American executives will ever be as group-oriented in their thinking as cultures where allegiance to the group is a central part of larger cultural values.

One of our most hotly debated issues this year was the color of our new logo. I liked red, but several executives worried that red is too aggressive, especially since we are already viewed as aggressive by our partners and customers. They suggested a more mellow color, like blue.

But I want us to continue being aggressive, and I want everybody here to understand that that's our philosophy. As long as there is consensus at the top about our basic vision, we are going to have agreement about every other issue. Those who don't feel comfortable with this vision shouldn't work here.

—*Michael J. Durham, chief executive officer, Sabre Inc.*[11]

My former boss at a publishing company used to make decisions "in the next 30 seconds." He would say, "We have to make a decision and move on!" It wasn't a question of knowing what we were talking about. If we couldn't figure out how to make everything fit within the budget, he would just cut a category: "We will have no supplies for this quarter!"

We pretended to go along with his decision but did our own thing, anyway. In the end his fast and wrong decisions eroded employees' confidence in him, and he eventually got fired.

—*Chan Suh, chief executive officer, Agency.com Inc.*[12]

DOING BUSINESS WITH GROUP-ORIENTED CULTURES

- Allow extra time for decision making and consultations.
- Remember the importance of giving and maintaining face.
- Introductions, establishing credentials, and relationship building are extremely important in group-oriented cultures.

AMERICANS VALUE GETTING THE JOB DONE OVER DEVELOPING RELATIONSHIPS

An American friend of mine told me the following story. When he was a child, there had been a great deal of tension between him and his father. At the age of 18 he was thrown out of the house by his father, and the two didn't speak for many years. When he was older, my friend tried to reestablish a relationship with his father, but when the two found themselves alone together they were uncomfortable and had little to say to each other. This situation continued until the father retired and decided to build a house in the mountains of Colorado. My friend took a summer off work and went to help him. As they worked together solving the various problems of building a house, the two became quite close. "We bonded in the American way," my friend jokes. "The only trouble is that now that the house is done we don't have anything to talk about anymore."

This story is typical of Americans' approach to others. They form relationships by doing things together. They have bowling partners or fishing buddies, friends from work, and friends from the PTA. This task-oriented approach to relationships extends to the workplace. Americans don't need to know each other to work together successfully on a project. American executives see relationships with other companies or individuals in terms of the task to be performed. When they first meet the other party about a proposed business venture, they are likely to start with a discussion of the precise phases of the project, what each party will be expected to contribute, what responsibilities each party will have, and how each party will benefit. Since the emphasis in American culture is on individual achievement and reward, accomplishment of tasks is a good measure of how successful a business relationship is. In a business transaction, if people are committed to the accomplishment of the task, then there's solid ground for them to interact and relate to each other.

Americans value their time highly, and they budget it. They always seem to be doing something. When I first came here from Spain, I would go days, sometimes even weeks, without seeing my friends. At first, this was hard to get used to. But then I realized something: It is not that people don't want to talk to you anymore or are not interested in your friendship. It's just that they are busy and assume that you are also, and they don't want to take your precious time.

—*Maria C. Garcia Garcia*

In American culture, "time is money." In traditional cultures, we could accurately say, "relationships are money." People need to feel comfortable in their relationship before they can turn their attention to specific tasks. This means recognizing people as individuals rather than treating them as extensions of the task at hand. In the tribal cultures of South Africa, for instance, establishing a relationship starts with a ritual recognition of the other person as a fellow human being:

> Recently, the Reverend Mvume Dandala of the Central Methodist Mission in Johannesburg opened his broadcast with the Zulu greeting "*Sanibonani*" ("*Sakubona*" in the singular). He explained that in literal translation it means "we see you." When Africans—in this case Zulus—meet someone, they begin by affirming that person's existence. The full sentence would be, "*Siyakubona ukuthi ungumuntu*"—"We see that you are a human being, as opposed to an unwelcome spirit."[13]

In Asia, Africa, Latin America, southern Europe, Russia, and the Middle East, it is considered essential to form a relationship before focusing on the specific task. People must feel that they like and trust the other side, at least in a preliminary way, before they can feel comfortable working together. Establishing a business relationship in these cultures includes a getting-to-know-you phase that can leave Americans confused or impatient. Instead of getting down to business, hours may be spent in rituals designed to "give face" or establish personal ties.

When I arrived in the United States from Brazil, my first job was in a travel agency. My manager insisted that we not spend more than five minutes on the phone with a client. "We must think sales," he would say to me. "Take the order and call back later." In my opinion, if you work

in sales you must spend a little more time trying to give good service instead of just thinking about the commission you'll make.
—Claudia McAchran

Although it may be frustrating, there are good reasons for this approach to doing business. Compared to Americans, group-oriented
cultures place more emphasis on the social context in which a project
takes place. Getting things done in these societies depends on a web
of relationships. Therefore, throughout their business lives people
cultivate and nourish these relationships, knowing they will come in
handy when needed. The time and effort spent maintaining this web
of relationships is not for mere enjoyment. It's a business necessity because a person is only as effective as the quality of his or her contacts
and relationships.

Figure 4.1 depicts the differences between task and relationship
orientations. In the West, with its well-defined legal system and standardized business practices, people are primarily concerned with the
task. They know that if things don't work out, they will be protected
by the legal system. In group-oriented cultures, people prefer to do
business with those they know or members of their clan. Until recently, the only contract in many cultures was a handshake or a bow.
(In the not-so-distant past, pulling a hair out of one's mustache was
the ultimate oath of honor in the Middle East.) Making sure the
other side is trustworthy—that the individual is also part of the web
of obligation and commitment—is the best insurance against a
breach of contract.

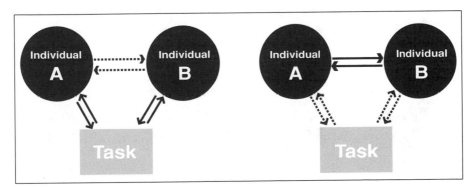

Figure 4.1　Task Orientation and Relationship Orientation

> ## BRIDGING THE GAP BETWEEN TASK AND RELATIONSHIP CULTURES
>
> - Take the time to form a relationship before getting started on the task at hand.
> - Schedule extra time for business meetings devoted to getting acquainted.
> - Remember the importance of social events in doing business in relationship cultures.

AMERICANS LIKE DIRECT COMPETITION

Americans are openly competitive—a fact that often irritates businesspeople from other cultures. American corporations encourage the open display of competitiveness and incorporate it as a central feature of both social and business interactions. American management theory assumes that different managers will be competing with each other and often sets up corporate structures to encourage this competition. The best way to get things done, from this perspective, is to let "survival of the fittest" determine who is strongest and best able to lead—a process euphemistically referred to by American companies as "discovering talent."

A GERMAN VIEW OF AMERICANS

American businesspeople have the reputation of being the toughest in the world, but they are, in many respects, the easiest to deal with. That is because their business philosophy is uncomplicated. Their aim is to make as much money as they can as quickly as they can, using hard work, speed, opportunism, and power. Their business decisions are not usually affected by sentiment but by the almighty dollar. This single-minded pursuit of profits results in their being seen as ruthless.

In business dealings, Americans show the following tendencies:

- They like to go it alone without checking with the head office. Anything goes unless it has been restricted. (In Germany, everything is prohibited unless it is permitted.)
- They become informal immediately, taking off their jackets, using first names, and discussing personal details.

- They give the impression of being naive by speaking only English and by offering trust and friendship too soon.
- They use humor even when the other side fails to understand or regards it as out of place.
- They put their cards on the table right at the start, then proceed on an offer, counteroffer basis.
- They have difficulty when the other side doesn't reveal what they want.
- They try to extract an oral agreement at the first meeting: "Have we got a deal?"
- They want to shake hands on it, even if the other side feels the matter is too complex to make an agreement on the spot.
- They don't like lulls or silence during the negotiations.
- They make up their minds in a hurry.
- They regard negotiations as problem solving through give-and-take based on each side's strengths. They do not appreciate that the other side may have only one position.

—Rene Zimmerli

This does not mean there is no competition in group-oriented cultures. The Japanese and the Chinese, for example, are extremely competitive in all aspects of business and life. For example, suicide is not uncommon among Japanese students who fail to make the grade. But competition in these cultures is expressed less directly. Students are not singled out for their individual accomplishments. Instead, group accountability is emphasized and group identification encouraged:

> In the collectivist classroom the virtues of harmony and maintenance of "face" reign supreme. Confrontations and conflicts should be avoided, or at least formulated so as not to hurt anyone; even students should not lose face if this can be avoided. Shaming, that is, invoking the group's honor, is an effective way of correcting offenders; they will be put in order by their in-group members. At all times the teacher is dealing with the student as part of an in-group, never as an isolated individual.[14]

The results for management practices in group-oriented cultures are evident. Rather than encouraging competition among individual managers, these cultures focus on group responsibility and group honor.

DEALING WITH COMPETITION IN GROUP-ORIENTED CULTURES

- Avoid self-promotion or outward displays of competitiveness.
- Don't put workers or managers from group-oriented cultures in a position where they must openly compete with each other.
- Avoid calling attention to individual members of a team—whether for praise or for blame. Direct praise and blame to the group.
- Blame is best conveyed indirectly rather than directly.

American Culture Values Equality over Hierarchy and Social Class

> *Americans . . . find it very confusing to shift from high to low status as the situation demands and . . . respond by a continuous endeavor to stabilize relationships. Their uneasiness often leads to an assertive attempt to either establish a superficially egalitarian ethos—as in the ritual use of first names for everyone, which is most disorienting to persons of many cultures—or else to attempt to establish hierarchies which are rigidly resistant to other considerations such as lineage and education.*
>
> —Margaret Mead[15]

American culture minimizes status differences and values equality over hierarchy and social class. Americans are proud of the egalitarian nature of their society and they tend to think it is a universal value. Even if they recognize that other cultures have social and institutional hierarchies, they tend to ignore them. They assume that all people will appreciate being treated as equals.

Asian, Middle Eastern, Latino, and European cultures are much more formal and hierarchical than American society is. In these cultures, titles and class position are very important. How you relate to other people is largely determined by these class relations. It would be inconceivable in France or Japan for the secretary to address the company president by his first name; in the United States it probably wouldn't even raise eyebrows. Americans abroad need to pay attention to the codes that regulate behavior between different classes or levels of status. Mingling with the workers or addressing the vice president of the company in a familiar way might be inappropriate or rude—even though it would be an expression of solidarity and teamwork in the United States:

> The managers of one American firm tried to export the "company picnic" idea into their Spanish subsidiary. On the day of the picnic, the U.S. executives turned up dressed as cooks and proceeded to serve the food to their Spanish employees. Far from creating a relaxed atmosphere, this merely embarrassed the Spanish workers. Instead of socializing with their superiors, the employees clung together uneasily and whenever an executive approached their table, everyone stood up.[16]

Their egalitarian ethos can cause problems when Americans set out to penetrate closed foreign markets. In U.S. culture, Americans are used to cold calling and doing business with strangers. The hierarchies and exclusiveness of foreign business cultures can be confusing (and even offensive) to those who are used to being treated on their merits.

In Mexico, decisions are usually made by one person. Mexican society and business are very hierarchical. Mexican businesspeople have a great respect for authority. The *patron* or boss does not accept much questioning. His managers are usually not delegated important decision-making authority. Even if they do have some authority, the boss has the final say.

—*Alan Ibarra*

In Spain, for instance, being well connected is essential for doing business successfully. Business contacts and relations take place through a system of *enchufismo*—a kind of Europeanized old boys' network. The problem for Americans is to find an initial entrance into this system. The person introducing you assumes an obligation to other members of the group by, in effect, promising that you are trustworthy. Once inside the system, you can have access to a whole network of contacts and connections. Without an initial connection, however, outsiders can find themselves talking to bureaucrats and underlings with no real power to help them.[17]

Equality-Oriented Cultures	Status-Oriented Cultures
Representatives are chosen for their perceived abilities.	Representatives are chosen by class, age, or family affiliation.
Informality and use of first names are the norm.	Formality and use of titles are the norm.
Privileges and status symbols are frowned on.	Privileges and status symbols for managers are expected and desirable.
Individual responsibility is important.	Respect for lines of authority is important.
Subordinates expect to be consulted.	Subordinates expect to be told what to do.
People are motivated by desire to demonstrate achievement and knowledge.	People are motivated by desire to defend status and privilege.
Authority is established by self-presentation.	Authority is established by introductions and credentials.
Decentralization is popular.	Centralization is popular.
People are warm on the surface.	People are cool on the surface.

SOURCE: Some of these attributes are based on and adapted from Geert Hofstede, *Cultures and Organizations: Software of the Mind*, New York: McGraw-Hill, 1991.

AMERICAN CULTURE IS FRIENDLY ON THE OUTSIDE

The informality of their culture may leave Americans unprepared for the standoffishness of many foreign people. In Asian or Middle Eastern cultures, strangers are less likely to acknowledge or talk to each other. If people haven't been formally introduced, they might feel no obligation to exchange pleasantries with one another. Because human relationships in these cultures entail a great deal of obligation, care, and concern, group-oriented people tend to avoid situations that might incur unwanted obligations. Therefore, although they are helpful and hospitable to foreign visitors, they tend to keep their guard up and it takes a longer time to establish close relationships.

The two circles in Figure 4.2 demonstrate the differences between American and Asian cultures in this regard. Americans' inner self or psyche is surrounded by a thin, easily penetrable outer perimeter but a heavily barricaded inner core. It is very easy to get to know Americans on a superficial basis, but the individualist core is very difficult to penetrate. There is always something at which they are protective, be it business or personal, and they will not make themselves vulnerable. Asians and other traditional cultures have a thick outer barrier but a fragile, less protected inner core. It is very difficult to penetrate the outer barrier. They use this outer shell as a way of deciding which people they will form a relationship with. Once the outer shell has been breached, however, there is little resistance in the center.

Many foreigners are deceived by the surface friendliness of Americans. They take the friendly smile of a classmate or the warm greeting of a coworker as invitations to a deeper friendship. They don't realize that this surface friendliness is often used by Americans as a way to keep people at a distance. Travelers from traditional cultures, in fact, often feel that despite their surface warmth Americans are actually cold or distant.

In traditional cultures, the structure is reversed. The thick outer barrier of traditional cultures is meant to keep strangers at a distance. But after the barrier has been broken through, group-oriented people are more open and vulnerable. This explains why people from traditional cultures may feel no obligation to deal fairly with people outside their group or clan. The feeling is, "If I don't know you I don't owe you." But after you have penetrated the heavy barrier there is a strong feeling of obligation and reciprocity.

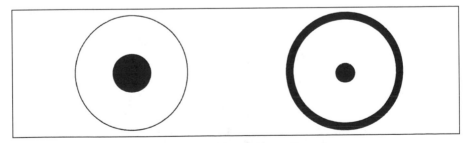

Figure 4.2 American and Asian Psychic Defense Structures

Source: Boy de Mente, Japanese Etiquette and Ethics in Business: A Penetrating Analysis of the morals and values that shape the Japanese business personality, 5th ed., Chicago: NTC Business Books, 1990, 16.

ADAPTING TO HIERARCHICAL CULTURES

- Dress and speak more formally than you would in the United States.
- Remember to use titles and to respect status distinctions.
- Act in accordance with your own titles and authority.
- Be careful with overtures to underlings.
- Don't be put off by the brusque outer shell of some foreigners.

Americans Prefer Objective Laws and Rules

In "The Tidy Secrets of Danish Freedom," the American humorist Garrison Keillor comments, "I come from a nation of jaywalkers. [Denmark] is a nation of people who wait for the green light to cross, even if it's 2 A.M. and the streets are deserted."[18]

Why do the Danes wait for the green light even if it's obvious there's no traffic and no police around to tell them not to walk? One good answer can be found in Fons Trompenaars's distinction between *universalist* and *particularist* cultures.[19] Universalist cultures emphasize rules and laws that apply to everyone equally, regardless of circumstances. Particularist cultures place more emphasis on personal relations and particular circumstances.

Denmark has a highly universalist culture. Rules are rules. The Danes feel obligated to obey the law, even if it doesn't apply precisely in a particular case. If you make an exception here, they reason, where will you draw the line? Particularists, on the other hand, notice the absence of traffic and walk across the street. They simply aren't worried—as the universalists are—that the whole system will collapse if someone makes an exception for the particular circumstances at hand.

Keillor's experience in Denmark can give Americans a feeling for the way much of the rest of the world views them. Although Keillor plays the particularist in this case, the United States is generally a universalist culture. Americans depend on the rule of law to guarantee that people are treated fairly. For Americans, justice is blind: The law should apply to everyone equally, and people feel an obligation to uphold the law, even if it conflicts with personal obligations. For universalists, applying the same rules and criteria to everyone ensures fairness.

Particularist cultures are less concerned with universal principles such as the law or abstract rules. In these cultures, fairness is situational and personal. Doing the right thing means taking account of the particular circumstances at hand and showing allegiance to one's friends and family. Particularists recognize rules and laws, but they are given less weight than they are in universalist cultures. If a law doesn't apply—or sometimes if it is just inconvenient—particularists tend to ignore it.

Trompenaars describes an experiment in which respondents are asked what they would do if they witnessed a friend hit a pedestrian while driving over the speed limit. Would it be right to tell the truth as the law requires or would it be more honorable to lie and defend one's friend? Those opting for the universalist response—telling the truth—range

Universalism	*Particularism*
Rules are important.	Relationships are important.
Contracts are immutable.	Contracts can change with circumstances.
Legal actions are used to settle disputes.	Mutual accommodation or intermediaries are used to settle disputes.
Established procedures are followed.	Established procedures are often ignored or subverted.
Allegiance is given to laws and abstract ethical principles.	Allegiance is given to people or groups.
What is right is absolute.	What is right depends on circumstances.
People appeal to rational, universal principles.	People appeal to interest and affiliation.
Treatment is given by merit.	Treatment is given by affiliation or special needs.
Business channels are formal.	Business channels, contacts, and intermediaries are informal.
All cases are treated the same.	Each case is judged separately.
People have faith in the system.	People are suspicious of the system.

from 26 percent in South Korea and 34 percent in Venezuela to 95 percent in the United States and 96 percent in Canada.[20] It is important to recognize here that the particularists also think of their response as moral: Isn't it right to stick by one's family and friends? Allegiance to one's friends and family is considered a virtue in our culture as well, but it has considerably more importance in particularist cultures and often overshadows the universalist framework of laws and rules.

Particularist cultures are generally suspicious of government power. What good are supposedly universal principles or the rule of law if their real function is to maintain the power of a corrupt elite? In such cases, personal relations and group solidarity are the only things people can count on to defend their interests. Being willing to stand by your friends is considered much more ethical than aligning oneself with a system of justice whose real purpose is to defend the interests of a few.

Trompenaars identifies four major areas where the split between universalism and particularism affects business relations: contracts, business trips, role of the head office, and job evaluation.

1. *The contract.* In universalist cultures such as those of the United States, Germany, and Northern Europe, contracts and lawyers are used to enforce agreements and make sure the other side does not renege. The best contract is one that foresees all possible contingencies and provides a stable framework which both sides can depend on for making future plans and operations. The sanctity of the contract—like the universal rule of law—guarantees that the system will operate in a dependable and fair way. Particularist cultures, on the other hand, pay less attention to detailed contracts. For them, a contract is simply an initial agreement on how a business relationship should be structured. As circumstances change, the contract should evolve to reflect those circumstances.

These differing views of what a contract represents are a source of enormous friction between universalist and particularist business cultures. American companies are horrified when the Chinese "go back on their word"—from the Americans' perspective, the Chinese have committed a breach of faith so their intentions from the beginning must have been devious. The Chinese, on the other hand, can't understand the Americans' refusal to look at the changing circumstances. For them, the Americans' inflexibility has violated the spirit of the relationship (which the contract merely formalizes).

Of course, the Chinese can sometimes use this fluidity to take advantage of others—both Americans and other Chinese. But for the Chinese, the problem with these breaches of faith is not the violation of the contract as much as the damage done to the spirit of the relationship and a company's reputation.

Our company won the bid to overhaul a Mexican company's large fishing boat. The boat had sunk in the Pacific Ocean, but was raised and towed to our shipyard in San Diego. The contract was negotiated between our sales representative, Chris, and their company's project manager, named John. The contract quoted new engines and electrical refitting for a certain price, and specified that other components and labor needed to refurbish the ship would be extra.

There were quite a few additional parts and repairs during the course of the overhaul. Unfortunately, we never received written change orders signed by John. Chris felt comfortable working with John, and trusted him to follow through on his word.

Before the overhaul was complete, however, Chris decided to retire and move back east. After we completed repairs, we sent an invoice to John for the original contract and the additional parts and labor. John responded that the invoice was too high and that the additional parts and labor were never authorized. We did not have a signed change order, and Chris was no longer there to defend our position.

Fortunately, we had filed for insurance with the Import-Export Bank of the United States on this customer. When we threatened to file a claim, the Mexican company decided we were right and paid the invoice. The point to be made is that relationships are important to promote and maintain business, but it is always wise to protect yourself to stay in business if relationships should fail.

—Ron Zeltman

---

2. *Business trips.* Particularism is closely tied to the importance of relationships in group-oriented cultures. Since the relationship is more important in these cultures, it is wise to develop personal ties in addition to arranging the details of the contract itself. This means allowing more time for getting-to-know-you meetings, social events, and other relationship-building activities. This doesn't mean you have to spend weeks making yourself a member of the family, but you do have to allow some additional time for good results. (See Chapter 7 for more on how to establish a relationship of trust quickly and effectively.)

3. *Role of the head office.* As companies go global, they necessarily become more universalist. Standardized procedures and policies are necessary for global companies to function effectively. The problem is that these universal policies are applied to the particular situations of different regional offices or subsidiaries—where things can be very different culturally and logistically. Particularist cultures tend to resist directives from the central office, while working to solidify the network of local customs and personal relationships in which they feel secure. Regional offices will sometimes fabricate a fictional front to satisfy the home office while continuing to operate according to their own local standards.

WHAT THE BOSS DOESN'T KNOW WON'T HURT HIM

When I started my career in pharmaceutical sales, I was assigned to cover the San Gabriel Valley in Southern California. My clients were physicians, pharmacists, and nurses from many different countries: Latinos; Vietnamese; Chinese from China, Taiwan, Hong Kong, and the United States; Japanese; Armenians; East Indians; blacks; and many others.

Pharmaceutical sales is different from other types of sales: It is almost entirely based on relationship building—with physicians and pharmacists but also with the nurses and staff who provide access and run the office. One of the biggest problems I faced was the cultural differences and expectations. It was not uncommon to go into a medical building and find physicians and staff from many different countries. Receptionists would often speak three dialects of Chinese (Cantonese, Mandarin, and Taiwanese), as well as Vietnamese, Cambodian, and Spanish.

I'm of Chinese descent (I speak fluent Chinese), but as a sales trainee I was taught American sales methods: (1) Be very aggressive. (2) Ask a lot of questions. (3) Close the sale. My sales manager at that time was Caucasian, born and raised in the Midwest. When he worked with me, he never took the time to understand the differences in cultures and what approach could result in the best sales long-term. He assessed my job performance based on what he was taught in sales training. In his view, I should have been more assertive in my sales presentation. The trouble was, when I used this technique I found that most of my foreign-born clients would not look directly at me and tended to give short answers to my questions. When I asked for their business, they would say yes, but later they would request additional clinical and technical information instead of placing an order. When I talked to the office managers about this, they told me I was too aggressive and that I was making the physicians uncomfortable.

Based on my knowledge of Asian culture, I devised my own guidelines for sales in my region:

- Avoid looking directly at the client.
- Present the products rather than myself.
- Explain how the products would help patients.
- Support my presentation with clinical data.
- Keep my voice low and offer a soft handshake (I am a woman, and this is expected in Asian cultures).
- Build a good relationship with the office manager (often the physician's or pharmacist's wife).

The problem was that my manager would periodically accompany me into the field to observe and critique my performance. I tried to explain to him that his techniques would not work with people from these cultures. In the end, I started apologizing in advance to my clients and explaining that I had to behave this way when my manager was with me. The physicians laughed and enjoyed playing along with the game, and I was able to return to my normal relations after the manager left.

What worked in this case was the opposite of what management wanted me to do. By not being sensitive to the needs of the customer, I'm sure the company missed out on a lot of business in other sales areas.

—Susana Lee

---

4. *Job evaluation.* Universalist cultures seek objective ways to evaluate job performance and related promotions and pay increases. The fairest way to evaluate an employee's performance, in this view, is to have impersonal standards that apply to everyone. This prevents favoritism and nepotism and helps maintain the merit system: Employees get what they deserve based on concrete achievements. In multinational companies, this system can cause conflicts. In cultures where the boss is supposed to be a benevolent autocrat, personal relations and specific circumstances are just as important as abstract evaluation criteria.

Suppose a member of an employee's family becomes seriously ill and he or she has to take time off work to deal with the situation. As a result, job performance is negatively affected. Using the objective standards of the universalist system, it would be inappropriate to take these special circumstances into account. It might be hard on that particular person, but to make an exception would threaten the stability and fairness of the entire system. In a particularist culture, however, it would be perfectly appropriate to take the particular circumstances into account. In fact, the boss's paternalistic role would almost require that he (or she) do something to help out an employee in his or her time of need. The employee's job performance might be off for that year, but there are reasons—and the family has even more need of the extra income. The company bonus for the year might be awarded despite a poor performance—an action that would seem normal and appropriate in a particularist culture but which might cause howls of protest in a universalist environment.

CONFUCIAN DYNAMISM: TRUTH VERSUS VIRTUE

> *If one should love one's enemies, what would remain for one's friends?*
>
> —Confucius[21]

In *Cultures and Organizations*, Geert Hofstede recounts the experience of Dr. Rajendra Pradhan, a Nepalese anthropologist who did a field research project in a Dutch village during the 1980s.[22] As part of his project, Dr. Pradhan spent a good deal of his time attending church with the "natives." After services, he was often invited to people's homes where the topic of conversation centered, naturally enough, on religion. According to Hofstede, "His Dutch hosts always wanted to know what he *believed*—an exotic question to which he did not always have a direct answer. 'Everybody over here talks about believing, believing, believing,' [Dr. Pradhan] said, bewildered. 'Where I come from, what counts is the ritual, in which only the priest and the head of the family participate.' "[23]

Dr. Pradhan's bewilderment at the Dutch preoccupation with belief led Hofstede to ask himself: If the question of belief is not a central value in Asian cultures, what is? Hofstede found an answer in the work of Michael Bond, a Canadian who lived and worked for many years in the Far East. Bond was worried about the way in which Western anthropologists studied Eastern cultures. If Westerners design their inquiries to look for Western values (such as belief in abstract religious truths), perhaps they are missing the values that are really important in Eastern cultures. To overcome this problem, Bond asked a group of Eastern researchers to assemble a set of questions about central Eastern values. What he found was a complex of values that revolved around the Confucian concept of *virtue*—a concept which Bond found to be equal in importance to the Western emphasis on *truth*.

The Dutch villagers studied by Dr. Pradhan, for instance, were preoccupied with belief in the universal and transcendental truths of Christianity. These truths stand outside the changing world of day-to-

day life and demand allegiance even when they are not socially or personally useful. The Confucian concept of virtue, by contrast, centers
on how to organize a harmonious society in a constantly changing
world. There is no universal truth guaranteed by an all-powerful God.
Confucianism is not a religion but a social philosophy based on the experience of its founder, who lived in a turbulent period of Chinese history dominated by competing warlords and rapidly shifting political
realities. His philosophy focuses on the pragmatic problems of attaining a stable social order in this life rather than sacrificing oneself in
the service of a religious truth that promises a reward in the hereafter.

Hofstede enumerates four central features of the Confucian concept
of virtue:

1. *The stability of society is based on unequal relationships between people.*
For Confucius, society functions best when people respect mutual and
complementary obligations, such as those between father and son, husband and wife, or senior friend and junior friend. Confucianism, that is,
focuses on the actual power differences that occur in the real world
rather than the theoretical equality under the law that dominates Western thinking. Westerners can recognize these Confucian relationships,
but they tend to subordinate them to the universal principle of equality.

2. *The family is the prototype of all social organization.* Confucian cultures are group-oriented. A person is first and foremost a member of a
family and a social order that reflects this basic organization. Harmony
within the family or social order is more important than individual
rights or freedoms. The Chinese approach to human rights and its frequent conflicts with the West reflect this preference for social harmony
over individual liberty.

3. *Virtuous behavior toward others consists of not treating others as one
would not like to be treated oneself.* This curious inversion of the Christians' Golden Rule is based on subtly different principles. The Christian
injunction to love your neighbor as yourself makes all people essentially
equal (we are all equal in God's love). The Confucian version implies
that people should be basically good to each other, but they are not necessarily to be treated equally. The Confucian rule would prevent a
prince from beating a commoner, but it would not imply that the commoner and the prince were equals.

4. *Virtue with regard to one's tasks in life consists of trying to acquire
skills and education, working hard, not spending more than necessary, being
patient, and persevering.* The difference between this outlook and the
Christian ethos is striking. The Western world can recognize these

virtues, but they are subordinate to the imperative to avoid sin and obey God's laws—regardless of the social or personal consequences. The Christian saint doesn't hesitate to create social turmoil if it is in the interests of divine truth—an attitude that is even more pronounced in Islamic fundamentalism. The Confucian concept of virtue, by contrast, focuses on working hard to acquire the skills that will help the individual to live successfully and harmoniously in an unstable and constantly changing world. There is no reference to a higher power or a universal truth. It would be impossible to imagine a Confucian Abraham sacrificing his son to prove his obedience to an all-powerful God; there would have to be some compelling reason in the here and now— social order or the well-being of the family—to justify such a sacrifice.

This pragmatism is also reflected in the other major Asian religion— Buddhism. One of the Buddha's most famous injunctions for dealing with life in this world was, "Avoid error." Unlike Christianity, Judaism, and Islam, the Buddhist formulation does not impose a law—it simply gives advice to help one get through the confusing intricacies of the world. Ignoring the Buddha's advice is likely to lead to increased suffering in this world, but disobedience is not grounds for punishment. The Christian form of the Buddha's injunction would be, "Do not commit error." For the Christian, violating the law is a sin in and of itself, and the perpetrator is liable to be punished in this life and the next.

Americans Are Direct in Communication

Tell the door so the wall can hear it.

—Persian proverb

In our culture we say, "Don't beat around the bush." Honesty in expressing one's feelings is valued and we "tell it like it is." When Americans have a problem they like to go straight to the source and get a straight answer. Americans admire people who speak their minds, even when this involves disagreeing with a superior. American schools train their students to question what they are told and to express their own opinions openly. And while American employees may be adept at playing the game, speaking one's mind is generally considered a virtue in American corporate culture.

In Asian, Middle Eastern, and Latin American cultures, people are more indirect in expressing themselves, especially when it concerns matters that reflect on specific individuals. Because business relations in these countries are intensely personal and based on human feelings, the expression of opinions or judgments that might offend others is carefully guarded. People routinely hide their true feelings in order not to offend.

Issues are often approached in a circular fashion, and direct "no" answers are rarely given. Rather than communicating information directly, these cultures rely on indirect or contextual cues to transmit much of the message. In order to communicate successfully in these cultures, careful attention must be paid to seemingly ambiguous words and gestures. Differences of opinion, negative evaluations, or refusals are usually delivered indirectly—a form of expression that sometimes leads to confusion for Americans.

These cultures rarely deliver bad news directly. They may deliver the message by means of an intermediary, or they may convey the message indirectly by saying, "It is very difficult," or, "Maybe." Bad news is delivered piecemeal and indirectly until one gets the picture. In the Middle East, if a relative you are fond of dies, the first call from your family tells you that the person is not feeling so well; the next call lets you know that the fever is worse; another call lets you know that the patient's condition is very grave. By this time, it's safe to assume that the relative is gone.

I once asked a high-level Malaysian official who had been involved in negotiations with many American companies what he thought was the biggest communications mistake made by Americans. His answer was that in his view the up-front and direct "no" that Americans often give during negotiations frequently causes an irreparable loss of face for one of the parties—an effect of which the Americans are usually completely unaware.

To Americans, this tendency to conceal one's true feelings can seem dishonest or hypocritical. In other cultures, it is more likely associated with tact and courtesy. The Japanese word *tatemae*, for instance, refers to the "surface communication" that maintains harmony and prevents relationships from deteriorating. The practice is similar to when Americans say, "We should have lunch sometime!"—without any intention of carrying through—or when we compliment someone on an outfit even though our true feelings are the reverse.

While open conflict and airing of differences is acceptable in the United States, open discussion of differences might irreparably damage a relationship in traditional cultures. People habitually suppress their individual feelings and opinions to conform to the group. Sometimes this deference to group opinion is hard to spot. In the Middle East, Latin America, or Russia, there is often a great display of emotions, loud discussions, and heated exchanges. These fireworks, however, are usually expressions of passion more than candor.

   While Americans are a lot more direct than Asians, Middle Easterners, and Latinos, they are not as direct as Germans and Scandinavians. I remember returning from a grueling business trip with an associate from Sweden. Although I preferred to close my eyes and relax for the duration of the plane ride, I felt it was polite to chitchat a bit. As I tried to say a few words he turned to me very seriously and said, "I am very tired and don't wish to talk to you for the duration of the trip." Although I felt the same way, I didn't find his honesty very pleasant.

HIGHCONTEXT AND LOWCONTEXT CULTURES

Anthropologists define cultures that depend on indirect communication as high-context cultures. In low-context cultures such as the United States, Germany, or Australia, stress is placed on saying exactly what you mean; the best communication is one in which the meaning of a message is conveyed by the words themselves. If you took a transcription of the words and gave them to someone who was not familiar with the situation, that person could understand what was going on. The meaning is in the words themselves.

   In high-context cultures, on the other hand, the words can be interpreted only by understanding the social, political, or personal context of the situation. High-context cultures also tend to rely more on nonverbal cues such as facial expressions or body language. Verbal skills are generally less important in these cultures. As Edward C. Steward and Milton J. Bennett comment: "Japanese leaders are not required to have highly developed rhetorical skills and may even be distrusted for too much verbal facility."[24]

MOVING FROM DIRECT TO INDIRECT COMMUNICATION

- Be more discreet about expressing your feelings and opinions.
- Don't be paranoid, but be prepared to read between the lines.
- Don't deliver a direct "no"—especially to a single individual. Using an intermediary or an indirect way of expressing refusal is preferred.
- Remember that "It may be difficult" or "We will try our best" may actually be tactful ways of refusing rather than heroic promises to do the impossible.

The American Concept of Time

If you wait long enough, even an egg will walk.
—Ethiopian proverb

You can only be a good egg for so long. After that, you have to either hatch or become rotten.
—American proverb

The pace of American business is fast, busy, and driving. We want to get things out of the way as quickly as possible. Efficiency and speed are equated. We are more comfortable with brief introductions and forms of social address. Contemplation or rumination before action isn't encouraged. We say, "When in doubt, do *something*."

American executives are under pressure from management to produce tangible results in clearly specified time frames. This can cause problems for executives traveling abroad. When Americans go to China on business trips, their Chinese hosts invite them to banquets and give long speeches in flowery language about future cooperation. But the Americans need to show their management what they are accomplishing during their time overseas. A long list of banquets and *qumpai* (bottoms up) is not a very satisfactory result in the eyes of bottom line–oriented upper management in the home office.

When I came to Los Angeles as a representative to McDonnell Douglas from Construcciones Aeronaúticas—a Spanish aerospace company—I realized there were ongoing communications problems. Both sides had been blaming the other. The root of the problem was two different senses of time. American businesses require answers to inquiries or requests in a very short time. In Europe, the response time is much longer. In order to help resolve this problem and improve our company's relations with McDonnell Douglas, I started to put pressure on management in my home office in Spain to respond more quickly. At first, this pressure was not well understood by different departments in my home office, but after about a year and half I was able to convince them of the importance of speed to be successful with McDonnell Douglas. Because of the time difference of nine hours, this often meant working almost 24 hours a day, but eventually we were able to improve communications and win additional contracts for our company.

—Victor M. de la Vela

In group-oriented cultures, relationships are the oil that lubricates the wheels of business. Connecting to the right relationship is more important than strict schedules. This makes people more flexible with time arrangements. Sensitivity to relationships makes interruptions more likely and focusing precisely on the task at hand less important. For example, people in Latin America or the Middle East often do not think of time and causality in the linear way that dominates American or German thinking. Events have a multiplicity of causes and individual responsibility is not as easy to determine.

MONOCHRONIC AND POLYCHRONIC CULTURES

Anthropologist Edward Hall coined the term "polychronic" for cultures that juggle many tasks at the same time and "monochronic" for those that organize single tasks into linear sequences.[25] Asian, Latino, Middle Eastern, Russian, and Southern European cultures are generally polychronic in their outlook, while Northern Europeans, Americans, Australians, and Canadians are more monochronic. Because American culture emphasizes individual achievement and a linear, rationalist approach to problem solving, the sequential allocation of time to discrete tasks seems like the natural way to get things done. Each individual becomes responsible for a sequence of events leading to a specified conclusion.

MONOCHRONIC AND POLYCHRONIC BUSINESS CULTURES

Monochronic	Polychronic
Linear planning sequences are used to reach goals.	Flexible implementation is used to reach goals.
Meetings follow an agenda and end on time.	Meetings are open and often spill over into socializing.
Relationships are subordinated to schedules.	Schedules are subordinated to relationships.
Polychronic businesspeople are seen as scattered and disorganized.	Monochronic businesspeople are seen as cold and rigid.

Monochronic cultures tend to see polychronic organizations as disorganized and scatterbrained, and their own style as organized and focused. It might be more accurate, however, to see polychronic cultures as an early model for the multitasking and decentralized team-oriented approaches that characterize the new management science.

Most gringos think that "Mañana" means, "I'll do it tomorrow." Not true. "Mañana" means, "I know this went wrong, but don't worry, I'll get it right tomorrow." The myth that Mexicans are lazy is just that. Mexican employees in our offices work far harder than their U.S. counterparts. Many days, they go for 12 hours without complaining.
—Eric Lesin

Polychronic cultures tend to see the monochronic style as heartless, mechanical, and money oriented. In our culture, time management experts advise managers to reduce office chitchat and give tips on how to cut people short. In Asian, Latin American, or Middle Eastern cultures, the time saved by cutting short an associate and being coldly focused on the task is likely to incur bigger costs down the road.

Mexican companies do not feel internal pressure to comply with time-related promises. You will almost certainly have to allow extra time for any deliveries or appointments. It may be vexing, but your time may not appear to be valued by Mexicans who supply services or meet with you as customers or partners.
—Eric Lesin

WORKING IN POLYCHRONIC CULTURES

- Allot extra time for relationship building and the other side's decision-making process.
- Pay attention to people as well as tasks.
- Use time to network and multitask.
- Recognize the role of tradition in the decision-making process.

PAST, PRESENT, OR FUTURE ORIENTATION

Another important dimension of differing attitudes toward time is whether a culture is past or future oriented. Americans are oriented to the present and near-term future rather than the past. Their approach to problem solving causes them to envision concrete sequences of events leading to a different (and better) state of affairs. For Americans, having a *plan* to change things is very important. Latin American and Middle Eastern cultures are generally more oriented to the past and the present, while Asian cultures are both past- and future-oriented; but in all these cultures change does not necessarily mean progress, and when change comes it generally comes slowly.

A Spanish friend of mine who had spent most of his life living in Canada went to São Paolo, Brazil, and opened a small clothing store. It took him quite awhile to adjust to doing business in Brazil, however. He had to get used to the fact that Brazilian stores close for lunch, most holidays, soccer matches, and after 6:00 P.M. But his biggest surprises came in managing his workers. They would leave at 11:30 for lunch and not return till 1:30. They were very relaxed and easygoing about workplace rules.

—*Airton Rossatto*

This does not mean that traditional cultures can't plan for the future. The Japanese often have business plans that extend 30 years or more into the future. They tend to see the future in terms of historical context and thus cast plans in terms of long-term historical trends or goals. Americans' sense of the future is much more immediate; looking more than a year or two into the future is rare. A good way to look at this difference is to liken it to the chess matches between Gary Kasparov and IBM's Big Blue computer. Kasparov looks at the overall plan of the board and thinks of the game in terms of long-term strategies. Big Blue calculates every possible move in a linear sequence. It can only look six or seven moves into the future—but it's a formidable opponent.

American attitudes toward time may be partly responsible for the high pace of innovation in this country. Americans do not feel constrained by the past, and they tend to think of innovation as a good thing in itself. Their "just do it" attitude encourages people to jump in

PAST- AND FUTURE-ORIENTED BUSINESS CULTURES

Past-Oriented	Future-Oriented
Relations are constrained by tradition and history.	Relations are viewed in terms of future possibilities.
Care is taken in implementing change.	Change is the essence of business.
Long-term planning is emphasized.	Short-term, bottom-line planning is emphasized.

feet first and take risks that would be difficult in a traditional culture. Of course, this attitude can lead to disaster when things don't work out, but for Americans a few business failures here and there are the sign of a vibrant economy.

To Russians, with their agricultural heritage, time is like the seasons—a time for sowing and a time for reaping, and a time for doing little in between. Communism reinforced this native disrespect for time because workers could not be fired, and there was no incentive to do anything on time. Russians are still notoriously not on time, but they don't consider themselves late, either. Patience, not punctuality, is a virtue in Russia. You should be punctual, but don't be surprised if the Russians are not. It is not unusual for Russians to be one or two hours late for an appointment.

—Janna Bronechter

Today, things are changing on both sides. Many foreign companies are adopting American production and problem-solving techniques as a way to improve efficiency. American-style punctuality for meetings and the assignment of discrete tasks with formal deadlines are becoming more common. On the other hand, Americans have found that sometimes slow is better than quick in the long term. American managers are learning to focus on personal relations and team dynamics instead of concentrating exclusively on accomplishing specified tasks.

And they increasingly recognize the value of devoting time to cultivating relationships.

THE RHYTHM OF BUSINESS

Perceptions of time are rooted in the natural rhythms of a country's national life. There are always bad times to negotiate in certain countries. Many European countries are basically closed for business during the month of August. Avoid Ramadan in Islamic countries and Carnival in Brazil. There may often be unofficial holidays to take into account. If an opposition political party has just called a general strike to protest the austerity programs imposed by the International Monetary Fund (IMF), it's probably not the best time to arrive with the name tag of a major American financial corporation on your suit jacket pocket.

A ROUNDTABLE ON TIME

This discussion took place during one of my classes on international business relations conducted at the University of California, Irvine. The participants are from the countries indicated.

Turkey: Punctuality is important, but things come up. Being late is not such a big deal, especially if there are only Turks at the meeting. Important people come late.

Thailand: Being late is okay: In Bangkok you just blame it on the traffic. People are usually late.

Italy: Everyone is *really* late.

Germany: Everyone has to be on time. In Germany, things are too organized for anyone to be late. I once arrived to work at 7:31 A.M. (one minute after work started) and was reprimanded for being late.

Sweden: Get there 15 minutes early and drive around the block to ensure you will arrive on time.

Saudi Arabia: Time is important. People try to be on time, though they don't always make it. If Americans are present, there is more sensitivity to time.

Colombia: It's fine to be a little late. If you're really late, you should call first.

Japanese businesspeople always take time at the beginning of discussions to exchange business cards, show the company brochure, and explain about their company. American businesspeople will often skip the exchange of cards and begin with specific business discussions; then, if both parties are interested, they exchange cards and give information about their companies. Americans say yes or no directly to proposals, while the Japanese usually do not state their opinions clearly. These vague answers often create confusion for Americans, who are not sure whether the Japanese are really interested in their proposals.

—Mariko Takenoshita

Responses and attitudes toward time vary widely from country to country. As business cultures around the world become more internationalized, however, these attitudes toward time are starting to converge. Americans should be sensitive to different attitudes toward time, but they shouldn't try to imitate what they perceive as the habits of the country they are in. Being two hours late for a meeting just because the locals do it is likely to insult their sensibilities—especially if it becomes clear that this is how you view their culture.

Table 4.1 provides a schematic outline of key differences in various cultures. It addresses the way people in these cultures approach categories such as time, space, status, and decision making.

Table 4.1 Personality/Cultural Standards by Country

	United States	France	Germany	Spain
Time	Time is scheduled and compartmentalized. People concentrate on one thing at a time. Time commitments are taken seriously. People want quick answers and quick solutions. People are future oriented; short-term planning is the norm.	Living with style and elegance (*savoir vivre*) is more important than abstract schedules or deadlines. Dealing with multiple issues is normal. Advance planning is minimal.	Punctuality and order are extremely important for Germans. Always be on time. Long-term planning and detailed schedules are the norm.	Attitude toward time is very relaxed. Counterpart may keep you waiting. Culture is present-oriented with importance placed on family and living. Dealing with multiple issues is the norm.
Space	Space utilization is generous. People value privacy. Personal interaction space is larger than that of Latins, slightly smaller than Asians'. Physical contact is restrained.	Space utilization is economical (smaller cars, apartments, and streets than Americans'). Physical interaction space is close. Physical contact and intense eye contact are frequent.	Personal space and home life are off limits. Office doors are kept closed; knock first. Space is highly organized. Direct eye contact, little physical contact, and no smiling are the norm in business interactions.	Home and business life often intermingle. Space utilization is economical (smaller cars, apartments, and streets than those of Americans). Close personal space, and frequent physical contact, facial expressions, and eye contact are the norm.
Equality/Hierarchy	All people are equal in principle. Informality is valued. People are uncomfortable with class or status distinctions. Use of first names is frequent.	People are equal in principle but divided by class and status in reality. Intellectual prestige and aristocratic lineage count more than money. Use of titles and formality is the norm.	Power is important in German business. Formal communication and use of titles are the norm. Informality is verboten. Intellectual prestige and aristocratic lineage are very important.	Society is hierarchical, with strong class barriers. Dress and communication are formal (but friendlier and much warmer than those of Germans). Intellectual prestige and aristocratic lineage are important.
Individual/Group Orientation	Culture is highly individualistic. People are motivated by individual achievement and advancement. Self esteem is central. Overt expression of ambition is common.	Individualism is highly valued—but so is loyalty to family, in-group, and company. Individual asserts him/herself through verbal proficiency and logical argument. Self-esteem is central.	Individualism is valued. Germans are team players but concerned to establish individual authority and power. Individual competence and mastery of issues are extremely important.	Individualism is important, but so is loyalty to family, in-group, and company. Asserting personal power is important—especially for men.

Establishing Trust	There is little personal loyalty in business dealings. People are accepted on how well they sell themselves. What people can do is more important than whom they know.	Loyalty is important. People are judged by how well they argue their case, but also by credentials and status. Whom you know is important.	Past performance is important. Perceived authority and credentials are essential. Dependability and long-term commitment are necessary to gain trust.	Perceived authority and credentials are essential. The *enfuschismo* system—having important people vouch for you—is an important part of doing business in Spain.
Communication and Persuasion	Communication is direct. "Telling it like it is" is valued. Indirect messages or nonverbal cues are often missed. Logical, bottom-line arguments are valued.	Communication is direct, but nuance and context are also important. Logical argument is important. Establishing general principles is more important than arguing from specifics.	Communication is more blunt than in the United States. Logical argument *and* mastery of details are necessary. Nonverbal or contextual cues are rarely used.	Indirect communication with much unstated contextual knowledge is the norm. Emotions are an important part of a successful argument. Direct confrontation is to be avoided.
Decision Making	Decisions are made quickly. Decisions are made by individuals who take responsibility. There is little group consultation. People are uncomfortable with delayed decisions.	Decision making is hierarchical. Communication between different corporate levels is poor. Identifying real decision makers is important.	Consensus decision-making is often slow and laborious. German business is compartmentalized, with poor communication between units. Decisions are firm; changes are disliked.	Top-down, highly centralized decision making. Lower-level employees have little input.
Forms of Agreement	A deal is a deal. Legal contracts are important. People are uncomfortable with renegotiations. Lawyers are often present at negotiations.	Only written agreements are binding. Agreements should be carefully reviewed. Verbal agreements can be changed without notice.	An initial verbal agreement may be given, but final agreement is in writing with all details worked out.	Written contracts are the norm, but there is also an unspoken understanding to cooperate in changing circumstances. Contracts are less detailed and more subject to change than American contracts.
Gender Issues	Women hold positions of responsibility and authority in business. There are legal protections against sexual harassment.	Few women are in top management positions. There are fewer legal protections against sexual harassment. Romance is an art form for the French; courtship in the workplace is accepted.	German women have less status in the business world than American women. Because of their culture, German women are often seen as forceful and authoritarian in other cultures.	Women have little power in the Spanish business world. Catalonia has more women executives than Madrid. American women need to take care to establish their authority.

(continued)

73

Table 4.1 (Continued)

	Japan	China	Korea	Brazil
Time	Punctuality is important. Business time and social time overlap. Long-term planning is important. More time is allotted for negotiations, meetings, and planning than is done by Americans.	Past (respect for tradition) and future (building the new China) are important. Dealing with multiple issues is normal. More time is allotted for negotiations, meetings, and planning than is done by Americans.	Punctuality is important. Respect for traditions and long-term planning are the norm. More time is allotted for negotiations, meetings, and planning than is done by Americans.	Attitude toward time is very relaxed. Dealing with multiple issues is the norm. Culture is very present-oriented with importance placed on family and living. Meetings and negotiations take longer than in the United States.
Space	Space utilization is economical (smaller cars, apartments, and streets than those of Americans). Personal space between speakers is large. No touching and very limited eye contact are the norm.	Space utilization is economical (smaller cars, apartments, and streets than those of Americans). Personal space between speakers is large. Avoid touching head or shoulders; have limited eye contact.	Space utilization is economical (smaller cars, apartments, and streets than those of Americans). Personal space between speakers is large. Avoid physical contact; have limited eye contact.	Personal space between speakers is intimate. Physical and eye contact is frequent. Space utilization is more generous than in European countries.
Equality/Hierarchy	Status and hierarchy are important. Age is an important indicator of status. Dress and communication are formal (use of titles and deference to authority are mandatory).	Status and hierarchy are important. Age is an important indicator of status. Real decision maker is often difficult to identify. Dress and communication are formal.	Status and hierarchy are important. Age is an important indicator of status. Dress and communication are formal. Intellectual prestige and family position are important.	Brazil is hierarchical—but informality after introductory period is the norm. Intellectual prestige and family connection are important.
Individual/Group Orientation	Culture is very group-oriented. Loyalty to company and office in-group is important. Overt expression of individual ambition is frowned on. Face rather than self-esteem is central.	Culture is group-oriented. Loyalty to in-group and family is important. Expression of individual ambition is frowned on politically but accepted socially. Face rather than self-esteem is central.	Culture is group-oriented. Loyalty to company, in-group, and family is important. Overt expression of ambition is frowned on, but self-interest is higher than for other Asians. Face rather than self-esteem is central.	Group-oriented culture combines with frontier individualism. In business, competition among individuals is common. Ambition is a recognized value.

Establishing Trust	Perceived authority, credentials, and background are central. References from powerful people increase credibility. Overt self-promotion is frowned on.	Perceived authority, credentials, and background are central. References from powerful people increase credibility. Overt self-promotion is frowned on.	Perceived authority, credentials, past performance, and background are central. References from powerful people increase credibility. Long-term commitments are valued.	Trust is built slowly. Perceived authority, credentials, background, and past performance count. References from powerful people increase credibility.
Communication and Persuasion	Indirect communication with much unstated contextual knowledge is the norm. Emotions are not expressed, but decisions are made by intuition as much as reason. Avoid open confrontation or a direct "no."	Indirect communication with much unstated contextual knowledge is the norm. Emotions are not expressed, but decisions are made by intuition as much as reason. Avoid open confrontation or a direct "no."	Indirect communication with much unstated contextual knowledge is the norm. Emotions are not expressed, but decisions are made by intuition as much as reason. Avoid open confrontation or a direct "no."	Indirect communication with much unstated contextual knowledge is the norm. Emotions are more important than logic in making your case; Brazilians are passionate in expressing themselves.
Decision Making	Consensus decision making (*ringi seido*) within top-down power structure is the norm. Details and long-term planning are important. Decision-making process is long.	Consensus on the surface but authoritarian behind the scenes is the norm. Long-term planning is important, but flexible response to rapid change is necessary. Decision-making process is long.	*Culture is paternalistic and autocratic*, though consultation with departments and planning bodies is frequent. Long-term planning is important. Decision-making process is long.	*Bureaucratic and hierarchical decision making is the norm.* Decision-making process is long. Brazilians like time to bargain and shop around.
Forms of Agreement	Written agreements, leaving room for flexibility as circumstances change. Intermediaries rather than lawyers are used to resolve disputes.	Written agreements are left vague to account for changing circumstances. Cooperation and mutual aid rather than lawyers are expected to resolve disputes. Changing contracts is accepted.	Written agreements are the norm; room for flexibility is left—but changing contracts is not as frequent as with the Chinese. Intermediaries rather than lawyers are frequently used to resolve disputes.	In small and medium-size businesses, verbal agreements are frequent, but a written agreement is a good idea. Lawyers are used to resolve disputes and work out details of agreements.
Gender Issues	Women have little power in upper Japanese management, but this situation is changing. Women should take care to establish credentials and lines of authority.	Despite communism, China is patriarchal. Taiwanese women are often important players behind the scenes. Women should take care to establish credentials and lines of authority.	Few women are in high positions of power, but Koreans accept women executives. Women should take care to establish credentials and lines of authority.	Brazil is patriarchal, but women have more power and prestige than in other Latin American countries. Women should take care to establish credentials and lines of authority.

CHAPTER 5

The Social Setting of International Business

As we saw earlier, people are usually willing to forgive mistakes in simple matters of etiquette and form, especially when they understand that the behavior is due to cultural differences. The trouble is, the rituals and customs in the outer layers of culture represent or express deep cultural values (Figure 5.1). The Japanese bow is a ritual form, but it is also the concrete expression of deep beliefs about deference to authority, humility, and the individual's obligation to sacrifice his or her own ego in the interests of social harmony. The Japanese recognize that Westerners can't master all the nuances of this ceremony. They may even get irritated with clumsy attempts to imitate it. But they respond defensively without thinking to Westerners who violate the *spirit* of the bow.

Consider the case of an American executive who comes into a meeting and first shakes hands warmly with a Japanese engineer he's been working with before greeting the Japanese CEO, whom he doesn't know, with an awkward bow. The Japanese are likely to react very negatively to this behavior—not because the bow was awkward but because the executive didn't recognize the importance of the greeting in establishing

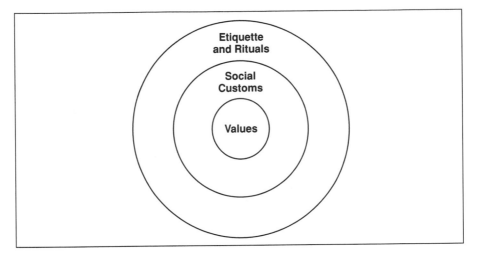

Figure 5.1 Layers of Culture

and maintaining social hierarchies. The handshake given first to the engineer implicitly placed him above the CEO, thus putting both the CEO and the engineer in an awkward position.

So do social forms matter or don't they?

The answer is: They do and they don't. They don't matter that much as mechanical rituals, but they matter very much as vehicles for expressing deeper attitudes, values, and beliefs, such as the ones we discussed in the previous chapter.

In Russia, food is considered a trivial topic. No Russian would bring up the topic during a meeting with foreigners, especially if there are important problems on the agenda. Russians are concerned to appear serious. They stick to art, literature, and politics when they make small talk.

Americans, by contrast, stick with easy topics that involve as many people as possible. When I first came to the United States, I was amazed to find that people immediately started talking about new food products, good deals on food in restaurants, or tips for healthy, easy-to-cook meals at home. I was even more amazed to find that they use lunches or dinners as motivational tools to market company products or create an amiable office environment.

—*Marina Volobueva*

For business travelers, the social environment can be broken down into two categories:

1. On the surface, as Figure 5.1 shows, are etiquette and other social rituals. These are expected social behaviors with openly stated rules. Examples are protocol, greetings, dining, exchanging business cards, giving gifts, and civil codes such as abstinence from alcohol in Islamic countries.

The mechanics of these surface rituals can be easily learned from books devoted to etiquette and protocol. Learning them will not necessarily clinch a deal, but familiarity with rituals can help smooth initial relations and reduce cross-cultural noise.

2. More deeply embedded are social customs. These include social expectations that are implicitly understood but not explicitly stated. Examples are social reciprocity, making friends, approaches to the opposite sex, hospitality, habits of speech, eye contact, and personal space. These social practices and behaviors are an important part of the "feel" we get about other people, but there are no explicitly stated rules or codes to guide us in this area. We simply have to learn a different mode or style of behaving and presenting ourselves.

This chapter—devoted to social customs—and the following one on etiquette outline some general principles for dealing with these outward expressions of culture. Many of these principles can be applied to a variety of cultures. Before going to another country, however, it's a good idea to get a guidebook and learn some of the customs and details of etiquette specific to that country. But it is even more important to think carefully about the deeper values and attitudes these customs and details of etiquette represent—for it is at this deeper level that a genuine rapport can be built.

Hospitality

Hospitality is an essential part of business relationships in Asia and the Middle East, and to a lesser extent in Latin America and Southern Europe. Hospitality reconfirms and reinforces the relationships that hold these cultures together. When you come to their country, you are likely to be overwhelmed by invitations to dinner or sightseeing trips, and being treated as the honored guest.

TAKING CARE OF GUESTS—EVEN IF THEY DON'T WANT IT

About two o'clock in the afternoon, we went back to our hotel in Kuala Lumpur. My husband Nate was off discussing business, and I had been left in the care of Neena, a lovely, very quiet, and very diplomatic Malay woman. Neena had been told to keep me closely under her wing, and she was forever at my side carrying bags and waiting on my every need. We had spent the day together shopping while the men worked. As an American woman who is very used to earning money and being independent, I found this constant attention difficult to adjust to.

I started to long for a moment to freshen up and rest alone for awhile, but that was not to be. Nate was supposed to be back at three, so Neena and I stationed ourselves in the lobby of the hotel to wait. Three o'clock, four o'clock, five o'clock came and went with no sign of Nate and the other men. Neena and I sat staring at each other and flipping through the pages of magazines that held no interest for either of us. I wanted to get to my room and work on the travel journal I was keeping of our trip. Neena had work waiting at the office and was eager to get back to it. We had exhausted our shopping needs and had little left to talk about. I watched her pace back and forth, periodically telephoning the office to see what was keeping the men.

Finally, with much exasperation in my voice, I told her that she could leave—I was a well-traveled person and perfectly able to take care of myself. In essence, I told her I didn't need a babysitter. That was the very worst thing I could have done—and one which I will never do again. It is very important in Malaysia to accept whatever your host or hostess offers, regardless of what you really want.

—*Rita Silvestre*

This hospitality forms an important part of doing business abroad. In Asian, Middle Eastern, and Latin American cultures, after-hours socializing is an informal extension of the formal business setting. It provides an opportunity to build relationships, and it also provides an opportunity for things to be said and ideas explored that would be difficult to pursue in a more formal setting.

The degree of hospitality encountered overseas can make Americans uncomfortable or even resentful. Americans don't like to be doted on, and they are used to a more precise division between work time and personal time. They value time to themselves, and—especially on short trips across a number of time zones—they can find a constant round of social events exhausting and disorienting. Social events may even be used deliberately to keep visiting negotiators off balance, or to build up a sense of obligation that makes it more difficult to say no during formal negotiations.

In Denmark, all the women are good cooks and restaurants are extremely expensive. All my business friends entertain at home when foreign customers and suppliers visit. They believe they can get closer to people when they meet at home than they could in a restaurant or some other public place.

The Dutch also like to entertain at home. It's a small country and everything is close to Amsterdam.

England doesn't have a home culture. There's some entertaining done in the homes, but the homes are are often cold and dark. People spend money on cars and clothes, but not on their homes. They have different values from Scandinavians, whose homes are beautiful and for whom entertaining is considered an art. The English often entertain in their local pubs. Almost all the pubs serve food now, and the food in England is not such a joke as it used to be.

Now, the French like to entertain in bistros, or sometimes in restaurants—although restaurants are expensive in Paris. The French don't invite strangers into their homes. But they have to know you really well to do business with you.

The Italians love noise. They can't do without it. People talk loudly. There's music playing everywhere all the time. And the motorcycles!

—*A Danish businesswoman*[1]

When businesspeople from group-oriented cultures such as Chinese and Japanese travel, they often expect the same kind of hospitality they extend to visitors in their countries. If they are new to the United

---

HANDLING HOSPITALITY

- Schedule time for socializing.
- Enjoy hospitality but remember that it is an extension of the business process.
- Remember that hospitality involves obligation and reciprocity.
- Don't let hospitality and obligation overwhelm your business judgment.

States, they may not understand the line Americans draw between work time and family time. Being asked to take a cab from the airport or simply being left to go back to their hotel after formal negotiations are over may cause a good deal of resentment.

Humility

A leader is best
When people barely know that he exists,
Not so good when people obey and acclaim him,
Worst when they despise him.
"Fail to honor people,
They fail to honor you;"
But of a good leader, who talks little,
When his work is done, his aim is fulfilled,
They will all say, "We did this ourselves."
　　　　　　　　　　　　—Lao Tzu[2]

At a 1997 news conference in Tokyo, executives of Japan's Green Cross Corporation were reading from a prepared statement explaining why their company had knowingly sold blood products contaminated with the AIDS virus. Without warning, a woman from the crowd interrupted and demanded: "Stop reading from that paper and make an apology from your heart. Do you understand the feelings of my son, who is dying from injections of poisonous medicine?" According to the *Los Angeles Times*, "The chastened executives set aside their prepared statement, walked around the table to face an assemblage of victims and relatives, dropped to their knees and touched their foreheads to the floor in a gesture of deep humiliation and apology."[3]

Humility is a virtue in the United States just like everywhere else. No one likes a braggart, and American movie heroes are usually modest until it comes time to blow the bad guys away. But try to imagine a group of American business executives showing the humility of the aforementioned Japanese businessmen.

One of the most common complaints about Americans abroad is that they are arrogant and pushy. This is partly the result of American business culture, which places a premium on confidence, leadership, and self-assertion. Americans are taught that they need to sell themselves, and that a strong leader is one who stands out in a crowd.

The situation is different in other cultures. In his book *Making Global Deals*, Jeswald Salacuse relates that "One experienced negotiator in China has his own rule of thumb—that the person who pours the tea for others is the leader of the Chinese team."[4] Humility is one of the ways group-oriented cultures express the importance they place on relationships within the group. Putting oneself forward too much is seen as a lack of loyalty to the group or, even worse, as a way to cover up for a lack of confidence in oneself. This is one of the most important places to meet the other side halfway. Americans should rein in their own tendency to sell themselves and recognize the importance of humility in many other cultures.

Americans are often unprepared for the frequent expressions of humility they encounter in Asian cultures. They may become impatient with the apologies of the Japanese, seeing them as a sign of weakness or obsequiousness. Takashi Kiuchi, a Japanese businessman who lived and worked for many years in the United States, points out the Japanese perspective on the same issue: "Few [American] employees apologize for minor errors or carelessness. They are extraordinarily reluctant to admit the mistakes they make." In Kiuchi's view, a "word of apology could have contributed to stronger teamwork."[5]

In a rather curious twist on perceptions of humility, the Japanese and other Asians often express surprise at Americans' willingness to say "thank you" for small things such as receiving change from a grocery clerk—a service not seen as needing acknowledgment in Asian countries. Similarly, Americans are much more effusive in showing their appreciation for a gift—and often rather miffed when Asians give a simple, formal acknowledgment in the same situation. As a rule of thumb, the Japanese are masters of the apology, Americans artists of the thank-you.

HAVE IT YOUR WAY!

On the second day of my stay in Japan, I went to a fast-food restaurant called Mos Burger and ordered a hamburger. Instead of putting lettuce on their hamburgers, they use shredded cabbage. I didn't find that appetizing, so I asked them to omit the cabbage—a perfectly normal request in the United States. I was totally unprepared for the reaction I got. I recall my dramatic body language as I tried to explain my request. In the end, after the cook and the manager had become involved, I received a hamburger *with* cabbage.

—Michelle Hobby

> ## HANDLING HUMILITY
>
> - Don't oversell yourself: Let your qualifications and accomplishments speak for themselves.
> - Recognize humility in opposing negotiators as a cultural value—not as a sign of weakness or indecisiveness.
> - In Asian countries, take the time to apologize for small mistakes.

The Concept of Face

About the time of the 50th anniversary of World War II, a story made the rounds in Japan. A German, a Frenchman, an Englishman, and a Japanese were each asked to define an elephant. The German took a tape measure and started calculating the dimensions of the animal. The Frenchman enumerated the different ways the elephant could be cooked. The Englishman talked about the role of the elephant in the 300-year history of the British Empire. The Japanese response: "What does the elephant think of us?"

According to anthropologists, societies where face is important are "shame cultures"—what other people think of a person is a central motivation. The United States and Northern Europe, by contrast, are "guilt cultures"—what counts is how the individual evaluates his or her own worth.

A QUESTION WITH NO MEANING

When I was first working in Asian countries, I would occasionally ask a question that would elicit gentle laughter and the comment: "That question has no meaning." After a time I learned that certain questions are not meaningful because they must always be answered in the same way—and are therefore not worth asking. For example, an instructor in Korea might ask if a student understands a question. But either way, this question must always be answered yes: The student will lose face if he or she doesn't understand the question, or the instructor will lose face because of the failure to explain adequately.

—Jon Thomas

The CEO of the company in charge of designing the recovery plan for Los Angeles County after the Northridge earthquake in 1995 was invited to speak at a conference on earthquake preparedness in Kobe, Japan. His speech came immediately after that of the mayor of Kobe, who outlined the 30-year recovery plan that had been developed for his city. The CEO of the company, who has a great deal of experience in international business, offered what seemed to him a complementary talk: bubbling over with American can-do spirit, he described all the recommendations and actions that his firm had already taken in Los Angeles in the year since the quake. At the press conference afterward, he was surprised by fierce interrogation from Japanese reporters about the quick pace of progress in Los Angeles after the quake. It turned out that the mayor of Kobe was under a great deal of pressure because of the slow pace of repairs in his city and the CEO had unwittingly caused him to lose a great deal of face.

—Interview by Dan Harwig

Face is a complicated concept that has no exact equivalent in the United States. It is a combination of the public persona one projects—how a person wants to be viewed by others—and his or her social standing, especially in one's own group. To "save face" means to maintain one's public worth or status. The concept is a product of group orientation and is indicative of sensitivity to others and where one stands in the estimation of group members.

Of course, even in the United States nobody wants to be humiliated or disliked by others. But the individualism of American culture dictates that what matters most is not what others think of us but how we feel about ourselves. The main concern is self-image and self-esteem: What I think of myself in the privacy of my own thinking. In this culture, we say that what you think of me is not my concern; in shame cultures what you think of me is everything.

In group-oriented cultures, the main consideration is the maintenance of one's image in a social circle. There is enormous concern about what others think. The need to maintain face ensures proper behavior through outside social pressures. People show a great sensitivity to other people's opinions of them. Americans interpret this as being thin-skinned and often think of it as a character flaw. Group-oriented cultures, however, may interpret the thick skins of Americans as a sign of insensitivity or lack of refinement—again a kind of character flaw.

THE IMPORTANCE OF GIVING FACE

As a Japanese-American employee of a Japanese trading company, I had a distinct advantage over my American manager. Not only do I understand Japanese, I was also raised with very traditional Japanese values such as honor, discipline, and saving face.

The issue at hand was whether a purchase order we placed was to be shipped in the middle of March or the beginning of April. Normally, these decisions are never debated. The Japanese warehouse simply ships out our orders when we request merchandise. However, the end of March is the end of our fiscal year.

Our Japanese counterpart insisted to my American manager that the shipment must be sent in March, while my manager wanted the shipment in April since he wouldn't be needing the merchandise until then and didn't want to add carrying costs to his inventory.

After a contentious 30-minute phone call between the two with no resolution, the company president finally took the matter into his own hands and decided to have the shipment sent in March instead of April. My manager walked away grumbling about how our president was more loyal to the managers in the Tokyo head office than he was to his own local staff.

But while I was listening to our president's conversation with the Japanese manager, I realized that his decision was based on much different and more important issues. The reason why he had decided in favor of the earlier shipment date was that the Japanese manager's projected sales figures for the prior year were dramatically lower and this large sale would put him close to meeting his sales projections. In other words, this sale was the Japanese manager's last chance to save face.

With this in mind, the president had negotiated a deal that allowed us to receive larger discounts and better terms and commissions on orders placed in the coming year. After this was explained, my American manager understood why it was indeed a win-win decision for both sides.

—*Ayumi Shiroma*

Asian cultures are often amazed at the amount of public abuse Americans are capable of taking without being fazed. American politicians level open and personal attacks on each other in a way that would be unthinkable in many other countries. And then they shake hands and act like friends after it's over. The same thing happens in our adversarial justice system: The lawyers on the two sides rip each other to pieces in court and then go out for lunch together afterward.

When I was a high school student in Iran over 30 years ago, one of my teachers visited the United States for the first time. When he came back he told us that the most amazing thing he had witnessed wasn't the Statue of Liberty, the skyscrapers, or the wonders of the American way of life—it was the way Richard Nixon and John F. Kennedy shook hands after their presidential debate! How could they say such unpleasant things to each other in front of the whole nation and then look one another in the eye, smile, and shake hands?

In cultures where face is important, this kind of behavior would lead to a permanent breach—perhaps even a prolonged feud. What Americans interpret as an open and forthright expression of their opinion can be interpreted as a personal attack. Americans abroad need to remember that the level of personal sensitivity in many cultures is much higher than it is in the United States. This doesn't mean you can't argue with the other side's position, but don't attack an idea outright, especially in a way that would single out specific individuals for blame. It is much better to suggest alternate ways to look at the situation or another approach to the problem.

The business cultures in many Asian and Middle Eastern countries include a ritualistic period of "giving face" at the beginning of a relationship. The participants on both sides comment on all the good things they've heard about the other, what an honor it is to meet each other, and so on. This may seem vaguely phony to Americans, but it is an essential part of the business process in cultures where face is a dominant cultural value.

Like most Asians, Koreans avoid confrontation and open disagreement. They are more likely to use compromise than direct argumentation to resolve conflicts. This desire to maintain surface harmony can make Koreans seem dishonest to foreigners. People may disguise their true feelings in order to keep harmony in the group.

—Byoung G. Kim

When doing business in South Korea, it is essential to be sensitive to both face and *kibun*. Face refers to a person's social and professional standing, whereas *kibun* refers to an individual's feelings, mood, and frame of mind. Both must be maintained, and great care should be taken not to cause loss of face or damage to *kibun*. Showing anger or hostility in public, or openly criticizing incompetence or mistakes, is distasteful to South Koreans. It is important to devise ways out of tricky situations that will enable all parties to save face and prevent shame or embarrassment.

—Nam Suk Lee

Since there is no exact equivalent to the concept of face in the United States, Americans are sometimes unaware that there is even a problem. For instance, in a country where face is important, delivering bad news to a member of the opposing team in the presence of his or her coworkers—say during a contract negotiation—might cause that person serious loss of face. In the United States it would simply be considered part of the give-and-take of bargaining, with no reflection on the individuals involved. Americans are generally thick-skinned, and they are used to disagreeing without taking things personally. Slights, especially if they are unintentional, are quickly forgiven and set aside. In Asian, Middle Eastern, and Latin American countries, loss of face and humiliation are not forgiven as quickly—people tend to remember personal slights and will keep score long afterward.

Americans also need to remember that *they* have to maintain face in foreign cultures—and that losing face can be disastrous. The CEO of an American company handling the management of large construction projects in a variety of countries commented on the importance of maintaining face in South Korea. At one point during talks with a large Korean firm, the Koreans demanded that he make a concession on a key point that he had earlier insisted was not negotiable. "I didn't really mind giving in on that point," he said. "But if I had, I would have lost so much face that it would have been difficult ever to get another contract in Korea." As it turned out, he held firm and made some concessions in other areas. After he got the contract, he was "in the network" and Korean companies started lining up to do business with his firm.

GIVING AND MAINTAINING FACE

- Be sensitive to the stakes different individuals have in negotiations or projects, and try to avoid doing things that would make them lose face, such as direct criticism or refusals.
- Take time to "give face" both at the beginning of a relationship and during the course of a business relationship.
- Giving face by making people look good can be a powerful bargaining chip.
- Maintain face on your side by insisting on proper protocols and sustaining the dignity and integrity of your position. Never allow yourself to be seen as inferior, weak, or needy.

Americans Fear Silence

The way we interact with other people is the result of ingrained habits that are part of the reality of each culture. For Americans, being together means talking. They are uncomfortable with silence. For them it signifies lack of interest or even deviousness. There's nothing more uncomfortable than a first date where the conversation keeps dying!

For Asians—especially the Japanese—taking the time to ponder on what the other side has just said is a sign of courtesy and interest. Jumping in with a comment right after someone has finished speaking means you haven't considered what the other person has just said. Asians don't communicate back and forth like a tennis match. They value communicating a lot with few words; they don't explain themselves or exchange arguments to establish their point.

Our Chinese counterpart helped me to understand that silence and small stature do not mean that a person is easily pushed around or does not have the ability to drive a hard bargain. She sat at the bargaining table, quiet and thoughtful, while I continued to talk and give her all the information she needed to drive a hard bargain.

—Danny Anderson

Besides its cultural connotation as a sign of respect, silence can be used as a tactical device to gain time to consider options and prepare a careful response. But many Asians have also discovered that silence can be an effective tool for extracting concessions from Americans at the negotiating table. Left in a prolonged silence, American negotiators can be tempted to offer concessions or volunteer information just to fill what for them is an uncomfortable breach of social norms.

The American style of conversation is like a tennis game; a Korean conversation is more like a bowling match. Americans can interfere when the other party is talking and respond as soon as the other person is finished. Koreans wait until the other person is completely finished; interfering would be considered extremely rude.

When I see American talk shows like Jerry Springer's, I'm shocked by all the people jumping into the conversation before the other person is finished. During a Korean talk show, people wait their turn. If someone does interrupt, the emcee stops the person and allows the first speaker to finish his or her thought.

—Yoon Tak Gwak

On the silence-noise continuum (Figure 5.2), Americans are somewhere near the middle. In Latino and Middle Eastern countries, there is often a great deal of emotion and back-and-forth argumentation to convince the other side. In the end, everyone ends up talking at the same time, and you have to fight to get a word in edgewise. To Americans, all

---

HANDLING SILENCE IN ASIAN COUNTRIES

- Don't interrupt Asian speakers; wait until they have finished speaking.
- Don't feel pressured to fill in awkward silences—especially with concessions.
- Learn to use silence as Asians do—to organize your thoughts and evaluate proposals.

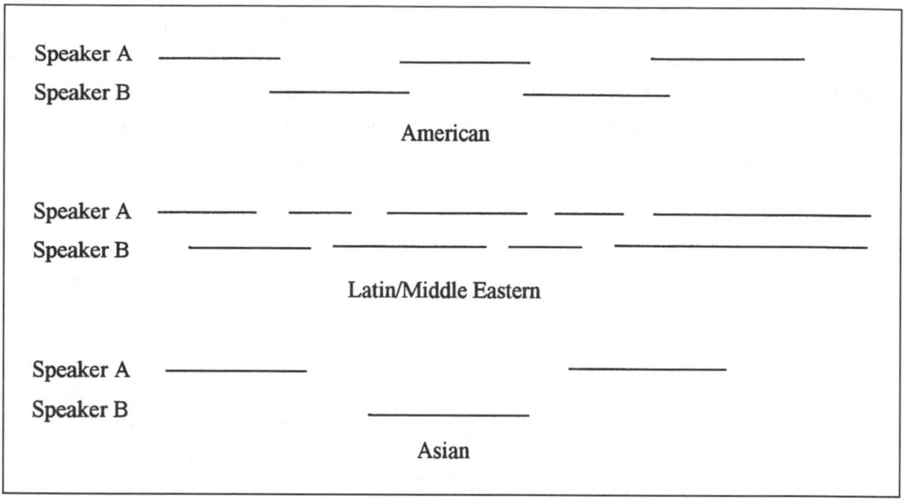

Figure 5.2   Patterns of Verbal Communication

this shouting and gesticulating seems like aggressive or rude behavior. This should serve as a reminder of how Asians feel when Americans fill every silence with trivial talk, even if they really have nothing to say.

American executives try to dominate the situation by speaking. However, effective listening skills reduce misunderstandings, sharpen concentration, and can actually be used to control negotiations. In the American mind, listening is passive. Silence indicates ignorance or lack of status. The truth is that listening is an active and powerful skill that Americans should learn to use in their negotiations with the Japanese.

—*John Graham, Ph.D.*[6]

Hierarchy and Respect for Authority

There are many subtle signs of social and business hierarchies that go unnoticed by Americans. A meeting room in Japan, for instance, has a "high place" or *kamiza* (at the head of the table as far as possible from the door) and a "low place" or *shimoza* (off to the side and/or closer to the door).[7] It is important for the Japanese to know in advance the status of different members of a visiting delegation so they can seat each person in the appropriate place.

Although Mexicans desire to be treated with respect as individuals, they recognize that Mexico is a land of unequal relationships. There are prescribed sets of relationships that acknowledge the subordinate-superior nature of most of these.

—*Alan Ibarra*

In status-oriented cultures such as those in Latin American, the Middle East, Asia, and some European countries, it is important to show proper deference to rank and social status. Failure to do so can cause hurt feelings or even loss of face for members of the opposing team, who have to maintain their status and authority within their own organization.

Many South Korean companies resemble large families, with a father figure who exercises almost total authority over family members. (Samsung and Hyundai are organized this way, for example.) The head of the company has absolute rights, but also absolute responsibilities. He must be obeyed, but in return he must provide for the people in his charge. Decision making is highly centralized. In many companies, the chairman or top executives (often family members) make decisions unilaterally or in small groups after consultation with the parties involved. Promotion within the company is usually based on length of service rather than skills or ability. This makes it difficult or impossible to promote a young highflier over the heads of superiors. Employees also have a strong feeling of loyalty to the person who originally brought them into the company.

—*Nam Suk Lee*

Hospitality and protocol are also important in showing the proper respect for status. One of my first experiences with the Chinese was when I was working for General Electric Trading Company. A delegation of eight visitors from China showed up in town unexpectedly. They called from a midtown Manhattan hotel asking to meet with me and demanded that I pick them up. I responded as if they were American businessmen: "It's only ten blocks. Take a cab." "No, no, you come and pick us up," the young interpreter insisted. In the end, I took a cab down to meet them.

We exchanged initial greetings and they gave me their business cards, but I was unable to figure out exactly who the different members of the delegation were. (One card said "Chief Engineer," another "Engineering Director," and so on.) The thought of hiring three cabs to take them back to the office seemed ridiculous, so I suggested that we go around the corner to a Chinese restaurant and have our meeting there. I thought this would be quieter than the crowded coffee shop in the hotel.

Although I didn't know it at the time, this was a serious breach of protocol. After they left, I sent a number of faxes asking for more information, but I never got any response from them. A year later, when I visited Shanghai for the first time, I arranged to meet with that organization (which turned out to be a very large enterprise employing thousands of people) and was treated much more coldly than anywhere else in China (where hospitality is usually quite lavish). I was led to a big meeting room where I saw a large portrait of one of the men I'd met in New York hanging on the wall next to a portrait of Chairman Mao Tse-tung.

It turned out that he was head of the entire enterprise—a very high-level person whose rank would have dictated an invitation to

---

HANDLING HIERARCHIES

- Treat opposing team members according to their rank.
- Use titles and formal forms of address until invited to do otherwise.
- Be careful about making end runs around authority figures or bureaucracies.
- Remember the role of hierarchy during social functions.
- Remember that the amount of responsibility subordinates will take on and the amount of direction they need varies widely among cultures.

meet people of comparable rank at our company and perhaps a banquet. I hadn't treated him in accordance with his rank and expectations. A restaurant might have been a quiet place to discuss business with an American colleague, but for a high-ranking Chinese official it was a social humiliation. In this case, showing the proper deference and respect was much more important than a comfortable place to talk.

Mexicans are extremely fond of titles that grant respect and authority and define or enhance status. In formal business settings, the title *Licenciado* (*Licenciada* for a woman) is a catchall title that acknowledges a person's qualifications. It implies that person is a university graduate, but that may not always be the case. It is also appropriate and preferable to use titles such as Doctor (the same in English and Spanish), *Ingeniero (a)* (engineer), *Achitechto(a)*, or other formal titles when the person's profession and credentials make it appropriate. Foreigners should make sure to use similar titles when they introduce themselves. If you do not know a woman's marital status, you should always address her as *Señorita*. Foreigners should continue to use a Mexican businessperson's title and last name until the person specifically requests that the relationship be put on a first-name basis.

—Alan Ibarra

Intermediaries

In cultures where maintaining relationships is very important, intermediaries are an important part of doing business. Intermediaries are useful for exploring an initial relationship, and they are especially useful when you must deliver bad news or mediate difficult disputes. The intermediary allows the other side to save face and provides a venue for exploring possible resolutions that might be difficult to broach in a formal setting.

Intermediaries can be especially useful when talks are stalled or one side has walked away from the table. The intermediary can explore each side's position and listen to grievances and frustrations without the element of confrontation and the danger of losing face—and then explore what each side's interests are and what is really possible for each side to do. If there are areas of overlap, the intermediary can find out what

---

USING INTERMEDIARIES

- In Asian and Middle Eastern countries, use intermediaries to mediate disputes or misunderstandings.
- Intermediaries can make initial contacts and help establish the terms and basic principles of difficult negotiations.
- In Asia, use intermediaries to deliver a "no" answer.

---

would be necessary to move each side in that direction and what kinds of public gestures or movements would be most useful.

Another form of intermediary is the use of an agent—a local person or company that will represent your product or service in another country. This is often a good way to break into a difficult market or smooth your way with manufacturers or suppliers. If you can find a company with credibility within the industry, this can make relations easier and save a good deal of time and expense—even if you give a little to the agent. Be careful to research the company you choose as a representative, however. Just because a company is from that country doesn't mean it is well respected or effective there. It's also a good idea to do your own market research to make sure it is doing a good job representing you. A small foreign company might have more interest in maintaining its local monopoly and ensuring its profits than in helping your company effectively penetrate a new market.

Social Obligations and Reciprocity

Americans have a nonchalant attitude toward social obligations. We may remember that someone owes us a favor or a lunch. Someone who is constantly accepting gifts without giving anything in return might come to be known as a mooch. But there is rarely a strong feeling of obligation involved in gift-giving or social hospitality. In fact, in the United States people who expect something in return for their gifts are looked down on as insincere. A gift should be just that—a gift with no strings attached.

The Korean business system is intensely personal. Human relationships are often more important than logic. Personal relationships are critical to doing business successfully in Korea. These personal ties can help solve problems when logic doesn't work. But these relationships also involve obligations. There are times when maintaining a relationship means doing something that is not in your best interest—at least in the short term.

—*Byoung G. Kim*

In traditional and group-oriented cultures, the codes governing repayment of favors, social obligations, and gifts are much stricter. Reciprocity is expected, and people retain a clear memory of favors or gifts they owe or are owed. This web of obligation and reciprocity is an essential part of doing business in these cultures. Since a great deal of time and effort go into building and maintaining relationships, the web of obligations ensures that these efforts are not wasted and that future benefits accrue to all sides involved.

It all started 30 years ago in the central highlands of South Vietnam. My grandfather decided to try his luck at growing coffee and rubber, and purchased some cheap land to start his venture. Within a short time, the plantation was a success and he acquired more land and a fleet of Land Rovers to help oversee the property.

My father had a different calling, however. He wanted to be a doctor, and after going to medical school he got a job in a hospital near the plantation.

One day he treated a little boy who had a rare, deadly disease that required expensive medicines. The child's mother was very poor and could not afford the medicine, so my father paid for the treatment.

After he was cured, the Communists took over South Vietnam, and the little boy came to Seattle, sponsored by an American gentleman who owned a large ship-construction company. My grandfather, however, was killed and his plantation taken over by the new Communist government.

The little boy grew up learning the ship-building business, and when the American passed away he left the company to his Vietnamese protég´. Last year, the new owner unexpectedly paid my parents a visit. He said his mother had always reminded him that one day he would have to seek out my father and thank him for saving his life.

Talking with my father, he found out that I was looking for an internship in a company. Without hesitation, he offered an internship to me whenever I wanted it. So now I'm going off to Seattle to learn the ship-construction business!

—*Tuan Ton-That*

> ## REMINDERS ABOUT RECIPROCITY
> - Remember when you receive gifts to reciprocate in some way.
> - Gifts symbolize the desire to establish a long-term relationship; they can be remembered years later.
> - Creating obligations can be used to build relationships, but also as a deliberate bargaining tactic.

The principle of reciprocity operates at both the business and the personal level. Americans should be aware that their international counterparts in traditional cultures probably view their relationship at least partially in terms of the personal and professional benefits it may have for them. For example, your Chinese counterpart may see beyond the present business transaction to the possibility of your help in sending a child to the United States to be educated, or to some other personal or business benefit beyond the scope of the present business interaction.

Obligation can also be used as a deliberate business tactic. A relative of mine owned a chicken fast-food restaurant that had a stable local business until a Boston Market moved in next door. Business fell off to the point that the restaurant's survival was threatened. The owner needed something to get customers back in the door, so he decided to give a free rice dish away to anyone who walked into the restaurant, even people who stopped to use the phone or look at the menu. The rice didn't actually cost much, but it created a tremendous amount of goodwill and an implicit reciprocal obligation. Eventually the owner boosted business back up to the point where he could compete with the corporate restaurant next door.

One of the reasons that Asians and other traditional cultures are so cautious about entering into a relationship is that they envision the future of reciprocal obligations the relationship will entail. Americans, on the other hand, enter into relationships more easily because they do not see them as entailing long-term obligations. This means that Americans should be cautious about establishing the level of a relationship. What seems like a casual, short-term gesture to Americans can be seen as an invitation to a much more serious and long-term set of obligations by the other side. It's a good idea to remember that casual invitations and offers are usually taken at face value and can entail serious obligations.

CHAPTER

6

International Business Etiquette

Whereas an American might refer to someone who acts in ways quite different from those of most other Americans as "a strange foreigner," in Japan the hen na gaijin *(literally "strange foreigner") is the one who acts too much like a Japanese.*

—John Condon[1]

You don't need to be a chameleon to do business internationally. Trying too hard to adopt local customs and manners—especially before you fully understand them—is likely to do more harm than good. Neither side should feel compelled to change themselves and their core beliefs when doing business together. It is best to be yourself but show an understanding of the other side's customs, expectations, and behavior. The most successful international travelers learn to "be themselves with an accent."

Being yourself doesn't mean you don't have to make adjustments, however. If your conduct violates deeply held cultural values—for instance, if you are perceived as arrogant or rude—this can have serious repercussions in the business realm. Cultural values are emotionally charged. Violating them even in small ways can cause a knee-jerk response in those on the other side. Frequently interrupting a speaker to ask questions might be seen as a way to express interest and demonstrate competence in the United States, but in Asian countries it would be seen as a serious breach of courtesy and respect.

One day soon after I'd moved to the United States from Korea, a delivery man was supposed to come to my house with a load of furniture. When he arrived, it turned out that the furniture had to be assembled. In Korea, we take our shoes off when we enter someone's home. I asked the delivery man to take his shoes off, but he surprised me by replying that he was "on duty" and couldn't possibly take his shoes off. I was unhappy and hurried him out of the apartment as soon as I could. It was only later that I realized this was the American custom and that the man had meant no disrespect.

—*Juhyung Czae*

You don't have to parrot the natives to be accepted. While it is important to be respectful and accepting, overdoing it in following local customs might be comical or leave you looking like a fool. Cross-cultural competence is not about becoming like others or teaching them to behave like you. It is knowledge and understanding of differences.

How to Handle Introductions

Manners are like the cipher in arithmetic—they may not be much in themselves, but they are capable of adding a great deal of value to everything else.
      —Freya Stark, French-born English travel writer
      and photographer[2]

Introductions are generally more formal in other countries than they are here. When you are abroad, conform to local protocols but don't feel obligated to reproduce local customs exactly. If you feel comfortable using the Japanese bow or the Thai gesture of clasping the hands together in front of the chest and bowing slightly, do so. People appreciate your effort to learn local customs and rituals. But if you are uncomfortable, feel free to use a handshake and a formal salutation.

Thai people are conservative, polite, and shy. It is unacceptable for people of the opposite sex to hold hands or kiss in public. It is against the law to publish nude pictures or broadcast movies that have sexual content. In the old days, every movie had to be approved by the King. Even now, Thais may look the other way if there is a kissing scene on television, and if a love scene is too passionate it cannot be broadcast.

When I first came to the United States, I knew that people here greet each other by shaking hands, by hugging, or even by kissing. I still feel nervous when my American friends hug me when we meet. Instead of shaking hands or hugging, Thais greet each other with a *wai*—putting both hands together as if in prayer and bowing slightly. There is a personal distance maintained between men and women in Thailand—although it is acceptable for people of the same gender, especially girls, to hold hands.

Modesty is very important in Thailand. Do not enter an office until you are invited, and do not sit until you are asked. People in Thailand are called by their first names, so most people you meet should be addressed by their title and first name. If a person does not have a professional title, simply use Mr., Mrs., or Miss plus their names.

—*Yuwadee Kiatbaramee*

The handshake has become a more or less universal business protocol—and the normal standard in many countries. When greeting a woman it is usually better to let her initiate the handshake. This can be awkward if both men and women are present, but if you hold back slightly the women will probably initiate the handshake or other gesture of greeting.

I was scheduled to meet a contact from Egypt to discuss supplying diving equipment for recreational scuba diving at resort properties in that country. Before the meeting, I researched some of the customs for doing business in Egypt. They were relatively minor points such as not using a person's first name until invited to do so and not using your finger to point at people.

The meeting was held in Miami during an international trade show. I introduced myself and, following Egyptian custom, addressed the contact using his surname. After conversing for a few minutes about topics other than business, he began using my first name and started talking about business. I was surprised to hear him use my first name, but since I was comfortable with this style I accommodated him.

The meeting lasted about an hour and the outcome was very positive for both parties. I got a verbal commitment from his company to purchase our products, and he was able to secure a complete line of items needed for penetrating the retail diving market.

In retrospect, I believe that the fact that I was prepared to negotiate using the Egyptian style impressed him and put him at ease. Since we were in Miami, he felt it was appropriate to use a Western style, but he felt comfortable because I had gone to the trouble to learn his customs.

—Bill Hamm

The exchange of business cards is an important part of introductions in many cultures. In Japan, Hong Kong, Taiwan, and Singapore, the card is offered with both hands, the printed side facing the receiver. This is accompanied by a bow, which varies in depth according to the relative status of the participants in the exchange. It is probably best for Americans not to try to duplicate this entire ceremony if they feel uncomfortable with it, but it is important to pay attention to the underlying values at work. The card is a representation of the person and should be treated with respect. When you receive a card from the other side, don't put it immediately in your pocket or leave it on the table and put your coffee on it. Read it carefully and put it on the table in front of you so you can refer to it during the meeting (Figure 6.1). When you give your card out, don't simply throw it on the table—a gesture that would be seen as quite rude.

Greetings in Brazil can be quite effusive. When meeting for the first time, Brazilians give extended handshakes, then progress to embraces once a friendship has been established. Women often kiss each other on alternate cheeks, twice if you are married, three times if you are single. (The third kiss is for good luck in finding a spouse.)

—Claudia McAchran

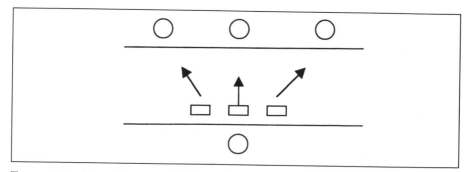

Figure 6.1   Use of Business Cards to Identify Members of the Other Team

During my second year in Brussels, I started to work at Rio Doce International, a subsidiary of Compania Vale do Rio Doce, a Brazilian mining company. I am Brazilian and speak fluent French, but I remember my first attempt doing business with the French. I was trying to reach someone in the European Commission to get information concerning the European steel market. The first time I didn't get the information and my counterpart on the phone was very unkind.

I was puzzled until one of my colleagues explained to me how phone calls work in the French business world:

1. After presenting yourself, you have to apologize for calling.
2. Then ask if you are disturbing the person at that moment.
3. Say why you are calling.
4. At the end of the conversation, tell the person how kind he or she was and give them a thousand thanks.

That was the magic formula! I had gotten used to speaking on the phone to fellow students at the business school I'd attended in Brussels, but this style was not formal enough for the French business world. Since that time, I've used the formula with great success—although, I must say, in Paris even this does not always work.

—*Luciana Vaz*

When making introductions, pay special attention to rank and seniority. Senior people should be introduced first, and in most countries they should be treated with more respect and deference than Americans might be used to. Use last names and titles when appropriate—the American custom of moving quickly to a first-name basis should be avoided.

Dining and Drinking

Eating and drinking are an important part of doing business overseas. Conform to local customs but don't do things you are uncomfortable with. For instance, in China they sometimes eat chicken and throw the bones on the floor. If they burp, belch, or slurp their soup, you needn't follow their example. But don't call attention to the issue with a comment about how "things are done differently in the United States," or, "that would be a rude gesture in my country."

Thais use knives and forks to eat, but they often eat only with the right hand because the left hand is considered unclean. A serving spoon is put into each dish for everyone to take food for their plates—it is impolite to use your own spoon or fork to take food. Sometimes we take food for others out of kindness. While eating, we usually don't talk since it is inappropriate to see food in other's mouths. It is considered courteous to wash one's hands both before and after eating.

It is common in America to put one's feet on the table, but this is a rude gesture in Thailand. Feet are regarded as dirty and should not touch things or people. I feel uncomfortable when I see a movie in which someone puts their feet on a chair. Stepping over a book is prohibited as well. Men should keep their feet flat on the floor; women are permitted to cross their legs while sitting.

—*Yuwadee Kiatbaramee*

Most Russian men like to drink and because they do it often they tend to handle their liquor better than foreigners do. While declining an invitation to drink probably won't sour your relationship, accepting will go a long way toward convincing Russians that they can trust you. But try to drink just enough to let them know you are not faking it. Becoming drinking buddies has implications that are not always conducive to the efficient conduct of business.

If you are a woman, the good news is that you will be under no pressure to sip more than a token amount. Indeed, your Russian hosts would think less of you if you seemed eager to knock back a few with the boys.

—*Marina Volobueva*

During my seminars I ask participants, "How many of you would eat monkey brains or fried scorpions if offered to you on a foreign trip?" The majority of sales professionals usually say they would eat anything to get the business, while purchasing professionals usually say, "No way! I'm not going to touch that stuff!" I guess salespeople are just hungrier.

Turkey is a very diverse country; some regions are poorer than Africa and others are richer than Paris. Our manager, Mr. Blake, and I were transferred from Istanbul to Sivas, in the poor eastern part of Turkey.

While we were touring the region, we were invited to dinner at the house of one of the local villagers. As we arrived at the house that evening, we were informed that they "never took no as an answer" and that we had to eat whatever we were served. After four or five cups of tea, we proceeded to the table, which was covered with kebabs and other local dishes. We chatted about the things we'd seen, and ate till we thought we would explode. I could see the pain on Mr. Blake's face. We were just thanking God that we had survived the meal when we saw an entire lamb coming toward our table. After that there was an entire dessert table. In the end, we spent the entire night eating, with no questions asked, just because they think saying "no" is disrespectful of their offerings. The two of us were quite sick for the next several days.

—*Akin Colak*

In most cases, you can get away without eating or drinking things you don't want. If they serve sea anemones or monkey brains, put a little on your plate but don't eat it. If you don't wish to drink, there are several tricks you can use. I often let my hosts fill my glass and then raise it to my lips during toasts or other ceremonial moments. A friend of mine who makes frequent business trips to Russia tells his guests that he has a heart condition and produces of vial of pills (Tylenol will work fine) to show them he can't drink. In general it is best not to make a big deal out of a refusal. If you do, people will ask you why you're not drinking or eating, tell you how good the wine or food is, and generally cause a commotion.

At meals in China, eat lightly at first because up to 12 courses are served. Your host will keep filling your bowl with food each time you empty it. Men will often drink wine in one draught. Women can ask for tea in place of wine. Do not stick your chopsticks straight up in your rice bowl. Hold your bowl near your mouth to eat or drink. Bones and shells are placed on the table or on a spare plate that is periodically replaced by the server. Try to show appreciation for exotic dishes that might not be that appetizing to you. Try not to openly show that you dislike something; the dish might be very special and expensive. Accept the food, but you do not have to finish it.

At the end of the meal, your host might apologize for not serving you well enough. This is a humble gesture commonly used by hosts. Just respond with more compliments to the host on the wonderful meal. Good topics of conversation include complimenting the host on his or her successful children or inquiring about the health of parents. Don't be surprised if you are asked personal questions such as how much you paid for something or what your salary is. If you don't wish to discuss something, simply tell them politely that it is not your custom to reveal such things.

—*Pam Kuo*

Pay attention also to local matters of table etiquette. In Japan, for instance, it is poor taste to put your chopsticks up and down in your bowl (a sign of death). In general, it is not polite to toast those who are older or more senior than you. If you smoke, always offer cigarettes to others before taking one yourself.

The Japanese, for their part, are careful to observe the nuances of American culture when doing business in the United States. The following list of recommendations by Takashi Kiuchi summarizes points on which Japanese businesspeople might stumble while interacting with American colleagues.[3]

- Say "thank you" often.
- Make direct eye contact when shaking hands or carrying on a conversation.
- Do not laugh meaninglessly.
- Do not close your eyes or doze off at meetings.
- Say yes or no clearly and do not act ambiguously.
- When you must speak with fellow Japanese in Japanese, first ask to be excused.
- Avoid belching, sniffling, and passing gas.

Gift Giving

In this culture we give a gift after the job is over as a sign of gratitude for a job well done. In other cultures a gift is often given up front as a way to ensure a good relationship. This can look like bribery, so you have to be careful.

Try to learn the Vietnamese way of doing things. It is important to the Vietnamese to get to know you and feel that you know them. It is important to get to know them personally. If they like you, everything comes easily after that. Whenever they invite you to go out, you should go. Deals are made more often in entertainment settings than at the office. Make sure you have a decent entertainment budget. Wining and dining are the fundamental tools for doing business in Vietnam. Don't expect deals to be made overnight. Sometimes it may take months, and you should be in for the long haul.

Here are some additional tips for doing business in Vietnam:

- Always smile and be as gracious as possible. The Vietnamese are a very friendly people.
- When visiting a friend or acquaintance, always bring a small gift (e.g., sweets or drinks).
- When being offered small treats—tea or wine—it is polite to accept.
- When someone pours you a drink, tap with the index finger as a way of giving thanks.
- Wait until the host offers the food before serving yourself.
- Ask about family, mutual friends and acquaintances, the weather, the country.
- Always take small portions.
- When drinking, control your alcohol intake. There will be many toasts, so take small sips.
- Try not to talk about yourself unless asked.
- Be humble and excuse yourself for being unfamiliar with the country.
- Don't bring up the Vietnam War.

—Tuan Ton-That

When you go abroad, bring some small gifts to give when conditions seem appropriate. Make sure gifts are thoughtful and tasteful. Smaller, less expensive gifts are probably best. But don't give anything flimsy or cheap—or anything made in the country you are visiting. A Japanese-American businessman representing an American company in Japan brought a case of T-shirts with a famous Japanese baseball player pitching for the Los Angeles Dodgers. They were a big hit. They bridged the culture gap but didn't create too much obligation. Many Asians take photos and send them as gifts. In Russia and Brazil, it might be helpful to bring a small gift to the secretary. She most likely has a lot of influence to facilitate the business interaction.

On a business trip to South Korea, it is a good idea to take a supply of small, wrapped gifts for the people you visit for the first time. On receiving a gift it is polite to ask if you may open it then and there. Etiquette requires that the giver apologize for the "humble gift"—no matter what the price.

—*Nam Suk Lee*

The form of gift giving is as important as the gift itself. The Japanese often wrap their gifts very beautifully, and presentation is an important part of the process. Unlike in the United States, gifts in many other countries are not opened immediately. This helps prevent potential embarrassment if the recipient doesn't understand the gift or lets some sign of disappointment or disapproval show. If there are several gifts given, it avoids awkward comparisons between gifts.

If you give a gift to one person, try not to give it in front of other people. It is probably best to pull the person aside at an opportune time and

---

NUMBERS IN ASIAN CULTURES

- **One** in the Chinese tradition signifies heaven, beginnings, and birth.
- **Four** signifies death to the Chinese, Japanese, Vietnamese, and Koreans. Don't give gifts in groups of four. House numbers that contain fours or groups of fours may be rejected by many Asians. A group of numbers that adds up to four might be considered unlucky.
- **Five** is a lucky number according to the Chinese and the Japanese. It is associated with the five elements of nature. However, in some dialects the word for "five" sounds like the word for "not," so some Chinese might not like it if a five is placed next to a lucky number. For instance, eight is a lucky number signifying prosperity. But 58—5 + 8—could equate to "not prospering."
- **Eight** is a very lucky number. Consider giving gifts in groups of eight. You might also consider using eights in counteroffers to Chinese clients.
- **Nine** is a very popular number with the Chinese, who associate it with longevity and dragons. However, for the Japanese, nines signify misery and suffering.
- **Ten** in Chinese sounds like the word for "sure" or "guaranteed." When 10 is combined with another number, it suggests a guarantee of that number's meaning. Fourteen—10 + 4—means "guaranteed death."

COLORS IN ASIAN CULTURES

- **Red** is auspicious and connotes happiness, warmth, and all good things in life. Deep reds and purples inspire great respect. However, some Chinese might not like to write with a red pen or sign their name in red ink.
- **Gold** and **yellow** represent wealth, authority, and longevity. Red and gold make a good combination.
- **Green** connotes tranquility, potency, and longevity resulting from healthy earth *ch'i* (life-force).
- **White** is associated with purity. It is an important color at funerals. Unbleached white muslin is worn by Chinese mourners and the funeral is decorated in yellow and white. White flowers or white and yellow combinations of flowers should not be given as gifts. Also, gifts should not be wrapped in white, or white and yellow wrapping paper.
- **Blue** is a secondary Chinese mourning color and is not recommended for use with white. Blue is often used with other colors, however. The Japanese especially favor blue.
- **Black** and **red** are lucky in combination. By itself, black signifies death and dark times and should be avoided.

give him or her the gift quietly. Or you can give a gift that can be enjoyed or divided by the group.

The American habit of giving gifts on the spur of the moment can cause confusion in cultures where social reciprocity is closely monitored. The person receiving the gift may spend considerable energy figuring out why the gift was given. Often a recipient will quickly give a gift in return, which can irritate Americans, who wonder why the other side can't just accept a gift without immediately feeling obligated to balance the ledger.

I was working for a company in Japan when one of our American clients heard that an employee in the company was getting married. It is the custom in Japan to give money in special envelopes during marriage ceremonies. The American client brought a beautiful white envelope with a black ribbon. He must have been shocked when I told him the next day that this kind of envelope is used only for funerals! The following day he went to a store I told him about and bought a wedding envelope.

—*Mariko Ishikawa*

Gifts are symbolic objects, and thought should be given to cultural meanings that might be associated with them. Knives make a bad gift in Japan because they symbolize the severing of a relationship (or even the hara-kiri suicide ritual). Groups of four are associated with death in many Asian countries. Three or five is better; in China eight is considered a lucky number. Clocks or watches are unlucky to the Chinese.[4]

Americans' informality about gifts and social obligations can get them into trouble in foreign cultures. In the United States, gifts are given (more or less) freely. The idea of expecting something in exchange would be considered ungracious. The same principle extends to social obligations. If you are invited to dinner at an American house, you might bring something to contribute such as a bottle of wine, or you might pitch in and help with the cooking or cleanup (something that would *never* happen in a traditional culture). Afterward, you might reciprocate with a dinner invitation of your own, but you would be under no obligation to do so.

In traditional cultures, on the other hand, gifts and social invitations always involve a measure of reciprocity. You are being included in a social network, but this involves a greater sense of obligation and quid pro quo than Americans are used to. Don't be surprised if the lavish dinner you had in Bahrain is followed six months later by a telephone call from one of your new Arabic friends who fully expects a tour of your American city. A friend of mine who does a lot of business in the Middle East recently received a phone call from an Arabic prince he hadn't seen in 10 years. The prince had a couple of extra days, and he took it as a given that my friend would drop everything to play golf, go out to lavish dinners, and recall old times.

Gestures

I used to travel to Brazil on business quite often. I don't speak a word of Portuguese, so when I wanted to express my satisfaction, I would circle my thumb and forefinger in an okay sign. However, this is a rude gesture in Brazil. They give a thumbs-up sign when they want to signal that everything is all right. But in the Middle East, where I come from, the thumbs-up sign means the same as the okay sign does to Brazilians: It is a rude gesture! Of course, everyone knew what was going on; we would all chuckle because we knew that no one meant any disrespect.

Every culture has its own gestures. When an Italian man sees a beautiful woman, he twists a finger into his cheek (as if creating a dimple). Greeks stroke their cheeks (because an egg-shaped face is considered beautiful). Brazilians form a tube with their hands as if looking through a telescope. A Frenchman might kiss his fingers and fling them in the air. Arabs stroke their beards. And some South American men pull down a lower eyelid with a finger ("Boy, that's an eyeful!").[5]

When in China, do not put your arm around another person's shoulder. Young children of the same sex will often hold hands, but it is inappropriate for others to do so. Do not make physical contact with people who are not good friends or family. Do not touch the head of another person's child; it is feared that intelligence may be damaged by careless touching. Feet are considered dirty and should not touch things or people. Take off your shoes when entering a house. People should keep their feet on the floor. Do not point with a finger; use an open hand instead.

—*Pam Kuo*

Learning the gestures of another culture (especially the ones to avoid) is a sign of courtesy and respect. Most people will understand if you've been in the country for two days and you accidentally make an obscene gesture, cross your legs the wrong way, or don't bow correctly during introductions. But if you've been there awhile, it's wise to pay attention to gestures and how they work. Avoiding rude gestures and learning the simple gestures of social interactions will show that you care about the people you are dealing with.

Communicating in Spain does not refer only to the words you say or write. Gestures are very important. Heads and hands are moving constantly when Spaniards have a conversation. To a foreigner, two or more Spaniards involved in a normal conversation would probably seem to be arguing. You can communicate important information with Spaniards without ever opening your mouth. In many cases, a gesture means much more than words—something very difficult to understand and master if you have not been brought up in Spanish culture.

—*Maria C. Garcia Garcia*

Some gestures are almost universally recognized as rude. According to anthropologists, "giving the finger" has been around for over 2000 years and is recognized in most cultures around the world.[6] The "forearm jerk," while not widely used in the United States, is easily recognizable as a rude gesture of defiance. Thumbing one's nose is recognized as a rude gesture in most cultures.

Other gestures change meaning from culture to culture. The okay sign is rude in Brazil, but in France it means something is worthless and in Japan it is used as a symbol for money. The thumbs-up gesture means "good luck" or "everything's all right" in the United States, but in Australia it signifies "up yours."[7] In Germany it means "one" as in, "Bartender, give me one beer." An American hitchhiker in Nigeria was roughed up by locals for trying to thumb a ride—not knowing that it was an obscene gesture in that country.[8]

Space

We normally think of space as the same everywhere. But the way we put objects and people into that space varies widely between cultures. For Americans the world is a huge grid—much like an American city. A friend of mine recently flew into Madrid and rented a car to get around the city. "I'm lucky to be alive," he told me. "All the lanes are in the wrong places, and they put these little bitsy stoplights off to the side about three feet off the ground." For an American, a stoplight's natural place is 10 feet off the ground and directly in line with the road.

The personal space people maintain between each other also differs widely among cultures. If somebody gets too close and invades this space, we tend to feel threatened or claustrophobic. Americans stand about an arm's length from each other when they talk. Middle Eastern cultures, Latinos, and some European countries stand much closer. Asians stand even further away, especially with people they don't know. When dealing with foreign-born clients, I usually let the other person decide what is comfortable and adapt to that. If you are uncomfortable with someone from the Middle East talking loudly, gesticulating six inches from your face, and following you each time you back away, try interposing a desk or table to increase the distance to a comfortable range.

The habits we have about touching other people also impact on people's personal space. During a news broadcast a few years ago, I saw an American congressman in Vietnam talking to an official (much smaller than he was) with his hand on his shoulder. He seemed oblivious to the overly familiar, patronizing attitude this gesture conveyed in Asia— where there is a lot of distance, except among family members and close friends. In Asian countries, it is best to avoid touching people on the head or shoulders.

Generally, Americans are not very touchy-feely. When they feel friendly with someone, they might slap that person on the back or put an arm on someone's shoulder, but they would never hold hands or kiss another man as they do in Middle Eastern countries. When I was in Brazil with a colleague, it was really funny to see the expression on the man's face the first time one of the Brazilians followed a handshake with a hug. I thought the man's head was going to snap backward off his body.

In Middle Eastern countries there is a lot of male-to-male touching or kissing but little male-female touching. When Henry Kissinger was in Saudi Arabia as Secretary of State under Richard Nixon, he would hold pinkies with Saudi ministers during press conferences—much to the amusement of the American press.

Women need to be especially careful abroad. You don't want to stand too close to men or have too much direct eye contact, touching, or smiling—it is easily mistaken for flirtation. In many countries, American women might notice that the men initiate less eye contact or handshakes with them than they do with the men in their group. This does not mean they are being discounted; it's just that many cultures consider extended eye contact with women to be rude.

Informal Behavior

Americans value informality. Introductions, dress, and day-to-day courtesies are easygoing. A good working relationship usually takes place on a first-name basis. One of the nicest things you can say about a superior in the United States is that he or she doesn't pull rank or demand special privileges. Informality is a way to make people feel more comfortable by removing barriers of social rank and unnecessary etiquette. Thus Americans will move quickly to using first names, and they often treat people they hardly know as if they are close friends.

As we saw in Chapter 4, this informality is closely linked to the egalitarian nature of American society. People may have higher or lower positions, but to the American eye they are all equal as individuals. The waitress in a coffee shop can talk to the president of the bank essentially as an equal: He's just another customer, and besides, he's in her territory.

AMERIKANA IN THE CLOSET

When I graduated from college in the Philippines, I decided go to the United States in search of the American Dream. One of the first things I did was go to a tailor and get my very first *Amerikana* or business suit. For me, this symbolized corporate America.

In the United States, I got a job with an investment company in Santa Monica, California. The company was very "California casual." People came to work in shorts, T-shirts, and tennis shoes. The atmosphere was: "You can do and wear anything as long as you get the job done." This attitude was a surprise to me because even in my college days I never wore a pair of shorts to school. I always wore a pair of slacks or jeans. In general, Filipinos love to dress up. They don't mind if they feel uncomfortable in their clothes as long as they look good.

Americans value comfort above anything else. This seems to go with the informality of American culture. Superiors are on a first-name basis with employees. In the Philippines, they have to be addressed as Mr./Ms. or Sir/Madame. Philippine culture is very conscious of rank and status within the company.

What happened to the business suit that was once the symbol of corporate America to me? Well, it's hanging in my closet now. I just use it for weddings and baptisms. I wear shorts to work most of the week. They're more comfortable.

—Erikson Magallona

Informality is likely to have the opposite effect on people from traditional cultures. Rather than making them feel comfortable, it can make them very uncomfortable. Overly familiar behavior, especially if it crosses the line between different social levels, is often seen as simply rude.

Brazilians are very fashion conscious. You should dress your best in Brazil to avoid perpetuating the stereotype of the badly dressed gringo.
—Claudia McAchran

Americans abroad need to use more formality than they are used to. Posture both sitting and standing should be more erect. Watch how you cross your legs, and don't keep your hands in your pockets. Pay attention to forms of address: Use titles such as Doctor or President when they apply. To be safe, call others by their last names and titles until they ask you to call them by their first names. Pay close attention to how others interact and the forms of address they use. For example, people in Vietnam and Thailand use first names (personal names) with a title of Mr. or Mrs. A little extra reserve in your dealings with other people will go a long way—especially in Asian cultures.

It is important to act in accordance with your own titles and authority. At the same time, accord other people the deferential treatment that their titles and authority call for. You should be especially careful when addressing people of higher rank or status. Pay attention also to status relations within foreign companies you are dealing with. It may be inappropriate, for instance, to invite individuals of different rank in the company to a social event where they would have to interact as equals.

In many countries, especially in Asia and Europe, businesspeople dress more formally than they would in the United States. Europe is still a long way from accepting the "casual Friday" as a normal corporate practice. Being too informal in these cultures can undermine your credibility. In case of doubt, it's safer to err on the side of formality—even if this seems strange and uncomfortable from an American perspective.

Jokes, Politics, Religion

Jokes don't translate well. Many Americans, and even people from some other cultures, will start a speech at a social gathering with a joke to put

---

The American executive had given a lot of thought to a joke that would break the ice at the beginning of his sales presentation, and it looked as if his effort had paid off. When the translator had finished, the roomful of Japanese businessmen laughed heartily. They showed no interest in the proposal, however.

"What went wrong?" the American asked a friend who had attended the meeting. "They laughed so hard at my joke that I thought I had them." The friend smiled. "People weren't laughing at the joke," he said. "What the translator told them was, 'This American has just told a joke that is very culturally bound and makes no sense in terms of our culture, and so, if you would, all please laugh *now!*' "

SOURCE: "Working with the Japanese 101," *Business Tokyo*, October, 1990.

people at ease. But this is almost always a mistake in another country. Jokes are rooted in cultural nuances and allusions that rarely make sense in another cultural universe. Of course, we've all met people from other countries who crack us up by cleverly using their accent or cultural perspective to make us look at things in a new way. But you had better know what you're doing if you try this in another country; if you're just a little off you can ruin the whole tone of a relationship.

Germans find it out of place to tell jokes during a business meeting or negotiation. Business is serious and should be treated as such, without irrelevant stories or distractions. If you do not concentrate on the issue, you are not showing respect for your interlocutor. In their eyes, kidding is not honest and creates confusion. They want to know about price, quality, and delivery dates—with some precision, please!

After business is over, Germans are quite willing to relax and joke with their partners in bars, in restaurants, and at home. Humor and anecdotes are more than welcome in these circumstances. Like business, relaxation and many other activities are strictly compartmentalized in Germany.

—Rene Zimmerli

Politics is a subject worth avoiding as much as possible. Politics can trigger violent emotional reactions. It's very difficult to gauge where other people stand, and this problem is exacerbated by cultural difference. No one likes Saddam Hussein, but if you're in Saudi Arabia they might not like you criticizing someone else from the region. I can criticize my brother or sister or child—but if you do it as an outsider, that's an entirely different matter.

Religion is a final area to avoid as much as possible. Don't assume that people have a certain religion just because they live in a certain region. Half the Koreans in the United States are Christian. The Middle East has Jews, Christians, and Moslems in most countries. When you get better acquainted, or if others bring the subject up, you can talk about it—but don't ever make assumptions.

7

Who Should Go to Assure Success?

The Myth of the Ethnic Business Representative

It's a myth that just because it's your experience you can't get it wrong.

—John Irving[1]

One of the favorite pastimes of American politicians is quoting Alexis de Tocqueville's observations of American life. De Tocqueville, a French intellectual who came to the United States as an observer and student, seemed to capture the essence of the "American spirit." By studying American life carefully and dispassionately, de Tocqueville was able to turn a disadvantage into an advantage. Since he was not caught up inside the American experience, he could see it and articulate it more clearly than Americans themselves.

American corporations doing business abroad can learn an important lesson from de Tocqueville. Just because you're an outsider doesn't mean you can't understand another culture enough to do business there effectively. When they first arrive, Americans are given a good deal of latitude, and they command a good deal of respect precisely because they are outsiders. Later, after careful study, they should be able to do business effectively within a new business environment. In many ways, it is no different from learning the protocols and practices of a new business in the United States.

Another lesson to be learned from de Tocqueville is that just because you come from a culture doesn't mean you understand how it works. Confronted with doing business in unfamiliar foreign cultures, many American corporations turn automatically to immigrants from that country. After all, they reason, immigrants know the language and customs of the country. And since they are also American they can "translate" foreign business practices for the home office.

But this strategy often backfires. A good example is Denny Ko, who was born in Hong Kong and raised in Taiwan before he came to the United States, where he received a doctorate and went to work. Twenty-eight years after he immigrated to the United States, he was sent to run the Taiwan Aerospace Corporation in Taipei. According to the *Wall Street Journal*, the "relocation became a disaster because local colleagues treated him as an interloper." Said Ko about the experience: "You look like everyone around you, but your thinking process is almost foreign."[2]

Immigrants representing American businesses in their native land face a number of obstacles. If they have been gone for a long time, they may be out of touch. Many left when they were children or students and never learned the business practices of their native country, or the business rules they learned are no longer applicable.

Immigrants may have partially forgotten their language or internalized American attitudes that seem alien to the native culture. When Seiji "Frank" Sanda returned to Japan after working in the United States for 22 years, he was chastised by the personnel director of Apple Japan (which had hired him as president) for greeting a cleaning lady. Mr. Sanda found himself caught in the middle between two different cultures: "If you ask the Americans, I was too Japanese. If you ask the Japanese, I was too American."[3]

I am Asian, but I was adopted as young boy and given an English name. I lived in the United States for over 35 years with an American father and an Asian mother. As the Asians in California describe it, I am like a banana: yellow on the outside but white on the inside.

The Asian countries I visited all had similar reactions, but the confusion was greatest in Japan. The Japanese are more homogeneous and find it more difficult to relate to an Asian with American mannerisms. I felt obligated to describe my background at each and every introduction. I felt caught in a no-win situation. In Asia, I am perceived as an American with no real authority, and in the United States I am perceived as an Asian who tries to be an American—again with no real authority.

At one point, I was sent with a white American associate to negotiate a contract in Singapore. We were both at the same level in the organization, but since the project was a manufacturing operation, I was the lead negotiator. When we first got there, I noticed that they were all focused on my associate. They didn't seem to understand that I was the actual leader of the team.

—Ed McCowan

Being caught between a "home culture" and a "home company" can divide the loyalties of employees sent back to their native land. I was once negotiating with a shoe manufacturer in Brazil using a Brazilian expatriate as an interpreter. The negotiations were hard-nosed, and the interpreter, trying to make both sides happy, constructed what were essentially two different versions of the agreement—one that made the Brazilians happy and one that made us happy. As you can imagine, this led to misunderstandings down the road.

Another problem is that immigrants returning to their native lands often face higher levels of expectation than a native American would. Since they are from the country and speak the language, they are expected to operate as natives. Often they encounter resentment because of the higher status (or salary) that goes with representing an American company. In international negotiations, the other side can take it as an insult if the talks are "farmed out" to immigrants rather than conducted by native Americans (who are perceived as having more authority).

Dr. Ko recalls that he was so resented when he was president of Taiwan Aerospace that his coworkers leaked secrets to his rivals. In his view, the dependence of American companies on poorly trained returnees "is partly why American companies are having trouble in China."[4] In another case, the *Wall Street Journal* reports that:

A major consumer-electronics maker hired a number of Chinese-born and Chinese-American new graduates from U.S. business schools for its burgeoning Beijing operation. But local colleagues resented the new junior managers because "they formed cliques and came across as if they were better trained," says Larry Wang, managing director of the Wang

& Li Asia Resources recruitment firm in Hong Kong. This year, he continues, the manufacturer asked the recruiters to locate ethnic Chinese "who aren't expecting special privileges and who realize they need to fit in immediately."[5]

Of course, in some cases it makes sense to send someone from the country in question. Advance work such as finding office space, setting up initial contacts, navigating government bureaucracies, or setting up the technical infrastructure of a foreign office, as well as preparatory work for negotiations can be done much more easily by someone who knows the language and culture. Gathering market information or doing initial research on a foreign firm's operations also calls for someone familiar with the culture and language.

Another option for companies involved in long-term relations with foreign subsidiaries or suppliers is hiring personnel locally. Many companies are moving away from expatriate American managers to oversee long-term operations in foreign subsidiaries and relying instead on local hires. According the *Wall Street Journal*:

> Local hires often display a more effective grasp of the nuances of doing business in their own country, and consequently are often more successful at it. Managers native to the city or country or region in which they operate are more skilled at solving local labor disputes, negotiating with regional suppliers, and anticipating consumer vexation.[6]

In the final analysis, the decision about who to send on a business trip abroad should depend on qualifications for the job at hand rather than ethnic or national identity. In both cases, however, training is important.

How Do Americans Select Who Should Go?

> *The clever combatant looks to the effect of combined energy, and does not require too much from individuals. He takes individual talent into account, and uses each man according to his capabilities. He does not demand perfection from the untalented. When he utilizes combined energy, his fighting men become, as it were, like rolling logs or stones. The energy developed by good fighting men is as the momentum of a round stone rolled down a mountain thousands of feet in height.*
>
> —Sun Tzu[7]

In international negotiations, Americans prefer to send a single person or a small team under the control of a single leader. This "John Wayne" approach to international business derives from the American tradition of self-reliance and individualism. The executive in charge is like a "lone gunslinger or a U.S. marshal going out single-handed to eliminate a gang of outlaws."[8] Since sending personnel abroad can be costly, the American style has the added benefit of keeping costs down.

As the complexity, scale, and stakes of international business increase, however, American companies should consider the advantages of using a team approach. Having a team allows the person in charge access to expertise in each area under consideration. Team members can provide valuable cross-checking to make sure that decisions are sound or that essential parts of the agreement have not been overlooked or misunderstood. Having a team also supplies valuable emotional and logistical support when the pressure is on. It is very difficult and intimidating for a lone company representative to hold out against a team of representatives from the other side—especially on their turf. As a rule of thumb, sizes of teams from both sides should be evenly matched.

There are three important areas to consider when selecting executives, managers, or negotiators for a foreign assignment: technical abilities, social skills, and attitude.

Technical abilities include scholastic achievement, scientific skills, legal training, business skills, and language fluency. Technical knowledge is, in general, easier to communicate than the strategic aspects of a business relationship or negotiation. Regardless of their cultural differences, engineers and scientists around the world speak a common technical language. But technical people often have less experience dealing across cultural lines, and they should be trained to deal with language and cultural barriers. The English proficiency of the technical people on the other side's team, for instance, might be much lower than that of the senior negotiators, and it requires special work to communicate across these accent and language barriers.

When choosing the technical people on your team, try to match them to the technical people on the other team. If the other side includes a specialist in chemical engineering or quality control, it's because they feel this issue is important. Having an equivalent technical person on your side will help ensure smooth lines of communication.

Social skills include status, social class, kinship, personal attributes, and interpersonal skills. (In many cultures, kinship and social class may be more important for a businessperson than they would be in the United States.) Be careful about including representatives who are glib but do not have credentials or status to back them up; they are likely to be dismissed as irrelevant in many cultures. Generally speaking, the senior people on a team should be chosen for their people skills and for their ability to understand the global structure of the project. It is their job to coordinate the technical people and develop the overall strategy of relating to the other side. The status of senior representatives should match that of the other team's.

A third component of selecting representatives to go abroad—attitude—is often overlooked by American companies. Many Americans end up on negotiating teams or in long-term foreign assignments simply because their jobs put them there, but the truth is that some people are simply much better suited to working abroad than others.

To really be successful in another country, companies need to find people willing to make the necessary commitment to working with and in foreign countries. Takashi Kiuchi, a Japanese executive who spent many years living in the United States, tells audiences how his company asked him to come to the United States to spend his life living and working here. He then asks, "How many of you are willing to live in Japan for 15 to 20 years? How many of you are willing to spend the rest of your life in Jakarta or Bangkok?" The response, he observes, is usually dead silence.[9]

WHO ARE THE BEST CANDIDATES FOR INTERNATIONAL ASSIGNMENTS?

- Immigrants from the target country are not a sure answer.
- Consider local hires for long-term assignments.
- Language familiarity and cultural knowledge are important but not determining factors.
- Candidates with a flexible life situation are best for long-term assignments.
- Credentials and technical knowledge are essential for establishing credibility.
- Candidates with a capacity to handle ambiguity and uncertainty tend to do better.
- Attitude is everything: A sense of adventure and willingness to learn are the most important attributes of successful expatriates.

How Do Other Countries Select Who Should Go?

In order to understand whom they will be facing when they go abroad, Americans need to understand how foreign companies select managers and negotiators. An American company might consider a powerful speaker to be an ideal representative, whereas such a person might not have such high regard in Japan or China. Age, status, social class, and connections are more important in the selection of representatives from many countries in Asia, the Middle East, Latin America, and Europe.

Following are some short descriptions of how selected countries choose their negotiators.

France: Negotiators are chosen according to their social and professional status, their family ties, and academic qualifications. Social and verbal skills are highly regarded.[10] The French respect those who can hold their own in a good argument, and verbal sparring is an important part of establishing position.

Germany: Germans are very competence driven and task oriented. Negotiators have an excellent grasp of the details of a proposal or project.[11] Over 40 percent of German managers have an engineering-related education and most have been trained in scientific business management.[12] Because of the compartmentalization of German business, negotiators may not have direct communication with other departments or higher levels of management in their companies.

Japan: Selection of negotiators is closely tied to corporate status, which in turn is based on age, seniority, and knowledge of the subject. The Japanese expect much more loyalty and sacrifice from their executives than American companies do, including willingness to acquire language skills and work for long periods of time in foreign countries. Long-term thinking, good listening skills, pragmatism, and a broad perspective are often more important than detailed technical knowledge or skills—though this is changing rapidly.

China: Selection of negotiators is often influenced by political loyalty, with expertise an important but secondary consideration. Chinese negotiating teams are often large and responsibility is often difficult to pinpoint. Because of the great number of international contacts currently taking place, Chinese foreign-language specialists and specialists with managerial know-how and technical expertise are often spread thin.[13]

Korea: Negotiators are chosen based on status, knowledge, and expertise. Because of the influence of Confucianism, respect for elders is of paramount importance. Senior negotiators are often in their fifties or sixties, though economic pressures are bringing in younger figures. These younger figures are usually very well trained and educated, and are often related in some way to corporation founders.[14]

India: Indian society places a great deal of emphasis on social harmony, but this is complicated by intense social stratification. Higher levels of management often have a paternalistic attitude toward subordinates, whom they do not always trust, and who are not trained to function independently. Teams usually include both technicians and negotiators from company management.[15]

Spain: Class standing is very important in the Spanish business world and in the selection of negotiators, especially at the senior level. *Enchufismo*—having the right connections—is an important consideration. Education is also important; senior negotiators often have attended an elite university in Europe or the United States. Women are rare in higher-level positions, but this situation is changing slowly with the internationalization of business.[16]

Brazil: As in Spain, status is very important in Brazilian society and business. Brazilian negotiators are likely to be highly educated social elites. Social and speaking skills are considered important. Many companies in Brazil are privately owned, and with smaller companies it is common to find oneself negotiating directly with the owner.[17]

The Importance of Establishing Trust and Credibility

A nation's well-being, as well as its ability to compete, is conditioned by a single, pervasive cultural characteristic: the level of trust inherent in the society.

—Francis Fukuyama[1]

Although technology has made it easy to contact virtually anyone in the world, it cannot determine the quality of that communication or guarantee a transaction will be a success. If anything, the ability to communicate quickly across time zones and national borders makes your personal skill at establishing a relationship of trust and credibility even more important. In the final analysis, the effectiveness and profitability of international business transactions depend on the quality of the relationship the different parties are able to establish.

In the United States we don't start out by focusing on building a relationship because we concentrate on specific tasks and rely on our well-defined legal system to enforce business agreements. Our culture values the written word above all else, and we depend on it to protect us so that we can concentrate on getting the job done. In group-oriented cultures, people have traditionally relied on the other side's word and character to ensure that they will fulfill their side of the bargain. Business relationships are based on establishing credibility and trust with the other side. They need to believe that you have the expertise to do what

123

you say you will, and that you will live up to your word, even if the going gets tough.

Style and Intent or Time?

During my seminars, when we begin to talk about building relationships overseas, someone invariably objects: "But I can't invest a lifetime to establish a relationship. I need to get my work done." Or someone will say: " I wish I had enough time when I go overseas to get wined and dined, play golf, and build a relationship, but I haven't!" The tight schedules and cost-cutting measures of modern business have made this problem even more acute. Business trips are shorter than ever before. There is a great deal of pressure from the home office to fly in, get an agreement, and fly back out. How does one build a relationship of trust in this environment?

Establishing a relationship in business doesn't mean that you are required to cultivate cousins, aunts, and uncles overseas. A solid business relationship means developing an atmosphere of confidence in which both sides can proceed without constantly looking over their shoulders. Will the other side honor its promises? Will each side be mindful of the other's interests and work to protect them? Will the other side have the capability and authority to deliver on promises made?

Building such a relationship depends more on intent and style than on the actual time you put into it. You could know someone over a period of time and still not trust each other. In some situations, the more you know about someone the more uneasy you feel. With others, a bond of trust is established quite early and forms the basis for a continuing relationship. Therefore, although you build trust over time, it is important to quickly establish the *basis* for a relationship of trust early on.

How to Build Trust and Credibility

> *Credibility: reputation, status; acceptability among one's peers.*
> —*Oxford Encyclopedic Dictionary*, Second Edition

Trust and credibility are two sides of the same coin: You can't have one without the other. To have the other side's trust means convincing them you have the character and integrity to carry through on your promises. Credibility means convincing them you have the authority, skills, and connections necessary to do the job.

Imagine that you're a trapeze artist hanging from another acrobat's arms high above the ground (Figure 8.1). The only thing keeping you from plunging to your death is the other person's grip. What will give you confidence that he won't drop you? I ask this question during my seminars and the typical responses are: First, "How strong is he? Will he hold on securely?" The second thing people want to know is: "What is his track record? How many people has he dropped previously?" Finally, "How much does he care about me? Does he like me?"

In international business, your counterpart wants to have the answer to a similar set of questions. First, what are the other side's qualifications? Do they have the skills and contacts to do the job? Second, what is their track record? Have they established credibility in this field through previous performance? Third, does the other side have a win-win approach to the transaction? That is, do they care about my interests as well as theirs?

First Impressions: Self-Presentation versus Background

In this culture we say, "You don't have a second chance to make a first impression." Americans quickly size up people and then pass a final judgment based on the person's performance. In the United States, we tend to trust others until they prove themselves untrustworthy. People

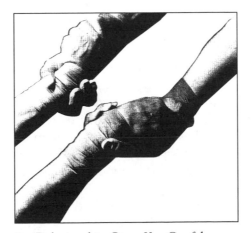

Figure 8.1   A Trusting Relationship Gives You Confidence

are "innocent until proven guilty." We make our judgments quickly based on first impressions gained from the way people handle themselves. Do they seem confident and comfortable? Do they look the part?

In most other cultures, first impressions are important, but trust is withheld until more is learned about background and qualifications. Trust is earned, not given. For Americans, this means unlearning ingrained and largely unconscious habits about how to sell oneself. Businesspeople are expected to talk openly about their qualifications and accomplishments—to sell themselves much as they would sell a product. We ask direct questions that call for self-promotion and then judge the other side by how well they make their sales pitch.

Mexicans are very distrustful of foreigners. Mexico has a long history of subjugation, foreign intervention, and revolution. There is suspicion and sometimes hatred of foreigners. They feel that foreigners do not take the trouble to study Mexican history and culture. Foreigners are also distrusted because they are seen as lacking deep religious faith, commitment to family, and a strong sense of morality.

Trust may be gained by showing interest in Mexico's history and culture, learning to be patient, and being sensitive to concerns expressed by the Mexican side. You should not insist that doing things your way is best, even if this is true. Egos can be hurt easily. Mexicans expect foreigners to take advantage of them economically, take their profits, and leave the country. Because of the long history of U.S. intervention, Mexicans are afraid of being taken advantage of by gringos. A business deal will work only if it is seen as a win-win situation for both parties.

—*Alan Ibarra*

In almost all traditional cultures in the world, this behavior comes across as arrogant. According to a Chinese proverb: "An empty bottle makes lots of noise." In Asian cultures, especially, humility is highly valued. Talking about oneself is seen as lack of confidence and authority. Businesspeople from traditional cultures have learned that appearances can be deceiving, and they usually reserve judgment until they have enough information to develop a full picture. You can help them in this process by conveying information about your education, experience, and position in the company.

Remember that Americans tend to be oriented toward the future, while many other cultures are oriented toward the past. During an initial meeting, Americans are likely to focus on future goals and objectives, trying to build a relationship on this proposed interaction. Their basic sales pitch is: "This is what I can do for you." Businesspeople from traditional cultures, however, are likely to be more interested in past behavior and relationships. Were you dependable and reliable? Have past relationships worked out for the best? Do you have mutual friends who could attest to this past behavior? They want to know your qualifications and background, and they want to work with people who have prestige and authority.

COMMUNICATE YOUR CREDENTIALS UP FRONT AND IN WRITING

An American company hoping to start doing business in Russia hired a Russian consultant to open initial negotiations with a potential Russian business partner. The consultant had moved to the United States after the fall of the Soviet Union, and with the help of his American wife he had set up a consulting business. An appointment was arranged, and the consultant went to Russia to meet with the director of the Russian enterprise. Upon arriving in Moscow, he called the director to confirm his appointment for the next day. The director wanted to give him directions about how to get there and where to park his car. The consultant told him: "I don't have a car, and I know exactly where you are located. I used to live in those apartments behind your office, and I know how to take the subway to get there."

When the consultant arrived at the appointed time, the director was gone and his secretary said he was not expected back. At first the consultant was astonished and upset. All that money and effort gone to waste! Then it dawned on him: Someone who didn't have a car and used to live in those dilapidated apartments wasn't worth the director's time. Rather than being impressed with the consultant's familiarity with Moscow, the director had dismissed him because he didn't seem to have the necessary prestige and authority. He would have done much better by establishing his credibility prior to his trip—for instance, by sending a letter of introduction from the president of the American company. This would have established him as an important envoy, not just a former resident of Moscow.

When you are interviewing for a job in the United States, the people who might hire you want to know one thing: Can you do the job? It's up to you to demonstrate your skills and expertise, and you will likely be judged on the spot by how well you convince your prospective employer that you are the man or woman for the job. In most parts of the world, your credentials are more important than your skill at selling yourself. Where did you go to school and what degrees did you receive? Whom have you worked for? Who can vouch for your expertise and integrity? What important connections do you have? What is your track record? Of course, these count for Americans, too, but they are often less important than they are in status-oriented cultures.

One of my first experiences in international business was when I was working as a sales representative for a company in Los Angeles. One of my clients was an American music company whose purchasing office was located in San Diego. I sold a variety of packaging components for its guitar string production facility, which was located across the border in Ensenada, Mexico. The operations manager in the Ensenada facility ultimately made the buying decisions.

My San Diego buyer thus functioned as a liaison who presented my products and services to the Ensenada office. The problem was that they communicated only by fax. Both my buyer and I had a difficult time conveying product innovations and changes in pricing structures effectively. If there were problems with a shipment that required input from the Mexican facility, it would often take days to iron out the problem.

I was anxious to establish a direct relationship with the Ensenada facility to help overcome these difficulties, but despite numerous requests I was unable to arrange a face-to-face meeting. This continued for some time until I learned that the San Diego purchasing office would be closing and I would be dealing directly with the Ensenada operations manager. I was delighted! I could make direct sales calls to the decision maker—the way things should be!

I knew the operations manager wrote and spoke English, so I faxed him a letter asking for a meeting at his facility on a specified date. I also suggested that we go out to lunch afterward, so that we would have some time to get to know each other. Since I am out of town frequently, I asked him to respond via my 800 voice mail. He did respond and agree to the meeting and—tentatively—to the lunch. I found out later that it is very difficult to make 800 calls from Mexico and that this was the reason for communicating by fax with the San Diego office.

During our meeting in Mexico, I learned that the facility needed fewer units of a certain product because production requirements had changed. I had to tell him that the new requirement fell well beneath our minimums, and that we would have to charge higher prices for special production. He immediately canceled the purchase order and made sure I knew that he had other vendors who would give him the product at the price he wanted. He seemed upset that my boss was not at the meeting and rather mystified that I could make important decisions about pricing without consulting my boss. After the meeting was over, I reminded him of the lunch we had discussed, but he politely refused.

—*Victoria Wilk*

Use education and titles to your advantage. People from status-oriented countries place great stock in titles and educational credentials. If you have an advanced degree or you've graduated from a prestigious school, let the other side know. You should also have a job title in your company that clearly conveys your level of authority. If you are young and without an impressive title on your business card, get the highest-level person in your company you can to write a letter of introduction for you.

GET A FORMAL INTRODUCTION

When you approach someone without an introduction, walls go up that are difficult and time-consuming to penetrate. But when someone the other side respects and trusts introduces you, the walls come down very quickly. It isn't necessary for them to know the person introducing you personally, as long as he or she has the necessary title and credentials.

For example, get a letter of introduction from a reputable bank, trading company, or government organization that can give a good account of the experience they've had with you as a business associate. This is especially important for independent businesspeople who don't have the benefit of a corporate name to establish their credibility. Trade missions led by important government officials can shorten the process of making initial contacts and help to establish instant credibility for visiting business executives.

South Koreans prefer to be introduced by someone already known to them. The South Koreans are great networkers. Westerners are often surprised that Koreans know who was in the classes above and below them at all levels of their education, who comes from their hometowns, and everyone who works in companies related to theirs. The reason is simple: Since the most acceptable way to arrange a meeting is through a mutual friend or acquaintance, the wider one's circle of friends and contacts, the easier it is to open doors in the Korean business community.

—*Nam Suk Lee*

ESTABLISH YOUR AUTHORITY

An American woman with her own import-export company and years of experience doing business in China went to Vietnam to meet with a potential trading partner. Before the first scheduled meeting, her Vietnamese counterpart phoned her hotel and canceled the meeting. Feeling that she was being brushed off, she insisted that he be there. The Vietnamese official agreed but then showed up an hour late. The relationship remained cold and distant the whole time she was there. Was she being brushed off simply because she was a woman? A more likely explanation was that she hadn't sent any advance material establishing her credentials or sought out someone of importance to introduce her. The Vietnamese official didn't know who she was, so he didn't take her seriously.

Association with people who have prestige and authority helps establish your importance. Although influence-peddling happens in this country as well, Americans are generally uncomfortable with the idea of using important friends or connections to get ahead in business. In many cases it may even be illegal. In Asia, Latin America, and the Middle East, knowing important people confers a great deal of status and forms an important part of your "portfolio." Americans were recently scandalized by the attempts of Asian businesspeople to "buy influence" by making large contributions after mingling with President Clinton or other important figures. In most cases, however, the influence they were after was not in Washington but back in Asia. A photo showing the recipient having lunch with the president of the United States confers a kind of status that many Americans would find difficult to understand.

> The attraction of a photo with a U.S. [president] isn't hard to explain in Asia: It conveys a proximity to power that can be useful in business or politics. Many businesspeople in China, for instance, crowd their office walls with pictures of themselves with top Chinese officials. When Chinese President Jiang Zemin earlier this year made a point of shaking the hand of Hong Kong shipping magnate C. H. Tung in front of the cameras at a reception in Beijing, Mr. Tung was seen by many as China's anointed choice to lead Hong Kong after July 1 next year when it reverts to China.[2]

ESTABLISH YOUR SPOT ON THE TOTEM POLE

A former colleague of mine was in charge of a delegation of negotiators in Japan. He was a relatively young man, and one of the other negotiators was considerably older. The Japanese, quite naturally, assumed the older man was in charge and treated him with greater deference than the actual leader. Since he was an American, the younger man hardly noticed the misplaced respect and deference, but when the Japanese found out who was the real leader it caused considerable confusion and loss of face. The whole problem could have been avoided by identifying the positions of the various members of the team before the negotiations began.

When Mexicans conduct business for the first time with foreigners, they tend to be extremely polite and go to great lengths to show their admiration and respect. Some outsiders might consider this behavior as overdone or insincere, but they will find that this posturing disappears once both parties have established their relative positions in the hierarchy. It is extremely important to Mexicans that relative positions be understood clearly. It is vital to determine and acknowledge the status of the person you are dealing with as well as to convey your own position clearly.
—*Alan Ibarra*

People from status-oriented cultures like to do business with people of authority. They are unhappy when they think they are doing business with errand boys or errand girls. They aren't comfortable unless they have a clear idea of where you fit on the totem pole. Before your first trip, it is helpful to send a packet with information about your company and your product, and a brief biography or curriculum vitae that explains your experience and education. Information conveyed in writing carries more weight than verbal information—especially in cultures where describing your accomplishments orally may be seen as bragging. Sending this information in advance will establish your credentials and let the other side know who you are before you arrive. This will help them feel comfortable that they know the person they are dealing with and save time in establishing an initial relationship.

Business cards are essential for doing business in Korea. Your business card is your company passport and should clearly show your place in the company hierarchy. It is a good idea to have your cards printed in English and Korean, with a Korean title that accurately reflects your place in the company.

Koreans will often supplement scrutiny of your business card with questions that seem blunt, even impertinent: "How old are you?" "Are you married?" "How many children do you have?" They may even ask how much you earn. Though they seem out of place to Americans, these questions help Koreans fit foreigners into their frame of reference. It is often quite difficult for Koreans to tell how old Westerners are, and they may be confused by Western job titles.

—Nam Suk Lee

EXPRESS A SENSE OF SINCERITY

In this culture we say someone is trustworthy if he or she is honest and straightforward. A good friend can be trusted to "tell it like it is." In traditional, group-oriented cultures, however, trust means having the other side's best interests at heart. This is likely to seem odd to Americans, especially in business relationships. We tend to assume that others can take care of themselves as long as they have all the facts. Being trustworthy means being forthcoming with the facts and honest about one's intentions. If circumstances change, we assume that each party will use those facts to look after its own best interests. In group-oriented cultures where attention to the human side of the equation is the norm, however, a relationship of trust means that you watch out for the other side as you do for yourself. Of course these cultural expectations are based on an ideal situation. In any culture there are opportunists who look for any chance to gain at the expense of the other side. And when the going gets tough, people always put their own interests first. But the *ideal* of trust in group-oriented and traditional cultures is still based on mutual aid, not honesty.

As we saw earlier, group-oriented cultures need to establish a relationship of trust before they can work comfortably with someone. This can create problems for Americans, who often assume that a relationship of trust will emerge simply from working together. But focusing on the job—a perfectly natural relationship-builder for Americans—is likely to have the opposite effect on people from group-oriented cultures, who are likely to feel that they are secondary to task and profit. One of the most common complaints foreign business executives make about Americans is that they are only interested in money. In his guide for Japanese businesspeople doing business in the United States, Takashi

Kiuchi, the former chairman of Mitsubishi Electric, America, comments: "The extent of some Americans' avarice for money is rather embarrassing to the ordinary Japanese. For many Americans, almost any problem can be solved with money."[3]

But *everyone* is interested in making money. Self-interest plays just as important a role in Japan or China—it is just that this self-interest is focused differently. Self-interest is achieved through other people in the group rather than by independent action focused exclusively on the task at hand. Self-interest is ensured by maintaining the right relationships and connections—making money cannot be easily separated from maintaining group relationships. The American style of expressing self-interest is up front and open. Other cultures, such as Asian, Middle Eastern, and Latino, are indirect and camouflaged.

In group-oriented cultures, it thus is important to establish a rapport by acknowledging people as important in their own right rather than treating them as just incidental to the task at hand. How do you accomplish this? It isn't that difficult or time-consuming. When the Japanese hand you a business card, take the time to read it carefully before putting it away. This shows that you really care about who they are and the time they have taken to present themselves. Don't jump right into business. Pay attention to others as people. Take time at the beginning of meetings to establish personal connections. Remember the importance of after-hours socializing in the conduct of business in many countries.

Even more important: Show that you care about *their* issues and problems. It's remarkable how often American representatives abroad conceive of their task as presenting their own position, needs, and interests. While it's important not to forget your own interests, showing concern for the other side's position will go a long way toward establishing trust. Ask questions that show you are concerned about their needs and listen carefully to what they say. As far as possible, structure proposals and presentations to show that you've given thought to their needs and concerns.

DON'T EMPHASIZE LEGAL DOCUMENTS IN PLACE OF HUMAN RELATIONSHIPS

Contracts are very important in American culture. And of course you must pay attention to a valid and viable contract. But remember that many other cultures are just getting used to detailed legal contracts. Calling in the lawyers too soon is seen as a sign of distrust. With the advent of globalization, lawyers and contracts have become the norm, but they are not liked or taken to heart. It's like a prenuptial agreement: It takes the romance out of the relationship.

I once asked a top official from the Malaysian consulate in Los Angeles for the best advice he could give to Americans doing business in Malaysia. His response: "Don't threaten with a lawsuit as soon as a disagreement comes up."

Generally speaking, it is better to get an agreement between people first and formalize this in contract form at the end of the negotiations. Asian, Latin American, and Middle Eastern cultures may prefer to leave agreements flexible so they can make adjustments if circumstances change. Although you want to be culturally sensitive, don't sacrifice legal clarity or enforceability. In the future, these legal clarifications and enforceability provisions will reduce conflict. If there are differences over the interpretation or implementation of contracts, it is a good idea not to threaten immediate legal action. Before you resort to these tactics, try to solve problems through go-betweens or established relationships.

A very successful executive from Fluor Daniel Corporation who often negotiates multibillion-dollar contracts recently told me that the secret to his success is that he understands the ramifications of his deals so well that he doesn't need to get a lawyer involved in the initial stages of negotiations. This helps him to establish a personal relationship with his clients before the lawyers get involved in the details of negotiations and drafting of a final contract.

AVOID PRESSURE TACTICS

Americans value hard-driving, aggressive executives, but this tactic can backfire overseas. Pushing the other side to make a quick decision undermines their trust in you. The more impatient you are, the more they want to stretch the process. If you are negotiating to sell them your product or services, they may want to shop around and consider other options. The way to get them to choose your company is to give them information that focuses their attention and helps them make a decision. Remember to be sensitive to the way decisions are made in their culture. If you let them have time for networking and consultation, they will take it as a sign of respect and trust. They will be happier with the deal, and you will have set the groundwork for a long-term relationship.

Brazilians don't like to be pressured to sign a contract, and they like to bargain about the price. If Americans aren't willing to lower the price, they probably won't get the contract. The best strategy is to start with a fairly high price so that it can be lowered during the bargaining process without loss.

—*Claudia McAchran*

Refraining from the use of pressure tactics does not mean making concessions or being soft. Businesspeople from cultures with a long history of trading have become very tough negotiators, and they will not respect you if you show weakness or capitulate easily to their demands. You need to be patient and polite but firm. Don't be thrown by the way people from other cultures present their demands. Asians tend to be self-contained, while Middle Eastern, Russian, Latino, and Southern European cultures are often quite emotional. Keep your emotions in check and be dignified at all times. Show patience and listen. But don't let restraint become weakness.

YOUR WORD SHOULD BE AS GOOD AS A WRITTEN CONTRACT

Keeping your word is the essence of building trust. With the globalization of the economy in recent years, the lure of quick profits and the temptation to take advantage of strangers have become common. In a world with hundreds of markets, why not make a quick buck and get out before the other side can do anything about it?

An American company, for instance, placed a large order with a Chinese company in the mid-1980s. This was the first international experience for the Chinese company. When the shipment arrived by boat for delivery, the Americans discovered that the distributor they'd lined up no longer wanted the shipment. Instead of alienating the distributor, who was essential to their future business, they decided to stiff the Chinese company and cancel the purchase order, knowing well the Chinese had no recourse. The huge shipment was left rotting on a pier in California.

This might sound like a smart decision in a hardball business climate, but it is ultimately self-defeating. Keeping one's word and banking the accrued trust will be more profitable in the long run. Your reputation is an important asset in international business. You may be able to put it over on others once or twice, but your reputation will eventually catch up with you. International business may have hundreds of markets, but it also has networks of information, evaluation, and gossip that move across borders and cultures.

MAINTAIN BUSINESS RELATIONS OVER TIME

In China, *guanxi* or connection is very important in business. Having the right connections can mean the difference between a deal and no deal. Though the Chinese custom of *guanxi* incorporates an element of graft, it is a common practice widely used by the Chinese people and should not be cause for offense. This is just how things get done in Chinese society. In fact, using *guanxi* can help you get things done faster and more efficiently if used properly.

—*Nadia Lee*

When doing business with traditional and group-oriented cultures, it is important to think in the long term. When these companies are deciding whether to do business with you, they want to know if they can count on you when the going gets rough—or, conversely, whether they would want to help you out if necessary. They want a relationship that can grow and adapt to new circumstances in a way that is mutually beneficial for both sides. Approaching the relationship as a long-term commitment will help convince people from these cultures that you take them seriously. Using this approach also helps to lay the groundwork for future win-win relationships.

Maintaining relations with individuals is also a valuable asset in international business. In many cultures, a mutual friend, a good connection, or a recommendation from an important person can help you out years down the road. Takashi Kiuchi has an interesting system for keeping in touch with people in the long term. Whenever he meets someone new, he asks for his or her business card. At the end of the year, he places all the cards he has collected in a photo album. He can thus go back through the albums and remember all the people he has met for each year.[4] Modern electronic organizers make this task even easier.

USE A SIMPLE RECIPE FOR BUILDING TRUST AND CREDIBILITY

The process of establishing trust and credibility can be summed up in four easy-to-follow steps. Although this chapter has been devoted to establishing personal credibility, the same recipe applies to the relationship between corporations and their customers.

1. Communicate your credentials and your facts up front and back them up with written documentation.
2. Establish that your authority comes from the highest level.
3. Be consistent; don't change your story in midstream.
4. Show that you care about the other side and their special circumstances.

Even the world's best-known brand blundered badly in the European market by violating these simple rules. Coca-Cola failed to move quickly to establish trust and credibility with the public in response to a contamination scare in Europe in June 1999. Due to a series of minor lapses in production and testing, batches of Coca-Cola from bottling plants in Antwerp in Belgium and Dunkirk in France were contaminated—either with fungicide used on shipping pallets or with contaminated CO_2 gas. A number of people, including children from several schools, became ill after drinking Coca-Cola with a "foul smell." Coke's response to the crisis was a classic case in botched public relations. After a number of complaints, Coke tried to mobilize a credible investigation. Shipments of Coke were sporadically recalled while local company executives assured people that their tests revealed no real health dangers—despite accumulating reports of illness and the fact that they had no confirmation of the safety of suspect shipments from their labs. When they finally brought in a credible expert—a toxicology specialist from Utrecht University in the Netherlands—they simply gave him data from their own labs to review. Based on this, Coke claimed that the levels of any impurities were too low to cause any health risks and implied that many of the reported illnesses were psychosomatic. But Coke's data came from only a small sample of the suspect shipments, and the original gas used was no longer available for testing.

Coke's handling of the affair effectively squandered its credibility with the European public. The executives started out by not presenting the real facts up front and documenting them. Then they left the verification of those facts to local managers who didn't have the authority or expertise to make claims about the purity of the product. They kept changing their story in midstream as new facts about the case emerged. Finally, they produced a series of conflicting versions of the event that were clearly designed to defend Coke—even going so far as to imply that sick schoolchildren were simply imagining their illnesses. As France's health minister, Bernard Kouchner, commented: "That a company so very expert in advertising and marketing should be so poor in communicating on this matter is astonishing."[5]

Principles of Successful Cross-Cultural Communication

The most immutable barrier in nature is between one man's thoughts and another's.

—William James

The Art of Persuasion

Rhetoric means surveying the available means of persuasion and choosing the best one.

—Aristotle

You can't argue a man into liking a glass of beer.
—Oliver Wendell Holmes

Aristotle's theory of rhetoric proposes three forms of persuasion (Figure 9.1): *logos* (an appeal to the listener through logical argumentation), *pathos* (an appeal to the listener's emotions), and *ethos* (an appeal to the listener based on the speaker's authority and the community values he represents).[1] Each of these persuasion strategies is appropriate in certain circumstances. The trick to communicating effectively across cultures is to judge when each is likely to be most effective.

Americans tend to rely heavily on rational arguments to convince others to adopt their viewpoint. This approach follows naturally from

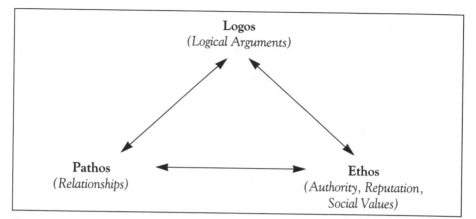

Figure 9.1   Aristotle's Mode of Persuasion

American management style, which relies on analysis and rational problem solving to achieve discrete, clearly defined goals. For many Americans—and Europeans from countries like Germany, England, France, and Scandinavia—rational argument is the ultimate means of persuasion. Once a speaker (at least one with the proper authority) has "proved" his or her point logically and presented a well thought out plan of action, the argument is assumed to be over.

When I came from Spain to work in the United States, I was astonished to see the degree to which my opinion was taken into account in the decision-making process. Although I had no previous experience working in the United States, my opinions (some of them—not all, of course) were taken into consideration and my supervisor requested my feedback on an ongoing basis. In Spain, relatively important decisions are made only at the top, by either the owner or the general manager of the company. Employees do not have much influence and their input is limited. These customs are starting to change, however, because companies are beginning to realize the advantages of having all levels of the organization participate actively in planning and decision making.

—Maria C. Garcia Garcia

Reason, however, is not always the only way to persuade someone else to see things your way. Rational arguments tend to put the other side on the defensive—forcing them to devise rational arguments of their own to defend their position. Instead of one side convincing the other through superior arguments, both sides get entrenched in their own positions.

"It is important to remember: The Japanese do not operate from here"—he pointed to his head—"but from here"—pointing to his midsection. I dutifully wrote down his remark but discounted it. After all, I thought, look at all their long-range planning, their obsession with statistics, their attention to detail. Doesn't all this suggest the Japanese are the ultimate rationalists, that the emotionalism and instinctual behavior Father Ballon was suggesting had no place in trying to understand them? He was right, of course. Sure, the Japanese can intellectualize with the best in the West. And they border on the obsessive with their demands for information on which to base judgments. But, in the end, they make those judgments much more on how they feel than on what they think.

—*Mike Tharp*[2]

Generally speaking, rational arguments are only convincing when they confirm what we already feel in our gut. Group-oriented cultures emphasize tradition or intuition as the basis of decision making. This does not mean these cultures are irrational or incapable of thinking problems through logically. They just don't think of reason as the bottom line of making a decision.

In practical terms, this means that Americans working abroad need to pay closer attention to *pathos* and *ethos*. From a business perspective, *pathos* can be understood as the quality of the relationship between two parties—the emotional or personal bonds that hold them together. Traditional and group-oriented cultures tend to see business as a set of relationships and obligations rather than a set of discrete, disembodied agreements and tasks. Persuading the other side to see things a certain way means convincing them to trust you. If they feel secure in the relationship, they assume that the logical details of the situation can be worked out. If they don't feel secure, they are likely to view what you say with suspicion regardless of the logical proofs you offer in your favor.

Another important principle of persuasion—especially with Southern Europeans, Middle Easterners, Latin Americans, and Asians—is an appeal to *ethos*. *Ethos* refers both to the authority of the speaker and to the norms and values of a society. Americans believe that a good argument speaks for itself. In traditional cultures, the authority of the speaker is often just as important as the internal logic of the argument itself. The speaker's connections and credentials guarantee the validity of the argument.

Ethos also derives from the social values of the audience. Tailoring one's presentation to appeal to these values can be a powerful rhetorical strategy. Martin Luther King Jr.'s famous sermons and speeches reached across the divide separating whites from blacks by appealing to democratic and religious values that formed the backbone of American political ideology. King was an excellent cross-cultural communicator. He realized that what was important was not proving his point but releasing the desired response in white audiences—in this case, mobilizing their belief in American values such as equality and the intrinsic dignity of man.

What Are the Impediments to Good Communication?

East is East, and West is West, and never the twain shall meet.
—Rudyard Kipling, "The Ballad of East and West"

Stereotyping assigns attributes to people based simply on their membership in a particular group. Often these attributes themselves are a result of myths or preconceptions that are of dubious accuracy. The idea that Asians are "inscrutable" or that all Arabs are Islamic extremists are examples of stereotyping. In today's world, most people claim not to stereotype others. But stereotyping is a largely unconscious process—part of the way we make sense of the world by putting things into categories. It was probably very useful, for instance, for primitive men to stereotype all lions as dangerous rather than having an open mind about each new lion. But in the communication process—especially across cultures—stereotyping can often lead to misleading impressions of others and false conclusions about their motives, actions, and goals.[3]

OVERCOMING STEREOTYPES

In 1989 I was hired to teach English at Kobe College in Nishinomiya, Japan. Despite the school's long-standing relationship with Americans, I was something of a pioneer: the first African-American to teach at Kobe College.

Socializing is an important precursor to doing business in Japan. Creating an atmosphere of harmony is achieved by dining together, or drinking and singing in a karaoke bar. But I often ran into stereotypes on these occasions. Many people thought that because I was black I was athletically inclined or an entertainer. I was often compared to Jackie Joyner or asked if I were in Japan as a singer or dancer. In Japan, African-Americans appear to be portrayed as great athletes and entertainers; there are no images of African-Americans as educators, doctors, or attorneys.

The challenge I faced working in Japan was competing against a stereotype I did not represent. At times, however, the stereotype worked in my favor. My students at Kobe College were fascinated by me, and I found I could use this to my advantage. I was like a celebrity and the students acted like fans of mine!

People in general were impressed that I had studied the language, and my language skills opened many doors. There were times, however, when people focused more on how I looked than on what I was saying. When I went to restaurants with Japanese colleagues, for instance, I would often order in perfect Japanese, only to be treated by the waiters as if I had spoken English. Even asking people for directions often elicited nothing more than a blank stare. The sight of someone so different from them meant automatically that I was not speaking Japanese but some language they could not comprehend.

—*Michelle Hobby*

The halo effect is similar to stereotyping, except that it moves from one positive attribute to other attributes a particular person or group might have. For instance, a friendly person with a bright smile might be judged also as honest, trustworthy, and genuinely interested in our well-being but—especially in the business world—this is often not the case. Like stereotyping, the halo effect is a largely unconscious process, and one that can easily lead us astray if we don't pay attention.[4]

Climate can either impede or improve communication. A defensive climate tends to chill the communication process. Judgmental or controlling speech, for example, will put the other side on the defensive, as will adopting a position of implicit superiority. It is much better to adopt a neutral stance that recognizes the other side as copartners in a process of exchange. Opening with upbeat remarks and a review of points of agreement can establish a positive climate for further discussion.

Emotionally neutral or strategic communication (communication that is part of a deliberate strategy to influence the listener) is likely to lead to a defensive reaction. Emotionally empathic, open, and spontaneous communication will help open up the communication process. Even in Asian countries, where expression of emotions is severely limited, a little extra warmth can facilitate the communication process.

Getting angry is a sure way to freeze the communication process. In my seminars I do an exercise in which I ask two participants to place their hands against each others'. Then I ask one of them to push. The other participant instinctively pushes back. People react instinctively when they feel pressure of this type, and they tend to become more entrenched in their position. Expressing dogmatic certainty is also likely to freeze the communication process. Express ideas provisionally, seek the other side's input, value their advice, and you can create a much better climate.

On the other hand, appearing to get angry can sometimes be a useful tactical move. If you have spent weeks being level-headed and reasonable and you suddenly lose your temper, it's sure to get the other side's attention and let them know you take this particular issue seriously. In emotionally expressive cultures such as the Middle East or Russia, a great deal of passion in expressing one's position is the norm—but be careful about directing this anger at specific individuals.

Designers from our team had been up all night completing clay models of the new product line for a group of visiting Japanese executives from Honda Motor Corporation. The presentation was the culmination of 18 months of intensive design work, but there were still many problems that needed to be ironed out. There was a general consensus by the design review board that costs were still too high, design was not up to standard, and that many small changes needed to be made in quality control and production. Our team understood that these changes were necessary, but the time frame expected by the Japanese seemed impossible to meet.

Our project leader had extensive automotive engineering experience with American Big Three manufacturers but no experience with Asian design and business practices. For the first part of the meeting, he defended our work in a calm and professional manner, but as the rather indirect criticisms of the review board started to accumulate, he reached his limit. Rising from his chair, he stormed to the overhead projector with the earphones used for translation still on his head with the wire dangling next to his chin. At the microphone, he broke into a tirade about how the requests from senior management were "fruitless." His temper rose as he began to rattle off his objections to the various criticisms and suggestions of the design committee.

I could sense the discomfort of the Japanese executives and those American members who had become "Asian-ized." Expressing disagreement in such an open manner—especially with superiors—was completely inappropriate in a Japanese business environment. The Japanese wore expressions of extreme disapproval, though they still listened patiently as his tirade continued. Needless to say, the objections of the Japanese were upheld and the project delayed until improvements were completed in an acceptable manner.

—Andrew J. Penca

Distractions are often a barrier to effective communications. During meetings, frequent interruptions can derail conversation. So can outside factors such as time pressures or conflicting obligations. Americans negotiating with members of polychronic cultures such as Arabs, Latinos, and Russians, people who habitually do several things at once, are at a disadvantage here. They are not used to the level of interruption that is the norm in these cultures.

Problems with meaning are especially important in cross-cultural communication. What you mean when you say something is not necessarily what the other side hears. Messages derive a large part of their meaning from their cultural context. In a cross-cultural communication, messages are composed or "coded" in one context, sent, and then received or "decoded" in another cultural context. In the United States when you say, "It will be very difficult," it generally means that there will be additional effort or expense required to achieve a certain goal. In an Asian culture the same words might mean that the person is unwilling or unable to do what is asked.

Status and power differences can often disrupt communication—a point often overlooked by Americans working abroad. Communication proceeds best between parties who have approximately the same status or power. If there are differences in status and power, it is important to show the proper respect and deference. In the United States, a low-level manager might casually mention to the company vice president that he or she has a brilliant new marketing strategy (a common theme in American movies), but an accountant from an American company who suggests that he or she has a better idea than the CEO of a foreign operation is likely to create a crisis.

OVERCOMING PROBLEMS IN CROSS-CULTURAL COMMUNICATION

- Avoid stereotyping, and instead listen to individuals.
- Don't generalize from one attribute (e.g., friendliness) to others (such as honesty).
- Work to establish the proper climate for communications.
- Gauge the level of emotion expressed and logical argumentation used to the cultural context.
- Never get angry—unless it's part of a deliberate ploy.
- Reduce distractions to a minimum, but be prepared to deal with distractions in polychronic cultures.
- Pay attention to the cultural context of messages.
- Respect power differentials when communicating in status-oriented cultures.

After several days of social events with little business, we met with a group of Japanese executives in one of their manufacturing plants to discuss the design of the product they would make for us. The first thing I noticed was that we were outnumbered two to one. It reminded me of negotiations for a peace treaty instead of a casual product specification review. The ranking manager was at the center of the conference table with junior workers distributed toward the ends of the table.

The meeting started out cordially enough but degenerated into a shouting match between one of my associates and the Japanese marketing project leader. At one point the verbal attacks on my associate were so intense that we considered leaving the meeting. Tempers eventually calmed down and we finished the meeting.

We all went out for dinner that evening, and it was interesting to see that the project leader who had attacked my associate was now unbelievably hospitable to him. We found out later that the Japanese executive's superior was in the meeting and that his verbal outburst had been a demonstration meant to impress his boss.

—Dennis J. Dureno

What Improves Communication?

Nobody ever listened himself out of a job.

—Calvin Coolidge

Listen more than you talk. This is especially important in Asian cultures, but all people respond well if they feel you are carefully listening to and evaluating their proposals. Taking notes is a good way to show that you are taking the other side's proposals seriously, and good notes always come in handy during complex international projects and negotiations. Be careful in Asian cultures not to interrupt speakers; wait until they are finished. If they pause or hesitate, resist the impulse to finish their sentences or supply missing information.

Do your homework. The more you know in advance about the people, the company, and the situation, the better you can communicate.

Build trust by sharing information (but be careful not to give away vital information on your needs, priorities, and limits). In cross-cultural negotiations, this might include information that is not considered relevant in the United States: In addition to data about your company and its plans, people from traditional cultures need to know who they are dealing with and what your credentials are.

Introduce new ideas slowly. When Newt Gingrich proposed the Contract with America, he made the mistake of showing his whole hand all at once. The ideas were new and different, and people didn't have time to absorb them and get oriented to this new way of looking at things. He also provided broad targets for his critics to attack, and since his whole program was exposed, he was unable to defend everything at once. Clinton, on the other hand, is a master of the gradualist strategy. He exposes new ideas gradually and only after preparing the groundwork, so that people can come around to his viewpoint slowly, without radical shifts in their thinking.

Americans like to think of themselves as risk takers. The executive willing to take big risks for big gains is admired in the United States—at least when the gamble pays off. Most people in other cultures are risk-averse. They don't like rocking the boat, and grand new policies that threaten the existing order are likely to be rejected. Introduce these new ideas gradually and one piece at a time.

Pay attention to nonverbal cues. Reading cues such as body language can give you valuable information about what the other side is thinking—but be careful to allow for differences in body language across cultures.

> ## STEPS TO IMPROVE CROSS-CULTURAL COMMUNICATION
>
> - Do your homework before face-to-face communication begins.
> - Listen more than you talk, especially in Asian cultures.
> - Build trust by sharing information.
> - Introduce new ideas slowly.
> - Pay attention to nonverbal cues.
> - Take notes.
> - Gauge the level of interruptions and the forcefulness of presentations to the cultural context.
> - Appeal to people's self-image.

Asians, for instance, often will not meet your eyes directly. They perceive too much eye contact as pushy, while Americans tend to think of too little eye contact as shifty.

Appeal to people's self-image. Many developing countries have successfully used Americans' image of themselves as saviors of the world as a way to extract concessions in aid or trade negotiations. The same can be done in business negotiations. One might appeal, for example, to a Japanese electronics company's sense of technological prowess or the Frenchperson's sense of superior rationality.

Brazilians consider themselves to be Americans—as do many Latin Americans. It is best not to use "America" as a term referring exclusively to the United States.

—*Claudia McAchran*

Style of Presentation

When I came to the U.S. three months ago I made presentations in a German way—I just gave facts and numbers. But how would Americans ever accept me if I was so dry? So I started my last pre-

sentation to a group of executives by telling a little story about myself. They liked it. It was as if I wasn't German to them anymore.
—Michael Muehlbayer, chief financial officer,
DaimlerChrysler Financial Services[5]

Selecting the proper style to make a presentation is an important consideration in business. Some cultures respond well to a show of professional competence with facts, figures, and graphs to back up an argument. For others, establishing an emotional connection is of paramount importance. There are times when it is best to be direct or even confrontational; other times it is better to proceed indirectly or avoid discussing substantive issues altogether. Following are some ideas for creating a persuasive style.[5]

Active versus passive participation. People are more likely to support a conclusion if they have an active part in formulating it. Invite input from the other side during negotiations and let them know they are active participants in your decision-making process. If possible, invite them to tour your place of business so they can see firsthand what your situation is. Getting people involved physically in a hands-on way can be quite effective in changing preconceptions. And getting the other side into your territory gives you a home-court advantage: You control the environment and agenda, and being a gracious host puts you in a good position when substantive negotiations begin.

Imagery and metaphors. A great deal of modern advertising is based on metaphor and imagery. The product is presented in association with some desirable image, whose attributes are associated with the product itself. People drinking soft drinks on television lead exciting lives full of beautiful people, great parties, and cute animals. Of course, we know drinking Coke isn't going to give us a great social life, but the association sticks in our subconscious and influences us when we get to the store.

Metaphors and images can also be useful for presenting ideas or facts in business negotiations, but they need to be used with care. Like jokes, metaphors don't translate very well. In another cultural context they may not make sense or even be downright offensive.

Unlike Americans, Mexicans enjoy wordplay. They are very fond of elaborate philosophical, political, and economic discussions with foreigners. This national pastime can be uncomfortable and intimidating for Americans, but it is a sure way to establish a strong bond with Mexicans.

Formal Spanish is extremely elaborate, convoluted and overly polite. Lavish praise and exaggerated emotion are part of Mexican identity. Humor is a great way to build personal relationships and connections. Among men, sexual jokes are very common, but they are never told in formal or family settings.

—Alan Ibarra

Intensity of language. Americans are about in the middle of the intensity curve in world cultures. Asian cultures are generally less intense in their expression than Americans. Conversely, Arabs, Russians, and Latinos are often much more intense than Americans. When you experience what seems to be the overbearing intensity of Arabs or Italians, remember that that is probably how Americans seem to the Japanese.

Tone is especially important when people are stressed—and people involved in international business dealings are often stressed. Try to gauge the intensity of your discourse to your audience. Take it easy dealing with Asians, but don't be afraid to up the decibels a bit when dealing with people from high-intensity cultures such as Latin America, Russia, or the Middle East.

Impromptu speaking versus prepared texts. It always amazes me to see how much time and expense companies will go through to prepare materials for a presentation, only to have it read verbatim in a monotonous voice by some executive with mediocre speaking skills, When your own executives speak, use props to liven things up. And do at least a little

---

ADJUSTING YOUR STYLE OF PRESENTATION

- Use an interactive approach to involve people in formulating your viewpoint.
- Be careful using images and metaphors.
- Gauge the intensity of communication to the cultural context.
- Don't read from prepared texts.
- Adjust your style of argument to the cultural context.

impromptu speaking. It may be a bit awkward—but it makes for a better connection with the audience.

This is even more important when foreign speakers address American audiences. I have attended lavish meetings sponsored by overseas governments to present investment opportunities in their countries to American businesspeople. But then, after all the preparation and expense, they have a series of speakers give long presentations filled with facts and figures in heavy foreign accents. If you have foreigners speaking to American audiences, coach them in how to do it. Make sure that speeches are short and to the point. Americans like show-and-tell and get impatient with long recitations of facts and figures. try to give them some backup in props, graphics or some other visual support.

Induction versus deduction. Americans generally use an inductive approach to presentations and problem solving. They start with specifics and executive summaries, then move on to background information and generalities. People from deductive cultures, such as the Germans, French, and Japanese, start with generalities and background information, then come to specific conclusions at the end of their presentation. Americans sometimes get annoyed or impatient with this type of communication. They want to have the bottom line up front before they hear the details of the argument.

10

Communicating across Language and Accent Barriers

A journey of a thousand miles must begin with a single step.

—Lao Tzu

The Importance of English in International Business

One of the most common misconceptions about doing business in other countries is that you have to learn the language in order to be successful. This is even more surprising when one considers that Americans normally pay almost no attention to learning languages. When it comes to doing business, however, they get rattled and feel they have to learn to speak the language.

Americans can let themselves off the hook. By happy coincidence, English has become the lingua franca of international business. It would be quite impossible, after all, for all the people in the world to learn all the languages of the people they do business with. When Germans and Japanese meet to strike a deal, the chances are the negotiations will take place in English.

An increasing number of people in the business world speak English. Many European companies require their employees to speak English as a condition of employment. In most parts of the world, children start learning English in elementary school. Generally speaking, as you go higher in the corporate hierarchy of a foreign company, more people speak English and speak it better. But even at lower levels, speaking English is an important skill in many foreign firms.

This is not to say that speaking another language does not give Americans an advantage. Learning even a little bit of a language is better than learning none at all. But most businesspeople working full time do not have the time it would take to become proficient enough to communicate effectively in another language. It would be nice if we could just take a pill and wake up the next morning speaking 10 different languages! But we all know this is impossible.

How to Work with Heavy Accents

A few years ago I ran into a friend who was working as a customs broker. To my surprise, she told me she was thinking of learning Chinese. Her business was handling more and more Chinese customers, and she often found it difficult to understand their heavy accents. If she learned their language, she told me, they could just converse in Chinese and the accent problem would be solved.

"But even if you spent years learning the language," I asked, "would your accent in Chinese be any better than their accent in English?" It would be a much better use of her time, I suggested, to learn how to understand their accents—a skill she could use for other foreign accents as well.

May Choi's China Chef restaurant was located in an area where many of the customers were Mexican. Most of the restaurant employees were Chinese and could not understand or speak Spanish. One day a Mexican customer came in to order dinner. During the order, the Mexican asked for *arroz*—rice in Spanish. May Choi, who was taking the order, thought the customer was asking for "a rose" and directed him to a florist located in the same mall. After this incident, May Choi hired a number of Mexican employees who spoke both English and Spanish to help communicate with her Mexican customers.

—*Sasivimol Suchinparm*

There is an art to communicating across language and accent barriers—a skill that one can learn with a little time and patience. Learning to understand heavy accents is an essential business skill when dealing with foreign-born people both abroad and in the United States. Repeatedly misunderstanding others, losing patience, or being condescending (by speaking pidgin English, for instance) can severely undermine the warmth and trust necessary for successful communication.

When we hear someone speak, we hear the cadence and the music of the language before we hear the words. And when the music is different or the rhythm and inflections of the words are unfamiliar, we get distracted. We listen to the music and the words pass us by without registering. This music is what gives many foreign accents their charm. As soon as our ears get used to the music, then the words start to appear as if by magic!

When I first came to the United States, I was 15 and my English was very poor. I spent the summer with an American family in Pennsylvania. One night shortly after I arrived, the family said a short prayer before dinner. During the prayer they mentioned what I thought was the name "Sasha." I had no idea who that was, and during the meal I finally got up the nerve to ask who Sasha was. Everyone stopped eating and tried to figure out what I was asking. After a good deal of confusion, I explained I heard the name in the prayer. They repeated the prayer, and it turned out that I had heard the "such a" in "such a nice day" as "Sasha." I was embarrassed, but they kept laughing about it. Eventually they started calling *me* Sasha, and even after I returned home I received letters from them addressed to "Sasha."

—Francis Prado

Here are some helpful tips for dealing with heavy accents:

Listen carefully. This may seem self-evident, but if you really listen carefully your ears get used to foreign accents. However, people aren't used to listening carefully. They usually have several different dialogues going on in their heads. They are planning the next day's activities or thinking about what to have for lunch while they are having a conversation. In order to increase your comprehension, you have to quiet these distracting internal dialogues and give your whole attention to the speaker.

I'm reminded of the story about three people traveling in a car. The first person looks out the window and observes, "It's pretty windy today." The next one says, "It's not Wednesday, it's Thursday." The last one replies, "I'm thirsty, too. Let's get something to drink.

Be patient. Take a deep breath and count to 10. Patience is an important part of conquering accent problems. Don't give up and pass the phone to the Indian or Chinese employee in the office. With time, accents come to seem natural.

When I ask foreign executives what they find most difficult about communicating with Americans, they often answer that Americans don't have any patience. As soon as they feel that they might have some difficulty in communicating, Americans' eyes get fuzzy and glaze over. They look as if they had been unplugged, like a television set disconnected from its cable.

Reduce anxiety. Hearing a heavy accent often creates stress or anxiety. This contributes to the distraction that keeps us from understanding what the other person is saying.

Listen again. If you don't understand, ask the other person in a polite way to repeat what he or she said. Rather than seeing this as an insult, most people will interpret this as a sign of interest and sincerity on your part.

Follow up with written memos. This helps assure that both sides agree on what has been said. Misunderstandings in oral communication can be cleared up before they become a problem.

Avoid using jargon, slang, and idiomatic expressions. American English is quick-paced and to the point. the aim is to communicate ideas that paint a picture and give a full impression of the situation as fast as possible. In order to achieve this, Americans take verbal shortcuts. People who use too many words to express an idea are considered boring. This contrasts sharply with languages such as Spanish, in which the use of complex, flowery expressions is considered eloquent.

American expressions such as "Let's get the show on the road" or "Let's get our ducks in a row" can quickly convey an entire administrative agenda. But these expressions may mean nothing to people who haven't lived in the United States for a long time, and they may lead to misunderstandings.

Corporations also have their own jargon. Insiders become so used to it that they forget it may have little meaning to outsiders. For instance, one American company calls all its top-secret government programs "black programs." After hearing this term used repeatedly, one group of foreign negotiators mistakenly thought the Americans were referring to special programs for African-American employees.

When I first came to Britain from Ghana as a student, I was concerned about adapting to the new environment—the weather, the food, and expressing myself well enough to be understood. But other things are important as well. I remember the jolt when I was summoned to the editorial board of the Bradford University student newspaper, for which I wrote a column. The editorial board wanted to discuss an article in which I'd used the phrase "Wham, bam, slam, her comes Pam" to describe the haphazard way a local restaurant prepared its food. The feminists on the board were up in arms after reading the article!

—Ato G. Imbeah

Don't be condescending. Don't laugh at someone's accent or simplify your own speech to pidgin English or baby talk. An accent does not necessarily mean that the person hasn't mastered the language. Many foreign-born people speak perfect English but still have an accent.

Don't raise your voice. When we feel we are having trouble communicating, we often raise our voices unconsciously. Unless you normally mumble, this won't improve communication, and it might insult your guest.

Be clear. If you think comprehension is a problem, speak a little bit more slowly and distinctly—but don't exaggerate.

Avoid using the telephone. If the other party is close by, suggest that you meet in person. If this isn't possible, follow up with a memo to clarify any points you are not sure about.

Remember that the biggest factor in communicating across accent barriers is motivation. Accents may seem incomprehensible at first, but after you get used to them they will be just as easy to understand as American English.

Working with Interpreters and Translators

China Grooms Itself for Fast Women
    —Headline in the sports section of the *China Daily*[1]

Communicating across language barriers is the biggest challenge when working in other countries. Despite the disadvantages, sometimes you have no choice but to hire an interpreter. Communicating through an interpreter, however, is like kissing through a screen door: You get the general idea, but it's just not the same thing.[2]

If you need an interpreter (for oral communication) or a translator (for written documents), get the best one you can. Make sure he or she is reputable and has good credentials. Mistakes or misunderstandings can be much more expensive than the extra cost of getting a professional. There simply isn't room for sloppiness when there are millions of dollars at stake.

Translation is more than simply transposing words from one language to another. A good translator has to convey an entire set of cultural norms and practices. An interpreter should understand something about the cultural nuances of both parties and have a good grasp of the subject matter being discussed.

During a negotiating trip I took to Brazil several years ago, I hired as an interpreter a young Brazilian customs broker I'd met during a previous trip. He spoke English without a trace of an accent. When I asked him where he had learned his English, he told me he had lived in Los Angeles when he was young.

We had barely gotten started in our discussions when the young man interrupted and asked, "What is 'marketing'?" As the meeting progressed, it became clear that he knew none of the vocabulary of business transactions. It turned out that he came from a poor family and as a young boy he was sent to live in the United States with an eccentric aunt. Instead of sending him to school, she kept him home as a companion, and he spent his days watching soap operas on television. It's a good idea to interview your interpreters before you use them in order to verify their abilities.

Another important point: Don't be too quick to ask for an interpreter when faced with a heavy accent on the other side. Show a little patience. The person you are dealing with may have been hired for his or her English-speaking abilities, and asking for an interpreter could cause a severe loss of face.

11

Political Ping-Pong

Politics: A strife of interests masquerading as a contest of principles.
—Ambrose Bierce[1]

In this country, politics are relatively unimportant in the business world. The person on the other side of the table might be a Republican or a Democrat or a Libertarian, but—if the issue came up at all—it wouldn't have any impact on the business at hand. People don't see each other as adversaries even if they do have differing political views.

The situation changes dramatically when you do business overseas. If you're working on a deal in China, it's impossible to ignore the latest Congressional attack on China's MFN (most favored nation) status. The political differences between the two countries are out in the open.

What can be done to minimize the problems caused by politics in international business?

Understand the Situation

All politics is local, as Tip O'Neill said. This may be true in the United States, but in international business, politics has global dimension as well. International trade agreements such as the rules of NAFTA (North American Free Trade Agreement) or GATT (General Agreement on Tariffs and Trade) or pressures from countries not directly involved in the deal may influence business transactions. Global environmental or human rights organizations may also influence the way business is conducted across international borders.

It is especially important that executives consider the local politics of both countries involved in a business transaction as well. On the American political scene, for instance, belief in free trade was a principle of the political center. But this bipartisan consensus has been fraying on both the left and the right in recent years. The ritual brawl in Congress that accompanies the yearly renewal of China's MFN status has caused growing alarm in the international business world, and companies need to consider how American politicians will respond to these pressures during the coming years.

Executives also need to study the political landscape of the countries where they plan to do business.

- Is the country hostile to American investment, or are its leaders actively seeking it? Until recently, much of the Third World was hostile to American business. Local governments thought of themselves as defending their people against American corporate imperialism. This situation is changing rapidly as developing nations rush to join the new global economy. But these attitudes remain in some pockets, especially in government bureaucracies and corporations where people's positions are threatened by privatization and globalization.

- What political forces are at play inside the other country? Are there labor or ecological movements that might have an impact on the business transaction?

- Is the country politically stable? Or is there the possibility of a coup or other change of government that might impact foreign businesses?

- Does the country have resilient institutions and courts that can ensure continuity during changes in the political climate?

- What local audiences does the other side have to take into account when making a deal or honoring its obligations?

Don't Make Judgments

Americans often think they have a monopoly on truth. After all, didn't we defeat the Nazis in World War II, bring prosperity to Western Europe with the Marshall Plan, and win the cold war? We've all seen countless movies depicting the triumph of straight-arrow American heroes over swarthy barbarians and knife-wielding ninjas swarming out of Latin America, Russia, the Middle East, or walled compounds on mysterious islands in the Orient. Captain Kirk's five-year mission to spread American values across the galaxy is part of our cultural inheritance.

These images have become so much a part of Americans' self-understanding that they can become preachy without realizing it. Americans have the distressing habit (at least for foreigners) of projecting their own values and hopes onto the rest of the world. This habit is reflected in the interventionist approach many Americans take to other countries. A survey by the *Wall Street Journal* in 1997, for instance, found that "Nearly two out of three Americans polled (62%) believe it is the world's responsibility to safeguard freedoms in Hong Kong."[2]

People abroad may admire many things about American culture, and they would certainly like to emulate their material prosperity. But this does not mean they are simply "proto-Americans." They have their own values and traditions, and they can get very touchy if others don't respect these. Taking a preachy or adversarial stance interrupts the flow of trust and goodwill necessary to establish good relationships—the backbone of any international business deal. People are often perfectly happy to criticize their own system, but they don't like someone else to do it. I can scold my own child, but I bristle if anyone else does it.

Distinguish People from Governments

We often equate people with the government of the country they come from. We take the latest news about what the Arabs or the Chinese are doing on the political scene and apply that knowledge to the people we meet from that country. But people from foreign countries without a democratic tradition often put little stock in their countries' official politics.

During a trip to China in 1986, I was constantly amazed at how much irreverence the young woman assigned as my interpreter had for the official politics of her country. Wherever we went, she openly ridiculed the official government propaganda (which adorned most public spaces in China).

As a child, she told me, she had to participate in "Red Book demonstrations"—propaganda events in which oceans of angelic children sang the praises of Chairman Mao and the Cultural Revolution. Each time she went to one of these, she told me, her father would complain that she "should be learning real things."

At the end of our trip, we attended a Chinese opera in Beijing. During the last act I was surprised to see that most of the people in the audience got up and left. When I asked my young friend what was happening, she told me: "The first part is the real opera. The last act is just propaganda thrown in by the government about the evil capitalist landlords. No one's really much interested in seeing it."

Avoid Talking about Politics

Politics come and go. The evil empire of yesterday is our buddy today. Political discussions will rarely make you friends—but they can easily make you enemies. The problem is that talking politics is a way of life in other countries. Americans make small talk about sports, or movies, or mutual interests. People overseas talk politics.

This can be disconcerting to Americans. During a business trip to Spain, one of my American colleagues and I went to lunch with a group of Spanish executives. The Spanish members of the group started criticizing the American role in the Spanish Civil War. My colleague, who wasn't used to intense political discussions, was taken aback.

Don't be alarmed if foreigners—especially Europeans, Middle Easterners, or Latin Americans—start talking politics. But be careful about being drawn into these discussions. It is important to be knowledgeable about local politics and be able to carry on a conversation about both local and global political issues. But there is little to be gained and much to be lost if you allow yourself to be drawn into an emotional debate.

Address Legitimate Political Problems by Creating a Joint Problem-Solving Environment

Of course, there are legitimate political problems that need to be addressed by executives working abroad.

For instance, Nike has been suffering an enormous amount of bad press because of the wages paid by its subcontractors in Indonesia. This is an inherently political problem. Nike can argue all it likes that its contractors pay more than other local companies or that it is simply obeying the law of the market. This isn't going to make the bad press go away (probably the reverse).

In contract negotiations with Indonesian subcontractors, this is a legitimate negotiating point: Nike has a business interest in this problem. The point is not to make it an adversarial issue. Nike's best bet is to present it as a problem to be resolved jointly by the two sides.

Maintain Confidentiality

Local news coverage can portray American companies as taking advantage of smaller, poorer nations. Host country negotiators are often playing for the local audience—they may need to act tough to please the home crowd. The best policy is to let representatives from the other country guide the news that is given (except in those cases where they release information as a deliberate pressure tactic).

It is also important to make sure that all members of overseas teams know what information is sensitive. A large American company recently landed in court because some of its engineers working in Russia divulged information that was considered a breach of national security. The engineers were simply trying to explain technical issues to their Russian counterparts—but the result was an international incident.[3]

CHAPTER

12

How to Deal with Culture Shock

Culture is simply the hospitality of the intellect. Your mind is open to new ideas and larger views; when they enter, you know how to receive them, and to entertain, to be entertained, and take what they have to offer without allowing them to dominate you.

—Thomas Kettle[1]

On a trip to China several years ago I met a businessman in the throes of culture shock. One spot on my itinerary was Guiyang, a small town in the Guizhou. There was little tourism in the region because of the concentration of defense industry manufacturing. When I arrived, I was brought to an old hilltop hotel with one of the most dramatic settings I had ever seen. The view from my balcony was stunning: a peaceful river wound through craggy mountains forming a picture as perfect as a Chinese painting. The rising mist from the river made it seem like the hotel was floating on a green island in the clouds.

One evening the hotel manager asked if I would like to meet another business traveler from the West who was staying at the hotel. A short time later, I heard a knock at the door and the hotel manager escorted a tall man clutching three enormous bottles of Chinese beer into the living room. He looked as though he'd had several bottles before he got there. An engineer from a Canadian company, he had been staying at the hotel for five months on his first foreign assignment for a Canadian company installing telecommunications infrastructure.

My first reaction was to ask him how he liked being in this exotic and magical spot. To my surprise, he responded with a tirade about how much he hated the place and how sick he was of China and the Chinese! His Chinese counterparts were impossible to get along with, he told me. He accused them of being "sneaky" and hard to deal with. He complained about the size of the soap (I hadn't even noticed the soap) and the roughness of the toilet paper. After work, he had nothing to do so he just sat in his room and drank. Fortunately, he was due to travel back home shortly. But he was worried that things were progressing so slowly that he might have to come back and stay for another year—a prospect that filled him with dread.

Just imagine how this man's state of mind affected his work! He was so depressed it was a wonder he was getting anything done at all. And he was so suspicious and resentful of the Chinese that working together must have been torture—both for him and for his Chinese counterparts.

Of course, not everyone experiences culture shock as severely as the engineer I met in China. There is a great deal of variation in people's ability to deal with different cultures. Some people can get severely depressed or hostile after just a few days in another culture. Others seem to thrive on the excitement of living in a new place and working with new people; they may only experience occasional irritation or confusion. Some people might adjust well to one culture but have a terrible time with another.

Fish out of Water

Living at home, we never think about culture. Culture to humans is like water to fish—the fish never stops to reflect on what it means to live in the water. It just swims and goes about its normal routine. But if you take the fish and throw it on a patch of sand, water takes on a whole new meaning. The fish flops around desperately looking for the water it never knew it had!

I was literally "stuck" on a train, all alone, on my way from Bangalore to Hyberabad—about a 17-hour train ride. All of a sudden I felt lost. I was in a foreign country where I did not speak the language and looked nothing like the dark hair, eyes, and complexion of all the bodies that surrounded me and continued to stare at me after four hours of being on the train with them. Feelings of fear, anxiety, complete unawareness of who I was, uncertainty of getting back to the ship, and a desire to see some familiar faces filled me. However, I knew I was on a train bound for another part of this country called India. How could I get back to Madras in a hurry before I had an anxiety attack?

—From Paul Pederson, The Five Stages of Culture Shock[2]

The experience of culture shock is similar. When you encounter a new environment, all the habits and behaviors that allowed you to get around and survive at home suddenly no longer work. Things as simple and automatic as getting lunch, saying hello to colleagues, or setting up a meeting become difficult and strange. The rules have changed and no one has told you what the new rules are.

When doing business overseas, suddenly all the habits you've developed for doing business in the United States seem out of place or positively wrong. You sell yourself and talk up your product and the other side think you're bragging. You try to establish a friendly rapport and they ignore you. You try to get to the bottom line and they seem irritated and uninterested.

Whenever we are faced with unfamiliar behavior, we go through varying degrees of culture shock. Symptoms can vary from confusion, loneliness, and anxiety to feelings of inferiority, fear, depression, and psychological withdrawal. Some people express intense hostility to another culture. Others simply shut down. Geert Hofstede comments that culture shock "returns us to the mental state of an infant."[3]

The effects of culture shock accumulate slowly. A few seemingly harmless negative experiences can end up poisoning your attitude about another culture. It is like Chinese water torture—the first few drops you don't even notice, but as time goes on the drip, drip, drip can drive you crazy.

Hostility, anxiety, or depression can affect a person's judgment and ability to communicate during delicate negotiations. Managerial duties can become a daily encounter with the enemy. Culture shock is a leading cause of early repatriations that can be quite costly for the company. The experience can be especially difficult for spouses or children who come along on overseas assignments. Without a job to give them direction and a stable point of contact with the other culture, they can feel lost and helpless.

SYMPTOMS OF CULTURE SHOCK

- Frustration
- Depression
- Fatigue
- Irritability
- Hostility to host culture
- Disorientation
- Anxiety
- Feelings of inferiority

The Stages of Cultural Adjustment

In *Cultures and Organizations*, Hofstede describes the stages one goes through while adjusting to another country (Figure 12.1). The first stage involves a romance with the surface features of a culture. Everything is new, different, and exciting, and feelings for the new culture are very positive. Most tourists and many short-term business travelers experience other cultures in stage one. The second stage of adjusting to another culture is culture shock, when the lack of familiar reference points and behavioral norms leads to overload and withdrawal. Feelings for the new culture become very negative. This stage often arrives for expatriates or business travelers after the initial greetings and ceremonies are over and they find they have to survive in a new culture on their own without being treated as the honored guest any longer. Culture shock can vary dramatically from person to person or situation to situation. One person can experience severe culture shock in a situation that would barely affect another. Some people barely experience culture shock on one trip and are affected severely on the next.

The third stage is a gradual period of acculturation during which the visitor learns to operate according to the norms and values of the other culture. This period requires work; learning about another culture means getting out and interacting in a meaningful way with other people in social and work settings.

The fourth and final stage is the arrival at a stable state of mind that marks the level of adjustment to the other culture. This stable state can remain negative (the person feels more or less permanently alien-

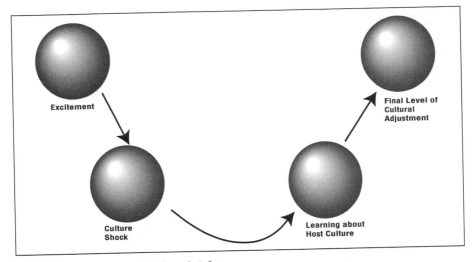

Figure 12.1   Stages of Cultural Adjustment

ated), neutral (a good healthy bicultural ability), or positive (the person "goes native").

What Can Be Done to Deal with Culture Shock?

The best defense against culture shock is knowledge of how other cultures operate. In *Culture Shock: Psychological Reactions to Unfamiliar Environments*, Adrian Furnham and Stephen Bochner point out that culture shock is not a psychological disorder but a lack of social skills and knowledge needed to deal with a new environment.[4] Even if things seem alien and disorienting, knowing some of the rules gives us reference points and a degree of confidence. One of the best ways to deal with culture shock is to look at the experience as an opportunity to learn—not only about the other side's culture, but also about specific factors that will influence doing business with them. *Dealing with other cultures is a skill we can acquire.*

The amount of time required for acculturation and how well you have adjusted at the end of the process depend largely on attitude and effort. Younger people generally have an easier time adjusting to new cultures and situations because they haven't formed a rigid framework for looking at the world and how things should be done. Adults who are set in their ways are more likely to see things that are different as deficient or threatening.

Approaching new ways of doing things with openness and curiosity can change the whole experience of being in another culture. It helps to remind yourself periodically to maintain a positive attitude and try things with an open mind. We often respond automatically to things that are different. It is possible to build up negative feelings about other cultures without being aware of it.

I had never heard of Libya before being stationed in Tripoli. About two weeks after I arrived in the country, Muhammar al-Khadafy overthrew the king in a military coup. I was assigned to work with a group of advisers to help the Libyans with their young air force. One of the first things I noticed was a strange physical feature: Many of the men had one bad eye. After some questioning, I discovered that the men had had their eyes damaged by their mothers as a way to keep them out of military service during the period when the Italians ruled the country.

Another thing that took getting used to was the way women only showed themselves in public completely covered except for one eye. When we went to visit the house of one of the Libyans we worked with, his mother brought the food to the door of the room and handed it to him without entering. We never did see her.

Later I saw the same man looking very depressed and asked what was wrong. He told me that he was getting married. This didn't seem like a reason to be depressed, until he told me that it was an arranged marriage and that he had a girlfriend he loved very much.

—Louis Krindelbaugh

The degree of culture shock you experience does not necessarily depend on how long you've been in another country. You don't absorb other cultures through osmosis. Going out to eat in local restaurants and buying souvenirs isn't enough. You have to get out and spend time with local people and learn about their perspective.

My fiance and I were in the United States with my mother and my niece working out the details of our engagement. We had spent the entire day working out the specifics of the agreement according to Taiwanese tradition. In the evening, the four of us were exhausted and no one felt like cooking. Although it is not considered healthy, we decided to order dinner at Kentucky Fried Chicken. We ordered an eight-piece dinner, but when we got home we discovered that only seven pieces had been included. My 12-year-old niece was quite upset; since she was the youngest person and the host she had to go without a piece of chicken. Afterward, she called the KFC 800 number and customer service immediately agreed to send her a special two-piece snack pack guest check.

During a summer vacation in Taiwan, I decided to meet several high school classmates at a KFC located there. I ordered an iced tea, but it was spoiled. I told the person behind the counter, but he simply said to me, "It is impossible for us to sell spoiled iced tea." Then he started to behave as if he were very busy and didn't have time to talk to me anymore. Although KFC is an international chain that tries to provide the same quality of food and service worldwide, it is obvious that Taiwan and the United States have different attitudes toward customer service.

—*Chun-Chu Lin*

There are immigrants who have lived in the United States for 40 years and still experience culture shock. They've brought their own culture with them; they shop in their own grocery stores and hang out with their own people. The same thing can happen to Americans overseas. You can be in a foreign country for years, but if you spend all your time with other Americans and don't interact with the native culture, you might never get over culture shock.

I interviewed a woman who had accompanied her husband on an overseas assignment to Poland. She was struck by the way Americans lived in expatriate ghettos where they stuck with each other and had nothing to do with the local culture. Associating only with your own compatriots is a sure sign of culture shock. It indicates that you are seeking the comfort of the known and the familiar rather than confronting and learning about differences. Really to adjust to a new culture you need to create a new framework for understanding the world. It might not be your framework, but unless you can learn to use it, you'll always be on the outside.

Overcoming the Ugly American Syndrome

When the husband of one of my friends was transferred to Spain, she followed with a great deal of excitement. Unexpectedly, her first encounter with Spanish culture tarnished the exhilaration and romance of a European assignment. A few days after their arrival, they were invited to an afternoon fiesta. They accepted, expecting a leisurely lunch and festivities in the town square. When they arrived they were shocked to find that the fiesta was really a bullfight! The atmosphere, she said, was a combination of an American football game and a slaughterhouse. Young children were there eating cotton candy while bulls were being butchered in front of their eyes. They found the idea of staying for this spectacle very distasteful but felt they couldn't walk out and offend their hosts. To do so, they believed, would have made them into Ugly Americans—culturally insensitive boors who travel the world trampling on other people's customs and beliefs. They ended up spending the afternoon looking at their shoes in extreme discomfort.

After hearing this story, I called a friend from Spain who lives in Southern California and works in a senior marketing position for a U.S. firm. I wanted to know his reaction and seek his advice as to what this couple could have done. His first reaction was that all of his American friends love bullfights (I wondered how many polite Americans he'd roped into seeing bullfights they didn't really want to see). But then he pointed out that Spaniards are very direct. "If you object to doing something," he said, "just tell them. They'll understand. Just don't preach to them about the unfairness or brutality of the event."

One of my first experiences in the United States was crossing the street in Evanston, Illinois. The moment the light turned green, I ran as fast as I could across the street, just as I always did in Taipei. I was so afraid that drivers would start honking at me from all directions or cutting in front of me. After I finished crossing, however, I felt surprised and embarrassed. I was embarrassed because everyone seemed to be wondering why I was running. I was surprised that none of the cars tried to smash me when I was in the street. They didn't even move while I was in the crosswalk. This was when I learned that the pedestrian is king of the road in the United States.

—Pam Kuo

The Flip Side of Culture Shock

Many people dread going on foreign assignments—sometimes even before they've gone on one. They hear stories about how exhausting and disorienting business travel can be. They worry about getting sick, getting lonely, or getting killed. They're afraid they won't be liked or that they won't succeed. But the fact is that for many people a foreign assignment can be the opportunity and thrill of a lifetime.

The *Wall Street Journal* reports the story of John Aliberti, who had spent his career working to become a midlevel manager for Union Switch in Pittsburgh, Pennsylvania. Aliberti seemed like an odd choice for an overseas assignment: He had no experience in international travel and business. But when he was chosen to represent the company as technical expert and representative in China, Aliberti responded with enthusiasm: "Back home, the work we do, it's been done for decades. In China you're breaking new ground. It's a milestone in the history of the world."[5]

By viewing his China assignment as an exciting adventure, Aliberti largely bypassed the negative effects of culture shock. According to the *Wall Street Journal*, "The crowds and chaotic lines don't faze him. He becomes animated telling stories of long train trips to out-of-the-way cities like Nanchang, where Union Switch is helping to build a railroad yard. . . . In the last four years, he has become an expert at dealing with the infuriatingly slow Chinese bureaucracy."[6]

Aliberti's enthusiastic attitude and his active interest in learning about the culture and business practices in China have helped him become a central figure in his company's China operations. His job in Pittsburgh is two rungs below vice president. In China, according to his boss, "He acts like a president or CEO. That's got to turn him on."

What Can Companies Do to Deal with Culture Shock?

Suppose your company is opening a subsidiary in another country and is planning to send a group of Americans there to help run the operation. Those Americans need to be trained because they'll be working constantly with people who have a different cultural framework. If they hang out just with other Americans and don't learn the rules of the other culture, they'll be fighting a more or less ongoing case of culture shock. This is likely to lead to both unhappy Americans (who feel alienated) and unhappy locals (who feel misunderstood or insulted).

Some people are simply much better suited than others for work in foreign cultures. Many American companies send people abroad because of technical skills or company organization. But it would be well worth screening people going abroad—especially on long assignments. A good point of comparison is the advice Takashi Kiuchi gives to Japanese companies about the kinds of people inappropriate for assignment in the

United States. The same advice is applicable to American companies sending people abroad.

> Unless the person is interested in the history and culture of the country it is quite meaningless to live here. Another condition of living in a foreign country would be to have a feeling of appreciation for the host country. I, myself, am very appreciative of the opportunity to live in the United States.[7]

Seek out people with a sense of adventure and the ability to adapt to new situations. These qualities can often be just as important as language skills or detailed cultural knowledge. As Aliberti's boss commented: "I wasn't looking for people who had studied Chinese at Harvard. I wanted someone who knew the product." According to the *Wall Street Journal*, Aliberti "found a common language with Chinese railway officials in the nuts and bolts of railroad signaling systems."[8] The success of an international project will depend ultimately on how well the people involved are able to communicate and work together to solve problems.

Careful preparation and training can also prevent costly problems down the road. Learning the proper skills for dealing with other cultures can reduce or eliminate the negative impact of culture shock. Intercultural education should be a regular part of corporate training programs—both for executives going overseas and for the domestic workforce. Such training helps the company work as a team on international projects.

It is also useful to seek out other people who have lived abroad. In many places you can find support groups to help expatriates get oriented to living in the country. After her experience with the bullfight, my friend in Spain was able to find a women's club of expatriate American women. Being together with them helped her to get her bearings and learn some of the tricks for getting around in her new environment. She also commented that her husband's company hadn't offered any training before they left, and that expatriates whose companies had offered training had a much easier time getting accustomed to the new culture.

I was living in the southern, Italian-speaking region of Switzerland. On Saturdays, everyone did their shopping and ran errands. Unlike in the United States, however, people really dress up for these small tasks: jewelry, scarves, hose, skirts. The problem for an American is that no one goes out looking like a bum. A person would definitely stand out wearing sneakers and sweats. Salespeople would give you dirty looks and maybe even be snotty to you if you came into their store like that.

Greetings also took some getting used to. Whenever you enter or leave a store, you are expected to use a full array of greetings and good-byes. There is *buon giorno* (good day), *arrivederci* (so long), and maybe *buona Domenica* (have a good Sunday/weekend). These are only a few, and the process can go on and on. Sometimes I just wanted to go in discreetly, browse around, and leave unnoticed. But in the smaller shops, this would be considered rude, if not positively uncivilized!

While I was there, I worked for a brief time as a secretary at a large steel-trading company. I felt quite resentful while working there that they wouldn't allow me to do anything other than answer the phones, fax, type telexes, and file. I had a degree in business and four years' experience as a buyer for TRW. It is true that I sometimes messed up handling calls in many different languages—often misspelling the names. They did not find these blunders at all amusing. And I frequently got in trouble for calling the traders by their first names (the other traders were on a first-name basis, but I was just a secretary). Europeans are very class conscious—something I never liked and probably never will.

—*Diane Fasoletti*

Culture Shock in the United States

Culture shock can also be an issue when doing business with people from other cultures here in the United States. Despite the popularity of American culture around the world, many foreigners experience symptoms of culture shock when they get here.

It is just as hard for foreigners to learn the rules of our culture as it is for us to learn how to get by in theirs. Can you imagine how hard it would be for Americans in Japan not to speak English during meetings? Americans can be impatient, or even uncomprehending, when confronted with behavior they don't understand.

If foreign visitors seem irritated or rude—or if they simply seem to be behaving strangely—they are probably experiencing culture shock. During a symposium on Japan, a member of the audience asked a panel of businesspeople consisting of Japanese and American executives who work with the Japanese this question: Why are the Japanese so hospitable and polite when one is either visiting Japan or doing business with them in their country, while sometimes they tend to be rude and have a herd mentality in this country? The answer from one of the Japanese businessmen was a single phrase: "Fish out of water."

After being stuck in the same job for years, I decided to go to school in the United States to improve my skills. I applied to UCLA and was accepted. Since I worked on the side as a preschool teacher in Brazil, I applied for a job as a nanny to make extra money. The family I worked for was great, and their daughter an angel, but as time progressed I discovered that Latin Americans are often looked down on in the United States. Relatives were amazed that I was going to UCLA. They seemed to think it was a waste of time since I was just a nanny. The father once asked me if I was recycling newspapers after seeing me every day with a copy of the *Los Angeles Times*. I asked him if I could read his *Wall Street Journal* and he laughed and said that I was the only nanny in the United States who read the *Wall Street Journal*. Many Americans seem to think that all Latin Americans are Mexicans. Especially odd is when I tell them I'm from Brazil and they start speaking Spanish to me! Others seem to think that coming from Brazil means that I'm some kind of "bad girl." One person even told the mother of the family I was working for to be careful because I might steal her husband!

—*Monica de Campos Gliemi*

Returning Home: Culture Shock in Reverse

In 1995, a *Wall Street Journal* reporter observed: "More and more, U.S. businesses are calling their expatriates home and staffing the top role at their foreign subsidiaries with skilled, local talent."[9] The homecoming of the these returning expatriates is often just as shocking as the experience of going abroad in the first place. Barry Newman reports in the *Wall Street Journal* the case of Ira Caplan, who came back to the United States after 12 years living in Japan:

> He had never heard of Rush Limbaugh: "I listened once and it was enough." He was so politically incorrect that he didn't know what "PC" meant: "I got a book on it." Prices astonish him. The obsession with crime unnerves him. What unsettles Mr. Caplan more, though, is how much of himself he has left behind.[10]

I was born in Hong Kong but spent most of my childhood living in Spain. I was raised in a traditional Chinese family, but I also learned to live in Spanish culture.

One Christmas, the father of one of my schoolmates came to our house and gave me a huge present. In Chinese families, it is considered impolite to open a present in front of your friends, so I said thank you and left the present in the corner. I can still remember the look of disappointment on his face. I didn't realize what was wrong; only later did I realize that he must have thought I was looking down on him.

Growing up in Spain, I learned to play two roles in my life—which was sometimes confusing for my friends. At Chinese functions, it comes naturally to me to be quiet, conservative, and polite, but when I'm in a Spanish environment my body system automatically changes and I become more friendly, talkative, and open-minded. My friends think that I fake these two different faces, but in reality it comes to me automatically, without any thought on my part.

—Linda Choy

Once people adjust to living abroad, they often find expatriate life exciting and glamorous. "I was running briefing breakfasts for congressmen and senators," said Caplan. Now he's just another midlevel executive in New York.

Coming back to their old job is often the most traumatic part of returning to the United States. Ways of doing business have been changing dramatically in the United States, just as they have all over the world. The old job usually doesn't exist anymore, and returnees often find they don't fit into the new scheme of things. After a time, many are laid off or simply quit.

The problems of adjustment and culture shock for returning employees can be as severe as those involved in sending them abroad in the first place. Companies make an enormous investment in their expatriates, and they should think carefully about how to utilize the expertise they have gained. As Caplan remarks about his experience: "You're a source of wisdom overseas. Once you get back, it's all over. Nobody can relate to your experience." Or, to quote from *The Marble Faun* by Nathaniel Hawthorne:

Now . . . they resolved to go back to their own land; because the years have a kind of emptiness when we spend too many of them on a foreign

DEALING WITH CULTURE SHOCK

- The best antidote to culture shock is knowledge of other cultures.
- Overcoming culture shock requires work.
- Don't be intimidated by foreign cultures or let the Ugly American syndrome prevent you from sticking up for yourself.
- Support groups can help ease adjustment problems, but you need to make friends to really adapt—especially on long-term assignments.
- Companies should seek out executives temperamentally suited to foreign assignments.
- Adaptability and a sense of adventure are more important than detailed cultural knowledge.
- Be prepared for reverse culture shock in returning expatriates. Companies should view foreign experience as an asset to be capitalized on.

shore. But . . . if we do return, we find that the native air has lost its invigorating quality, and that life has shifted its reality to the spot where we have deemed ourselves only temporary residents.

Thus, between two countries, we have none at all. . . . It is wise, therefore, to come back betimes, or never.[11]

13

Understanding the Gender Gap in International Business

We are learning that contrary to the widely held belief that female expats can't hack it in foreign assignments, we're finding just the opposite.

—Executive from Eastman Chemical Company[1]

The massive wave of global competition has carried businesswomen, despite the ambivalence of their companies, to the forefront of international business. Far from being passive bystanders, women have been proactive in accepting and meeting these challenges, and have succeeded in all areas of international business.

In a study of women expatriate managers conducted by Nancy Adler of McGill University, 97 percent of women working overseas rated their assignments as successful.[2] According to one female consultant who works in countries around the world: "I've found that international experience, decision-making authority, and sound judgment are valued everywhere—and far outweigh any consideration of gender when it comes to getting the deal done."[3]

These sentiments are reflected in the upward trend in women's assignments in international business. Before 1993, only 3 percent of overseas assignments went to women; by 1999, this number had increased to 15 percent. This trend will continue as myths about the problems women face overseas are shattered. A recent survey of human resources managers at global companies found that 70 percent expected to send women on overseas assignments in the next five years.[4]

Myths about the Obstacles Women Face Working Abroad

There are three myths about women's success in tackling international business opportunities. The first myth is that women themselves are not interested in international business or in taking managerial assignments overseas. Some feel that women are intimidated by the prejudice they may encounter working with people from male-dominated cultures. Others cite the predominant role of women in child-care and family duties that might interfere with international travel.

This myth has been overturned by several studies that show women are just as interested in working internationally as men. Women who aspire to high-level positions in global companies understand that international experience is necessary to their advancement. And women have found that many fears about the problems of working overseas are overblown. Responding to a column in *Fortune* about the new ascendancy of women executives overseas, a woman banker working in Kyoto exclaimed: "The experts you cited were right on. Girlfriends, come on over."[5] When Nancy Adler, professor of management at McGill University in Montreal, asked graduating MBAs about their desire to work on overseas assignments, she found no significant difference between men and women.[6]

A second myth is that American companies are reluctant to send women abroad. There is some truth to this myth. Although they have faith in women's managerial and negotiating skills in the United States, corporations often hesitate to send women overseas because they fear they will be poorly received in male-dominated cultures such as those in Asia, Latin America, and the Middle East. Since higher-level corporate positions are held almost exclusively by men in these countries, the fear is that women will not be taken seriously, or that they will not have the authority to forcefully represent their company's position. One American businessman told me that women could be a "jinx" during negotiations with foreign businessmen. Many corporations also worry about women's vulnerability to sexual harassment in countries that have different social codes and fewer legal protections than there are in the United States.

Although corporate resistance to sending women overseas persists to this day, women have worked to establish themselves as effective global executives. Susan Farber, for instance, had to ask her employer, AT&T, for an international assignment. Although she already had an MBA from George Washington University, Ms. Farber took steps to improve her credentials. She took a one-year leave of absence from her job and went to France to learn the language and culture. She returned to the company as treasury manager and several years later was sent to Paris as director of international services charged with building a sales and marketing organization for France.[7]

Our negotiating team to Saudi Arabia included one woman. Everyone had been carefully briefed on the technical details and maximum and minimum positions expected by the home office. The negotiations had progressed quite well and agreement was about to be reached at a figure significantly higher than our minimum. Prior to the Saudis' final agreement, there was a protracted period of silence. All of a sudden the female negotiator blurted out a figure less than our minimum position. We renegotiated and eventually settled at our minimum position.

After the talks were over, the woman was unable to explain why she had blurted out the lower figure. She was a seasoned negotiator, but the pressure of negotiating in such a male-dominated environment had put extra pressure on her.

—From an interview by Skip Spence

Despite challenges, many women are working very effectively in countries where the local business culture is dominated by men. The biggest problems women face, in fact, often come from male colleagues in their own company. Robert Moran and John Riesenberger found that women returning from abroad "report the biggest barriers come from within the corporation, rather than from situations actually encountered during foreign assignments."[8] If men are convinced that their women colleagues will not do well, they won't offer the proper support and give them the authority they need to operate successfully.

A third myth about women working abroad is that male-dominated local cultures are biased against women, which makes it difficult or impossible for women to do their jobs effectively. But experience has shown that if women establish their competence, experience, and authority, they will be taken seriously and treated professionally by foreign executives. Foreign businesspeople realize that women play an important role in American companies. When asked if she had experienced any negative consequences overseas as a result of being a woman, Suzanne Danner, a partner in Price Waterhouse's Audit and Business Services in Warsaw, Poland, responded that gender actually afforded her advantages that allowed her to be more effective on the job."[9]

One of the best ways to transcend the home-grown gender biases of male-dominated cultures is for women to emphasize their distinctiveness as foreigners. This effectively exempts them from many of the rules that govern the conduct of local women. In effect, they are treated as foreigners rather than as women and business relations can proceed on this basis. A woman manager from Hong Kong commented: "It doesn't make any difference if you are blue, green, purple, or a frog, if you have the best product at the best price, they'll buy."[10]

Focusing on gender discrimination and sexual harassment in other countries tends to fuel negative stereotypes. This can discourage women from entering international business or create a negative atmosphere that makes failure more likely for those who do. Sensational stories in the media often contribute to an exaggerated image of the problems women face working abroad. A *Los Angeles Times* article captures the view many have of women's lives overseas: "Before Japan knew the term 'sexual harassment,' Yuko Watanabe put up with her boss's back-room maulings as part of the job. The Tokyo hotel executive would call Watanabe, then a 20-year-old information guide, to the VIP lounge, cover her with kisses, and laugh as she struggled."[11]

While these kinds of things may still happen, sensitivity about sexual harassment is spreading rapidly around the world. The *Wall Street Journal*, for instance, records the following admonition from an instructor training Japanese executives for managerial jobs in the United States:

"Race," he writes with a felt-tip pen on the white board, "Color," "Sex," "Religion."
    "Avoid discrimination based on these things," he tells his charges, who sit at conference tables smoking cigarettes. "But particularly watch out for the gender hazard in the United States."[12]

Although various myths about women working abroad often contain a grain of truth these obstacles haven't seriously impacted the number of women seeking jobs with international responsibilities or adversely impacted their success. Anne Fisher comments: "The best reason for believing that more women will be in charge before long is that in a ferociously

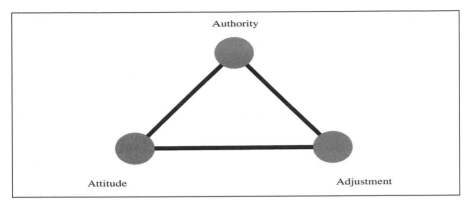

Figure 13.1 Women's Triple A Triangle for Success Abroad

competitive global economy, no company can afford to waste valuable brainpower simply because it's wearing a skirt."[13]

To help understand the most important factors leading to success for women working abroad, I use the Triple-A Triangle (Figure 13.1). The three vertices of this triangle work together to create a solid foundation upon which women can meet the challenges they will face in international business.

Authority

People from traditional and group-oriented cultures do not accept strangers at face value as easily as Americans do. This may create special problems in countries where women are generally not viewed as authority figures. To compensate for this, women need to establish their authority both officially and unofficially as quickly as possible.

PERSONAL AUTHORITY

Women can use their personal skills in addition to the clout that they gain from their official position to bolster their authority. On the personal level, qualifications and life experience, self-presentation, cultural knowledge, and sensitivity will create instant respect and acceptance. According to Betty MacKnight, vice president of global procurement, Asia/Pacific and China regions for Lucent Technologies: "One of my Japanese colleagues paid me a very large compliment when he said that the art and balance of humility and professionalism that I had learned helped to gain me tremendous respect with the Japanese people." [14]

There is clearly a glass ceiling for women in the new Russia. Though women in positions of power were common during the Soviet era, they have suffered since the collapse of the old system. Only about 5 percent of senior management positions in Russia are filled by women. But while the men drown themselves in vodka and self-pity, Russian women move on and up. Universities report more women enrolling in business and economics courses. Foreign companies in Moscow say that their new women hires are less picky about where they start and are more open to transfers. Russian women are more inclined than men to take an entry-level position and look for opportunities to move up.

—Marina Volobueva

Women should take special care to communicate their credentials up front and in writing. A young woman working overseas told me, "I lose points when I walk through the door without laying the groundwork. Businessmen tend to assume that I don't have the necessary background information, and they try to backtrack and explain the basics if I don't establish first that I have a thorough understanding of the subject matter."

Women need to take special care to master the details of their work. There's nothing like competence to create respect. Men in some cultures will be less aggressive about challenging a woman if they feel they are equally matched.

Proper dress is important to women's success overseas. Group-oriented and status-oriented cultures pay much more attention to clothing and appearance. In this country, the trend is toward casual Fridays and more informal office wear. Overseas, dress is more formal and conservative, and the quality of clothing is more important. It's best to take it easy on the red power dresses and the latest fads. These may work in New York or Los Angeles, but they are often inappropriate in conservative foreign cultures. Longer skirts and higher necklines are a good rule of thumb. The conservative rule applies to sightseeing trips and entertainment outings as well: Avoid bikinis, halter tops, and short skirts or shorts.

Individual authority can also be enhanced by how much you display the trappings of power and authority. Staying in a first-class hotel and choosing fine restaurants for social meetings will go a long way toward establishing you as an authority figure.

Gender itself can be used to establish authority. Lorna Larson-Paugh, a vice president for the Asia region of Allergan, Inc., claims that being an American woman is an advantage since it inspires "awe" in her Asian counterparts who automatically assume she must have special skills and authority to be sent on overseas negotiations.

Avoid placing yourself in situations in which your credibility might be undermined. Inviting visiting foreign business associates to your house for a home-cooked meal could be a plus. However, donning an apron, cooking, and cleaning for them could cast you in a homemaker's role and undermine your business credibility.

Women can also increase their personal authority by means of cultural knowledge and sensitivity. According to Sully Taylor and Nancy Rapier, women are better at building interpersonal relationships compared to their male colleagues. "They tend to remember and ask about personal matters, such as the graduation date of a client's son, and show appreciation for small favors and courtesies."[15] This attention to personal relationships can be critical in many foreign countries. According to John Graham:

> Women executives are often more successful because they are more sensitive in communication. Two female executives at Ford Motor Company won business from a group of male Japanese executives simply by inviting them into their family lives. They cooked dinner for the Japanese one weekend and went fly-fishing on another day. When one of the women was reassigned, the Japanese manager requested another woman executive to work with, saying he felt he could trust them.[16]

When I went to Taiwan, I brought a tall, blond female engineer with me to help with the testing process on the project. The Taiwanese didn't know what to expect of her. At first, they did not treat her with respect or disrespect. The male engineers were more patronizing in their attitude than anything else. They were more interested in making her comfortable than in her technical abilities. After the initial meetings, however, the engineers gained the utmost respect for her once they learned how capable she was. I got constant requests for her skills.

—Ed McCowan

In traditional cultures, there is often a great deal of respect given to older individuals. Age is seen as a sign of experience, wisdom, and authority. In fact, age is often more of a barrier to Americans working abroad—both men and women—than is gender. This does not mean that younger women should throw away their creams and lotions and work on acquiring wrinkles, but it does mean that they have to take additional steps to establish their authority.

POSITIONAL AUTHORITY

Positional authority derives from the your job title and position within the company. When I traveled to countries such as China, Turkey, Spain, and Brazil to visit factories and source products as a part of General Electric Company's counter-trade offset programs, my official position, my clear and specific mandate, and the fact that I represented a prestigious company gave me instant credibility and great deal of legitimacy. The fact that I was a woman was never a disadvantage. I was always treated the same as my male colleagues. In fact, I often felt that my familiarity with different cultures and sensitivity to their ways gave me an edge.

A woman doing business internationally should have a letter of introduction, preferably from the president of her company or the director of her division. The letter should spell out her decision-making authority and her position in the corporate hierarchy. *World Trade* magazine, for instance, reports the case of Diane C. Harris, vice president–corporate development at Bausch & Lomb, Inc., whose CEO sends letters of introduction on her behalf—"partly because I'm a woman . . . to add credibility just in case of questions."[17] Harris also compiles a packet that includes the company's annual report, translated business cards that define her title, and an organizational chart illustrating her hierarchical ranking.

It is also important that women be given clear titles and job descriptions. Dr. Sully Taylor, a professor at Portland State University who has done extensive research on women expatriates in Japan, observes that "the vague title of 'manager' does not have any real meaning for Japanese clients or suppliers and may undermine their confidence in the woman's ability to make major decisions."[18]

The support of male colleagues is a key ingredient for women's success on overseas assignments. If women are treated with respect by male colleagues from their own country, executives from the host country will follow suit. Taylor and Rapier report the case of a woman executive in Japan whose "U.S. male colleague, when introducing her to a new client, never fails to mention her highly successful legal work in New York and her prestigious university pedigree."[19] Women should be careful never to let the men in their group challenge their authority in public. This can cause irreparable damage to their credibility.

Attitude

Scientists have long been puzzled by the case of the bumblebee. According to the laws of science, the bumblebee shouldn't be able to fly. But the bee doesn't know anything about the laws of science—it just flies and doesn't worry about it. Similarly, women who focus on the task at hand have an advantage. If they expect to succeed they are likely to do so.

When Mardi Mastain graduated from college, she couldn't find a job in the United States. After a short stint at the Chinese consulate in San Francisco, she decided to go to China, learn Chinese, and look for business opportunities. Ten years later, she had a successful consulting and import-export business with offices in both Shanghai and California. When I asked her if she had encountered any difficulties as a woman in China, she replied that being a woman and being young opened the doors and gave her visibility.

International businesswomen should remember their advantages. My own experience and research shows that most women find their gender to be more of an advantage than a disadvantage. Foreign executives are often very curious about American professional women, and women can turn this visibility factor to their advantage.

Maintain a positive attitude about your hosts, even if you are sometimes treated differently than you would be in the United States. In her study of women professionals working in Japan, Dr. Taylor found that "women who perceive positive attitudes in their Japanese bosses, colleagues, subordinates are significantly better adjusted to working in Japan."[20] Rather than defensively looking for possible problems, it is important to enjoy and learn about the culture of the host country.

It is easy to distort things by seeing the situation from your own cultural perspective. An American woman, for instance, once received a fax from a company in a Middle Eastern country that wanted to study the market in Brazil. The woman fixed a date to meet with the company's representatives; however, two days before the meeting she received a call advising her that during the meeting she should refrain from shaking their hands or looking in their faces. The American woman's response: "I told them I did not accept that and they would be welcome if they respect my culture, because I would not respect a culture that humiliates women. They didn't come."[21]

This response, however, imposes American values onto foreign cultures. There was no reason to assume that the Middle Eastern representatives were trying to humiliate her. They were simply asking that religious prohibitions against touching women in their culture be respected. If they had asked her to cover herself in a black shroud in order to meet with them, I could understand her point. The best strategy in such circumstances is for women to keep their eyes on the ball and not lose sight of their business goals. Women working abroad are not activists trying to change other cultures but rather businesspeople representing their companies' interests. One women working for Domino's Pizza in Saudi Arabia commented: "I was there to sell a franchise, not to change a culture. You learn not to take things personally."[22]

Americans are sometimes perceived as having an air of superiority. This is especially true in the case of women's issues. Businesswomen should be especially careful not to patronize women in other cultures. One Japanese woman commented that she preferred being patronized by Japanese men to being "matronized" by American women.

Adjustment

Although it is wise to be sensitive to cultural differences, you are not required to adopt the culture of your international counterparts. The trick is to maintain your own cultural identity and conduct yourself with "an accent." In fact, the more you differentiate yourself from local women, the more you will escape any disadvantages they might face.

After-hours business entertainment can pose interesting challenges for businesswomen working abroad. Entertainment is an essential part of doing business overseas. Don't be intimidated by going out, even if the rest of the group is comprised of men. But use good judgment and intuition. If you feel uncomfortable with the men in the group or the kind of entertainment, you are not obligated to go. Give a credible excuse and bow out.

A young woman who works for Rockwell International was invited to go out after dinner with her boss and several other men while on a business trip to Korea. This included a visit to a karaoke bar with pictures of nude women projected on the wall. Though she said that the entertainment didn't bother her, it is evident that as more and more women go along on business trips this kind of entertainment will fall by the wayside.

Regardless of how comfortable you feel with local culture, refrain from trying to pass as a local. When in Rome you don't need to become a Roman. Keep your identity as a foreigner but be sensitive to local culture and make an effort to adapt to local norms of behavior. If you are naturally boisterous and outgoing, tone yourself down a bit in Asian cultures. On the other hand, if you are quiet and low-key, you may need to be more expressive or demonstrative in Russia, Spain, Italy, or the Middle East.

Darinka Despotova, a general manager of Kraft General Foods in Bulgaria, offers the following advice: "To be successful in international business, a woman must follow four rules: Look like a lady, act like a girl, think like a man, and work like a dog."[23] This is good advice, except for the part about acting "like a girl." Although overtly aggressive behavior is not tolerated from women in many cultures, women shouldn't be submissive, girlish, and self-effacing, either.

Always maintain self-control and show patience and poise. Don't take offense if older men are paternalistic or protective. If special respect is accorded to older people in that culture, you should conform to this custom. Be careful not to offend older people in the organization, even if you hold higher rank or status.

Women have come a long way in the past few years. Leadership qualities are no longer viewed as exclusively male attributes—even in countries where men are still dominant. Pakistan, India, Turkey, and Malaysia, for instance, all have women at or near the top of their governments. Education has done much to bolster the leadership role of women in these traditional societies. The prevalence of education and new technologies is rapidly changing the situations of women all over the world. As John Naisbitt comments in *Megatrends Asia*, "The new technology is gender-blind."[24]

14

Negotiating across Cultural Lines

Negotiation is one of the single most important international business skills.

—Nancy Adler[1]

What Is Negotiation?

When most people think of negotiation, the image that comes to mind is a group of people sitting around a table. The setting is formal and the game is played according to clearly defined rules that everyone understands in advance. Like a game of chess, one side will walk away the winner, the other side the loser.

This image of negotiation comes largely from the media. We turn on the television and hear about the U.S. trade negotiator facing down the protectionist *keiretsus* in Japan. During the cold war, we spent 40 years watching the United States and the Soviet Union jockeying for position: The goal of negotiations was to gain or lock in a tactical advantage.

In the reality of the business world, however, negotiation is not generally a win-lose contest of wills taking place during a single meeting. Negotiating is part of the process by which companies position themselves in the global marketplace. Coming eyeball-to-eyeball with the other party over the negotiating table is the culmination of a process that includes gathering information, considering options, making contacts, forming a relationship, and agreeing on a mutual course of action. From the moment you are in contact with the other side, the information you give and get and the way you present yourself influence the other side's perceptions and impact the negotiating process. Nor does negotiation end when you all leave the table: As long as the relationship lasts the negotiating process continues.

Why Do People Negotiate?

Parties negotiate when they have issues *in common* as well as issues *in conflict*. If they did not have some common interests, negotiation would be impossible.[2] If they had no differences, negotiation would be unnecessary. The goal of negotiation is to reach an *agreement* that increases what the two sides have in common while reducing the areas of conflict.

International negotiations are more challenging than domestic negotiations because cross-cultural differences create noise and interference—making the detection of needs and interests more difficult. For instance, different cultures deal with conflict differently. These different forms of handling conflict are neither good nor bad, but the way they are managed across cultural lines can have positive or negative consequences. Ways of defining common interests also vary from culture to culture, and misunderstandings in this area can result in an agreement based on confusion, risk avoidance, or maintaining surface harmony rather than on an authentic meeting of minds.[3]

Effective negotiators connect with the other side and increase common interests by determining the other side's needs and concerns. Ineffective negotiators try to impose their perspective on the other side. In the worst-case scenario, the overlapping areas of interest disappear altogether and negotiations break down. Many international negotiators returning to corporate headquarters back home are like the knight who staggered into the king's court all disheveled and bloody. When the king asked with astonishment, "My good knight, where have you been?" the knight replied: "I've been killing, raping, and pillaging your enemies to the west." "But I don't have any enemies to the west," the king said in surprise. "You do now!" the knight responded.

Being Mexican and working for a large American company has allowed me to make some interesting observations about how Americans negotiate with people from other countries and cultures. I have often seen potential international deals fall through due to a lack of investment in developing personal relationships. Many American negotiators have an excellent education in law, finance, or accounting. As a result, their general approach to negotiations is linear, fact driven, and numbers oriented. They are often impatient and the contract is their central focus during negotiations.

Based on these observations, I would give Americans the following advice for negotiating abroad:

- You need to care about people. Faking interest or following a 10-step program will not win the trust of the other party. If you can't be genuine about your interest in the other party, find another field.
- Be a good listener. Look for verbal and nonverbal signs of what the other side is thinking and feeling.
- Break the ice. Find common interests.
- Don't be arrogant, no matter how big your title or company.
- Don't underestimate the other party's ability to negotiate and understand the underlying power issues.
- Be patient. Don't focus on numbers and contracts until you have established a relationship with the other party.

—*Cenmar A. Fuertes*

The Challenges of Negotiating across Cultural Lines

There are truths on this side of the Pyrenees which are falsehoods on the other.

—Blaise Pascal[4]

Several months ago, the $125-million Mars Climate Orbiter flew too close to the red planet, fell apart, and burned. As it turned out, the Orbiter was fed data by the scientists in pounds, the English unit of force, when it was programmed to receive data in newtons, the metric unit.[5] Likewise, many international deals crash and burn because messages sent from one cultural context are received and decoded in another, where their meaning may be completely different.

Every negotiation is cross-cultural in some way. People come from different perspectives and there is always a gap in communication, even with people who work closely together or come from the same family. However, when we negotiate with people from other countries, that gap can become as wide as the Grand Canyon. In order to narrow the gap and bridge the differences, we need to understand the other side's perspective—the way they see the process and approach the issues.

For example, resolving conflict is an integral part of the negotiating process, but different nations deal with conflict in different ways. Americans find conflict natural; both parties are expected to give their best and fight for what they want. Disagreements and differences are expressed openly, though tactfully. Discussions of differences are generally kept unemotional and impersonal—often being cast in terms of problem solving rather than personal conflict.

The new Russian business managers are traders. Many got their start in the black markets of the old Soviet system. They will promise you the world, but these promises often lack substance. Although they are inexperienced in Western business practices, they are often very shrewd negotiators. In many instances, the stubborn Russian negotiator gets the best of his Western counterpart who is in a rush to close a deal.

However, those who live in Russia and get used to Russian bargaining techniques often come to enjoy the intricacies of negotiating there. Formalized games of power politics and posturing can provide hours of enjoyment for the entire office staff. To negotiate successfully in Russia, you must be thick-skinned, bullheaded, and warmhearted. And always remember that Russians are the world's greatest chess players.

—*Marina Volobueva*

Asian cultures, on the other hand, avoid conflict—especially conflict that reflects on individuals. Asians are likely to express differences of opinion indirectly and try to maintain a facade of surface harmony. Expressing differences of opinion openly is likely to be considered rude at best, and in the worst case it can lead to a breakdown of the negotiating process. Unlike Asians, the French enjoy emphasizing distinctions and differences even more than Americans. They take a blunt and logical approach to conflicting points of view that can seem antagonistic to people from other cultures. The secret to working with the French is not to get drawn into a debate or a tug-of-war. Passionate expression of differences is common in Middle Eastern and Latino cultures—though in order to save face and preserve dignity, people from these cultures tend to deal with conflict much more indirectly than Americans do. The Russians are also more personally and emotionally involved in the negotiating process, and they often engage in a great deal of posturing and theatrics. It is not uncommon for them to get up and lumber out several times during the negotiation.

Understanding these different forms of communication will prevent your team from being surprised and help make you aware of how best to communicate with the other side. To be a successful negotiator, you need to know the difference between "sending the right message" (conveying your view of facts and issues) and "releasing the desired response" (producing understanding and acceptance in the other side).[6] This means figuring out the best way of delivering a message in any particular culture. Negotiation is not simply an intellectual debate of issues; it is a deliberate attempt to persuade the other party to move from their position to yours.

Building a Framework for International Negotiations

Diplomacy is letting someone else have your way.
                                        —Lester B. Pearson[7]

During one of my seminars at the American Graduate School of International Management, a Slovenian manager told me: "The whole war in Bosnia was a result of mismanaged communications. It wasn't ancient hatreds so much as bungled negotiations."

As in international relations in the political realm, negotiation is the critical element to succeeding in global business. You can do the most thorough market research and assemble capable experts on international finance and law, but if you can't strike durable deals where both sides benefit, then all this specialized knowledge will do you no good. Negotiation is the knot that ties everything together.

The following checklist will give you a framework for preparing for the negotiating process.[8]

DETERMINE THE OTHER SIDE'S ABILITY TO COMMIT

Before starting negotiations, it is important to determine the other side's willingness and ability to make a commitment upon reaching an agreement. In the international realm, it is sometimes much more difficult to make these determinations than it is in the domestic marketplace. Does the other side have the resources to deliver what you need? Can they finish within the specified time frame? Does the person or persons you are meeting have the authority to make these commitments?

During the initial stages of negotiations, you may need to look carefully in the other side's organization to find the person who has the authority to make a commitment. If you try to go over people's heads to get to the real decision maker later in the process, this is likely to cause loss of face and alienate the other side.

Finally, you should also think about what you need to do in order to be prepared to make a commitment.

DETERMINE BOTH SIDES' INTERESTS

There is a story about twin girls fighting over an orange. The mother enters the kitchen and sees the two girls fighting. Without saying a word, she cuts the orange in two, hands one half to each twin, and walks out. After she leaves, one sister takes her half, peels the orange and eats the flesh. The other peels the orange and uses the peel to make a cake. If the mother had taken the time to understand the interests the two sides had in the negotiation, she could have come up with a more sensible solution. One sister could have gotten the whole peel, the other the whole inside. Both would have been complete winners instead of achieving only half of their objectives. Determining each side's interests ensures that negotiations are efficient and meet both sides' needs and goals. In this way everyone gets the best deal.

Interests are the basic, even instinctual, motivating forces behind the other side's actions. If you can meet these basic underlying needs, you are likely to be more successful than if you stay at the surface level of prrices and terms. Even in negotiations within a single culture, interests are often not fully verbalized; across cultures discovering true interests can become a complete enigma.

Interests exist at various levels in a negotiation. They need to look good in front of their superiors and other members of their team, and it often costs little to take these underlying human needs into account.

During negotiations I conducted in China during the mid-1980s, for instance, I found out during informal discussions and socializing that several of the Chinese negotiators were interested in coming to the United States. The only way the Chinese could come to the United States at that time was if they were invited by an American company. At a subsequent meeting, I casually asked them if they would like to come to the United States to visit our company. The response was an enthusiastic yes! Upon my return I wrote a letter of invitation on company letterhead clarifying that they were responsible for their own expenses and cleared the visit with company lawyers. Several months later they arrived for a visit, but at the same time they had a chance to visit other companies and go sightseeing.

Americans are very time-conscious and might hesitate to entertain foreign representatives without a pressing business purpose. But American negotiators should realize that paying attention to the human side of the equation is likely to pay off over time, even if it seems inefficient in the short run.

Different departments or goverment agencies may also have specific interests in the negotiation, and it can help enormously to pinpoint these needs and think about how they could be addressed.

What is the best way to determine interests in an international setting? People from traditional cultures tend to be indirect in communication. They may hide their true needs and values, or talk about needs that are not truly important to them. They are careful not to reveal their true needs for fear that it will give you power over them. The best way to find what is truly important across cultures is to establish an atmosphere of respect and trust. Spending time together, especially in relaxed social situations, will give you a chance to find out what their underlying concerns are. Listen, show interest, and, when necessary, gently probe the other side. Don't put them on the spot or interrogate them.

It is also a good idea to take a look at your own underlying interests. Identifying and prioritizing your interests will help you to see ways to be more flexible while still advancing your high-priority interests.

FOCUS ON INTERESTS, NOT POSITIONS

Positional struggles are especially perilous in international negotiations because of the danger of miscommunication due to cultural differences. American executives who present a hardheaded list of demands to their Indian counterparts may see themselves as being firm and straightforward, but the message received by the Indians might be that of a personal attack. Hanging tough on positions tends to involve the egos of the negotiators, preventing them from focusing on their common interests.

Looking at underlying interests expands the list of options. Consider the Camp David negotiations between Egypt and Israel in 1978. Israel had occupied the Sinai during the Six-Day War in 1967, and Egypt insisted that the Sinai be returned to it as part of the peace process. Israel wanted to keep part of the Sinai as a security buffer. The two sides drew and redrew maps of possible borders, but as long as they focused on positions, peace was impossible.

The key to resolving the impasse lay in shifting the emphasis from positions to the underlying interests of the parties. The Israelis' underlying needs were security and recognition. They didn't have any real need for the Sinai itself. The Egyptians, on the other hand, needed to reestablish their sovereignty before they could make a peace with Israel that was not perceived as a defeat in the Arab world. By focusing on these underlying interests, the negotiators were able to come to an agreement that Egypt would demilitarize the Sinai and recognize Israel in exchange for a return of the entire territory.

To move from positions to interests, it is important to recognize that each side has *multiple* interests—not simply those reflected in the immediate negotiation. Looking at the entire range of underlying interests can help generate options that would not emerge from focusing on the positional debates of the negotiations. Impasses should be viewed as problems that both sides must cooperate in solving. This allows you to separate the relationship from the impasse. If necessary, you can even make this explicit by going to the other side and assuring them of the strength of your relationship and asking them to work with you to resolve the specific problem at hand.

RELATIONSHIPS ARE EVERYTHING

In international negotiations, developing and maintaining a relationship is an important part of the business process. Every negotiation involves both a people aspect and a substance aspect. Personal issues can easily spill over into the substantive part of the negotiations. Of course, some people *are* more difficult to deal with than others are, but it will not advance your cause to view the negotiations as a personal contest of wills.

When oil prices plunged in the spring of 1998 after an unusually warm winter, the oil ministers of Mexico, Venezuela, and Saudi Arabia desperately needed an agreement to limit produciton in order to save their treasuries from disaster. According to the *Wall Street Journal*, the ministers "looked on in horror as national revenue imploded."[9] The problem? Bad blood between the parties made discussions almost impossible. According to the *Journal*: "The Venezuelans weren't talking to the

Saudis. The Mexicans and Venezuelans were kind of talking—though they disliked each other."[10]

Finally, Mexico's new oil minister, Luis Tellez, asked a neutral party—Robert Mabro, head of Britain's Oxford Institute for Energy Studies—to give the Saudis a call and ask if they would be willing to talk informally about an agreement. Tellez had already established a friendly personal relationship with Venezuelan oil minister Luis Giusti and secret talks were soon underway. Tellez had managed to make an end run around the animosities present in official channels and build a set of relationships that allowed the parties to focus on their underlying interests.

A good working relationship does not necessarily mean that everyone is best friends. It is a mistake to give in on issues just to get the other side to like you. A good working relationship simply means the two sides are comfortable enough working together that they can deal with differences in a sensible manner. This allows issues to be resolved on their merits rather than diverting them into a series of personal triumphs or favors.

During the two years I worked for an American company in Argentina, I had the opportunity to observe some of the differences between the business customs of the two cultures:

- Americans love to start work early, arriving in the office by 7:30 or 8:00 A.M. Argentinians arrive late in the morning—9:00 or 10:00. Americans also leave as soon as their eight hours are over, while Argentinians will stay until the job is one.
- Americans don't pay much attention to lunch. They eat a hamburger in the car or fast food at the office desk. For Argentinians, lunch is an important time. People take an hour to go to a restaurant or meet with friends and colleagues.
- During negotiations, Americans like to go straight to the point and finish business as soon as possible. They delegate responsibilities and establish objectives to fulfill. They love to know who, when, how, how much, and so on. Argentinians may spend twice as much time negotiating, and at the end things may still be unclear.
- Americans are often frightened when they drive in Argentina, where traffic is always a mess. When I arrived in the United States, I was surprised to find that people respect each other and have the patience to wait while a traffic jam is cleared. They don't get crazy with their horns like many Latin American drivers so.

—*Martin Estrada*

CREATE THE RIGHT ATMOSPHERE

Informal contacts and the overall feel of a relationship have an important influence on the outcome of international negotiations. The good negotiator understands how the negotiating process can generate frustration and works to build an atmosphere free of turbulence where negative feelings can be overcome and deals can happen.

I grew up outside my native Indonesia but went back to do an internship in the family business. One day I had the privilege of accompanying my father during a fairly important negotiation. We met first for lunch, but we never discussed the business deal at all. Instead, the person my father was meeting spent the entire time asking questions about my education in the United States. Apparently he intended to send his son to school there. After spending what seemed to me two unproductive hours, we agreed to play golf that Saturday morning. Afterward, my father told me that most important business deals take place on the golf course. That Saturday, we met on the course, but it was not until after the 10th hole that they finally got around to discussing business. After the game was over, they agreed to meet again at the office to finish up the details of the deal.

—Aidil A. Madjid

Avoid losing your temper or showing anger, especially with Asians. Latino, Middle Eastern, and Russian negotiators tend to negotiate with passion and great displays of emotion. Weakness is not respected in these cultures, and you should not back down easily. You should, however, maintain decorum and balance. Be patient but firm during negotiations. Don't corner the other side or cause them to lose face. It is often better to skip over sensitive issues for future discussion, or use informal channels such as a go-between or a private meeting away from the negotiating table—where personal relationships can smooth the way.

Using emotional common denominators will often take you a lot further than logical arguments. Generally, trying to win an argument logically can cause the other side to dig in their heels, or to spend their time looking for weak links in your argument. Although doing your homework and presenting a logical, well-researched position is important, by itself a superior argument can often spoil the negotiating atmosphere and lead to deadlock.

GENERATE A VARIETY OF OPTIONS

One of the best ways to pursue win-win solutions is to generate a variety of options. This is especially true in the rapidly changing international arena—where the possibilities for creative new ways to do things are multiplied. Currency differences, conflicting laws and tax codes, different consumer habits, the logistics of manufacturing and distribution, differing cultural norms, and many other obstacles in international business can be opportunities if looked at from a new perspective.

Jeitinho Brasileiro or the Brazilian way refers to the flexibility Brazilians use to solve problems. They are not intimidated by the idea that it can't be done and immediately look for some way to improvise a solution. To use the Brazilian way, you have to be creative, but not too concerned about the rules. You have to find alternative ways of doing things that apparently have no solution. Brazilians all over the world are known as "experts of improvisation."

For instance, in Paraná in southeastern Brazil, a woman came into the hospital with a rupture in the side of her heart. The surgeon tried all the standard techniques for repairing the damage but was unsuccessful. Suddenly he had an idea. He sent his assistant to a nearby store to buy some Super Bonder—a glue used for household repairs of metals, wood, and glass. The patient is still living, and the doctor is now famous for inventing a revolutionary new surgical technique.

—*Anna Carolina Aranha*

Unfortunately, many negotiators do not include a search for options as part of their regular procedures. Roger Fisher and William Ury point out four reasons why this is so: (1) Negotiators tend to make premature judgments that hinder the imagination and lock a certain set of possibilities in place. (2) People tend to search for a single answer, which leads them to progressively constrict the range of options rather than expanding it. (3) The assumption of a fixed pie locks people into a win-lose mind-set. (4) Negotiators concentrate on the home side's problems and needs instead of considering both sides' problems and needs together.[11]

Increasing the list of options also increases the power of negotiators. The problem is that these extra options are not always immediately visi-

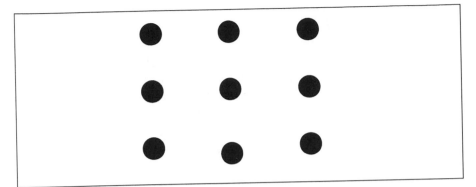

Figure 14.1   Connect the Nine Dots with Four Continuous Lines

ble. Habits, precedents, and lack of imagination limit the number of available options. Consider the well-known puzzle in Figure 14.1. How can you connect the nine dots using four straight lines and never taking your pen off the paper?

In order to solve the puzzle, of course, you have to go *outside* the box that contains the dots (Figure 14.2). Negotiators who train themselves to see options outside the box will gain an advantage over those inside the box.

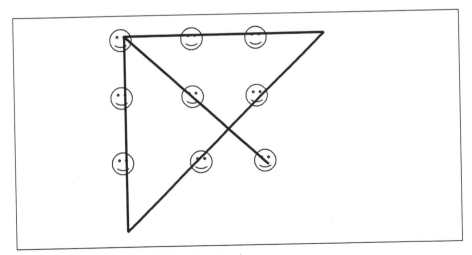

Figure 14.2   Solution to Nine-Dot Puzzle

BUILD LEGITIMATE SUPPORT
FOR YOUR POSITION

During the Law of the Sea Conference, India proposed that companies mining the seabeds in national waters pay an initial fee of $60 million per site. In India's view, this fee would help compensate Third World countries for the use of resources used by multinationals from industrialized countries. The United States rejected any fee, arguing that it would destroy incentives for exploration. Both sides dug in and the negotiations appeared to be headed for an impasse.

At that point, a study of the economics of mining the seabed by the Massachusetts Institute of Technology was discovered. The study provided a model for evaluating the impact of user fees on mining, exploration, and development. This model showed that the enormous fees proposed by India would indeed make exploration almost impossible, but that a moderate initial fee was economically feasible—and would increase revenues for both sides over the long run. The study moved the negotiations from a win-lose contest of wills to a discussion of the economic reality of the situation, and made it possible for the two sides to reach an agreement that was beneficial to both.[12]

People who come from a bargaining tradition are wary of being exploited or ripped off. Knowing how others in similar situations have fared will ensure them that they won't come up short compared to others. Use of an external standard or benchmark will help prevent agreements that are perceived as unfair by the other side—which will help ensure better long-term cooperation and performance.

If the other side proposes standards, however, it is important to verify that those standards are legitimate. A good example of this principle is the New York artist who was having trouble selling his paintings. He decided to have a show in Paris and gave a friend of his money to buy a painting for much more than he could have sold it in the United States. On his return, he used this sale as a standard to sell his other paintings for a great deal of money.[13]

PREPARE FOR COMMUNICATION

Negotiating in our own culture, we rarely think about the process of communication. It is simply taken for granted. But across cultural lines it can become tricky. Behavior that might seem odd and inexplicable in our culture might be quite normal and rational within the context of another culture. For a novice in international negotiations, a Russian's display of anger and aggression might be embarrassing and unsettling. And the Japanese's lack of emotion and stony-faced silence might be even more intimidating than the Russian's anger and emotional outbursts.

Negotiators can be taken off guard by these different styles of communication. Americans sometimes deal with the discomfort of the silent treatment by talking and may inadvertently give information that they otherwise would not give. Or the American need to produce quick and tangible results can clash with Asians' slower pace and long-term outlook.

Americans, Germans and other northern Europeans like to negotiate in a linear manner, one issue at a time. Asians, Middle Easterners, and Latinos tend to keep all the issues up in the air and discuss them simultaneously. It isn't necessary to adopt their style, but understanding these different approaches will help prevent frustration that breaks down the lines of communication.

NEGOTIATING IN KOREA

- Outsiders are often not given the same respect as Koreans.
- Be prepared for almost anything, including intimidation, unrealistic promises, and strategies that obviously benefit the Koreans.
- A common negotiation tactic is to delay major negotiations until the foreign team is about to leave the country, then tack on unreasonable demands and conditions.
- If you have a product that Koreans want and cannot get elsewhere, emphasize its unique value.
- Be prepared to walk away. You will gain respect from making it clear that you would rather have no deal than a bad deal.
- Don't give things away. This will be seen as a sign of weakness. Every agreement should be reached by give-and-take. Always get something for what you give.
- A signed agreement does not necessarily mean negotiations are over. Koreans will keep seeking to improve the terms of the bargain, and they may sign agreements that they have no intention of keeping.

—Nam Suk Lee

Managing the Negotiating Process

Every negotiation is a crafted solution designed to achieve a particular outcome. There is no off-the-shelf style that can be recommended for negotiating abroad. But there are some general guidelines that will help you choose a negotiating strategy that is more likely to lead to success and mutual satisfaction.

HOW DO YOU CHOOSE A NEGOTIATING STYLE?

Our preconceptions about international negotiations often lead us to think of them in win-lose terms. The image we have in mind is the hard-nosed German, French, or Asian negotiator who hangs tough, keeps delaying, and waits for the soft American to capitulate to unreasonable demands. With this image in mind, many American companies seek out tough, John Wayne–style negotiators and load them up with firepower to outgun the other side.

But this strategy is often counterproductive. Negotiators need to control their natural impulse to try to win the game and take a hard look at what the appropriate negotiating strategy is for a given situation. Even though the negotiation looks competitive on the surface, the underlying dynamics might be such that a cooperative strategy can lead to an outcome that will bring value to both sides for many years. A competitive approach might damage the relationship and further entrench each side in its position. What determines the style you should use is not the outward behavior of the other side but the internal dynamics of the negotiation and the context within which it takes place. Even in situations where the other side does take a very tough and seemingly competitive approach, you don't necessarily need to adopt a similar stance.

When I first started my consulting business, I received a call from the sales director of a prestigious company who was looking for someone to speak at its national sales meeting. He asked me how much I would charge for a presentation of several hours. When I told him my fee, he let out a gasp and said, "I don't want to hire you for a week! I just need someone to talk for a few hours." Then he told me that many speakers would be happy to come and speak for free in order to get the exposure and references. He asked me to call him back if I would be interested in speaking for a small honorarium and abruptly terminated the conversation.

Although I was offended by his blunt approach, and I knew that I didn't want to set a precedent by working for a low fee, I felt that I should take a cooperative approach to this negotiation. After all, he needed my services. If he didn't, he wouldn't have called. And he was perfectly right: I did need the exposure and the reference.

I tried to think about how the negotiation could be reformulated in win-win terms that would help satisfy both our needs. After a few days, I called him back and proposed that I would be happy to speak for free provided that participants have an opportunity to purchase my valuable workbook if they chose to. This proposal changed his attitude completely. During the presentation, he introduced me as a high-priced speaker and suggested that participants buy the workbook. Since there were over 120 participants, I ended up making more money than my initial fee. In the end, we both came out as winners.

A cooperative approach becomes even more imperative working in the international marketplace. Because of the cost and effort involved, most international negotiations aim for long-term relationships that can be harmed by a competitive approach.

During our negotiations with Mitsui/Masushita, the Japanese assumed that I did not have the authority to decide whether to close the contract. When it became clear that I had more authority than the previous representatives sent by my company, their attitude changed. Up to this point in the negotiations, I had been seated off to the side of the table. Now I was asked to sit at the center of the table next to the highest-ranking manager. It was clear they had not done all their homework prior to our arrival, and there was a slight note of embarrassment on their part.

—*Dennis J. Dureno*

There are several strategies you can use that will take the focus away from the competition and create a cooperative environment for negotiations. First, the other side often needs to be educated about the benefits of a cooperative approach. They might also have an unrealistic view of the alternatives available to them. These alternatives may not be as rosy as they think. If you know they are too optimistic, let them know without insulting them.

Another way to bring them down to earth is to inquire about the rationale behind their position. What is the standard on which their position is based? Coming to an agreement about standards will help move the negotiation from a hard-nosed contest of wills to a more cooperative approach.

Finally, from the initial stages of an interaction, skilled negotiators work to create an atmosphere of respect and trust. Developing a cordial relationship provides an environment in which you can point out the benefits of working together and jointly search for options.

There are times, however, when negotiations are more efficient if handled competitively. When there is no concern for a future relationship and you simply need to come a quick agreement, then both sides may benefit from a competitive strategy. And using a cooperative approach when the other side is resolute about using competitive tractics can be foolish.

Several years ago, I had an experience that illustrates the dangers of using a win-win approach when the situation really calls for a more competitive approach. I had an exclusive agreement with a Brazilian company to market its products in the U.S. market. After two years of attending trade shows, developing promotional literature, and meeting with company representtives, I had succeeded in landing several large accounts and had lined up the two largest American distributors to handle the product.

At that point, I heard through the grapevine that the owner of the Brazilian company was grooming his nephew to come to the United States and open an office. But how was he going to do that if we had an exclusive agreement? I decided that the issue was important enough to fly to Brazil and negotiate.

I left with a win-win agenda. After all, I thought, our aims and goals were the same. I had developed contacts in the United States, and the more I sold the more money his company made. Before leaving, I devised a series of possible options for how his nephew could play a part in my U.S. operation and had them translated into Portuguese.

I got there a few days before the meeting so I could do a little preliminary information gathering. I had friends in the Brazilian company, and I called one of them—a production manager—and asked him if he knew anything about the situation. He told me that the head of the company had talked with some Italian customers several days before about his intentions in the U.S. market. We gave them a call and invited them out for dinner. It turned out that the company's owner had a rather inflated impression of the U.S. market and felt it was "wrong for one person to make all that money." His real goal, according to the Italians, was simply to push my operations to the sidelines and set up his own distributorship in the United States.

With this information, I realized that my original perception was wrong. The decision was already made, and he had no intention of honoring our agreement. My attitude and strategy changed. During the negotiation, he portrayed the new office as a way to support my operation and help me make more money. Because of the inside information I had obtained, however, my attitude and negotiating strategy changed. Instead of cooperating, I kept my cards covered and responded as little as possible. When I got back to the United States, I hired a lawyer, stopped any payments, and forced him to renegotiate. In the end, he purchased my U.S. operation for a reasonable sum. But if I hadn't known when to start playing hardball, he would have simply crowded me out of the market and I wouldn't have gotten anything at all.

COMPETITIVE NEGOTIATIONS

Buying a car is the quintessential competitive negotiation. The only thing really in dispute is the price—the margin of profit the dealer will make versus the savings the buyer can get by lowering the price. Such a negotiation is openly competitive. For each gain on one side, the other side loses. Both sides are bargaining over a fixed sum and there is no concern for the future of the relationship. The idea is to get the best price you can and declare victory.

During win-lose negotiations, the tendency is for people to take extreme positions. This is especially true in countries where bargaining is a way of life. Starting with an extreme position accomplishes several things. First, it lowers the other side's expectations. If you are trying to sell your house for $300,000 and the other side comes in with an offer of $200,000, you might not take the offer completely seriously, but it works to lower your aspirations and force you to rethink what is possible. Unconsciously, you tend to lower the bottom line.

Extreme offers also test the other side's resolve. During arms negotiations in the cold war, the Russians were masters of the extreme position. They would start out with a set of numbers that both sides knew was out of the ballpark, and then they would stick to it. The famous Russian *"nyet"* was designed to test the West's will, and its repeated use allowed underlying tensions in the U.S. position to surface—hopefully in the form of concessions.

The risk of using extreme offers or proposals is that they can undermine your credibility. If you offer someone half of what the going market value is, and they know very well they can get near-market value, they're likely to dismiss you either as a shyster trying to put one over on them or as an incompetent who doesn't know the market.

People in competitive negotiations tend to be tough and stubborn. This lets the other side know they are serious about getting the best deal possible. Russians or Middle Easterners will sometimes threaten to end negotiations, or simply walk out. This lets the other side know they are willing to live without an agreement rather than get one that doesn't give them the best deal possible.

Competitive negotiators tend to hide their true needs and intentions—often by using straw issues. The Chinese are masters of this tactic. They make a barrage of demands to disguise the issue they really care about. If the other side can't figure out what the real needs of the Chinese are, they can't use the leverage that knowledge would give them.

Finally, win-lose negotiators usually make concessions as seldom as possible. This lowers expectations by communicating to the other side that there is little room for negotiation.

COOPERATIVE NEGOTIATIONS

In my seminars, I have put hundreds of individuals from different countries around the world through simulated negotiations. I have found that the majority of people, regardless of where they come from, see the world as an essentially competitive place. Their first instinct is to stake out a competitive position rather than looking for cooperative solutions for issues. In some cases, this response may be due to lack of negotiating experience or the fact that it is easier to negotiate over a single quantifiable factor such as price. But I suspect that competition is a natural human instinct that extends across cultures.

In order to help participants in my seminars find alternatives to this competitive approach to negotiation, I conduct a simulated negotiating session between an American seller and a Chinese buyer in which the price is set by the selling company's global strategy. Although the Chinese buyers initially try to negotiate price, they soon find that they had better explore other options. The aim of the exercise is to move the focus of the negotiators from the single quantifiable issue of money to a joint search for options and solutions. During the debriefing everyone enjoys hearing the other teams' creative solutions.

It is important to realize that competitive behavior usually comes from the perception that we are competing for the same things. In real life, however, people are different and come from completely different situations. With a little patience, negotiators can find complementary needs and create solutions in which both sides can benefit.

In a win-win or cooperative negotiation, you have a vested interest in a long-term relationship. Aims and needs are not necessarily in conflict. Don't assume that what you want and what they want are opposed. You can often get what *you* want by giving them what *they* want. If resources are not fixed—that is, if cooperation can produce more resources for both sides—a confrontational, win-lose approach can be counterproductive, especially if you are planning a long-term relationship. Win-win negotiators are careful to balance the benefits of long-term cooperation against the short-term benefits of a quick kill.

Consider the case of a corporate executive getting back from a long business trip. All he wants to do is take off his shoes, lie on the couch, and eat some home-cooked food. His wife, who has been eating fast food with the kids after work, wants to go out for dinner. This could easily become a win-lose negotiation. Either they stay home and the wife loses, or the exhausted husband has to get dressed up and go out to one more public function.

But this dilemma can be reworked in win-win terms. The wife needs a night out; the husband wants to dress down and relax. Perhaps they can eat at home and then go out to a movie. By expanding the options, both sides can measurably increase the possibility of enjoyment.

One of the greatest opportunities for win-win negotiating is when priorities on the two sides differ. Effective negotiation is a process of "creative collaboration."[14] One side may place a great deeal of value on Just-in-Time delivery of parts. For the other side, having a long-term contract to ensure stability in its production facilities might be more important. The two sides may both be able to get what they want at little cost to the other. These opportunities for creating increased value for both sides always exist, but it takes a skillful negotiator to find and use them.

Power

The nice thing about being a celebrity is that when you bore people, they think it's their fault.
—Henry Kissinger[15]

During the recent Asian downturn, an American electronics company had a chance to buy out one of its suppliers at an almost incredible discount. The Malaysian company was overextended on credit and its Asian markets had collapsed. Selling to the Americans offered it a chance to lease back some of its factory space and start to reconstruct the business. The only other option was foreclosure by creditors and bankruptcy. The *Wall Street Journal* described the final stages of the negotiations:

> "I see this as very one-sided," [the Malaysian negotiator] says.
> The Yanks are unmoved. "It could be worse," one says. "We could squeeze you even more."
> [The Malaysian negotiator] is speechless. An American laughs. The purchase price is 50% *lower* than the American's boss authorized him to accept. It is about half the cost of building a similar factory from scratch.[16]

Power is a function of need and depends on options. The side that has more options has more power. Going into negotiations it is important to know what other alternatives you have. Knowing what else is available protects you from making unfavorable agreements or from passing over a really good deal.

Power in itself is neither good nor bad. Power is the ability to get something done, to move from point A to point B. It is a means, not an end. In business negotiations, power means the ability to influence outcome. Both sides usually have various sources of power. Identifying and using those sources of power determine the outcome of the negotiations.

The importance of different sources of power varies greatly among cultures. In the United States, connections and having powerful friends are important, but in Asian, Latin American, Middle Eastern, and Southern European countries, having important connections is much more valuable. The prestige associated with your brand or company also goes much further in bestowing bargaining power to your company in these cultures. Risk avoidance also motivates foreign businesspeople much more than Americans: An established track record can be an important source of power.

The following checklist identifies some of the major sources of power available to you in cross-cultural negotiations.

Power of understanding cultural differences: Many executives naively assume that, although there are cultural differences, these problems can be handled right on the spot. After all, aren't all people different everywhere? Aren't negotiators from Dallas different from New York negotiators? Many executives assume that understanding people is easy. We do it all the time, so what is all the fuss about?

People who have traveled overseas are especially prone to have more confidence than they should. The problem is that their knowledge generally focuses on surface aspects of culture that have little impact on the negotiations. Bungling an introduction ceremony in Japan won't break a deal. But not understanding how the Japanese differ from Americans in sequencing the negotiations might create frustration to derail the whole process.

It is just as important to understand the way foreign negotiators are programmed to approach issues as it is to understand the substance of the issues at hand. Understanding cultural differences is a critical source of insight into the other side's behavior and mind-set.

The power of avoiding strereotypes: Understanding cultural differences does not mean slotting foreign negotiators into stereotypical categories. When negotiating in other cultures, it's easy to think of the other side as a monolithic block of stereotypical qualities: the Japanese as silent, "inscrutable," and relentless; the French as cynical rationalists; and Latin Americans as emotional and excitable. But the people you face at the negotiating table are individuals, not just representatives of their cultures. There is often as much variation *within* cultures as there is between cultures. There are talkative, outgoing Japanese and quiet, analytic Latin Americans.

When they are working abroad, many Americans forget the basic skills they would use automatically when meeting a team of American negotiators: sizing up the members of the other team, thinking about who they are and what motivations they have. Thinking carefully about the other side as *people* is an important source of power in negotiations. Taking culture into account is an important part of this process, but so is coming to understand the individual character of each negotiator. Balancing these two factors will give you an accurate picture of the other side's strengths and weaknesses and help you decide which negotiating strategies are likely to be most successful.

The power of walking away: You don't need to threaten, but if you have backup options that allow you to walk away from negotiations, you can say no or draw the line with more confidence. Many foreign negotiators are acutely aware of this form of power. Asians, for example, like to shop around and thoroughly investigate other options before they come to the negotiating table. China's potential buying power is an 800-pound gorilla that provides it with many alternatives.

In the fall of 1994, I renegotiated a contract with an Algerian oil company to change the isolation valves on their three main liquefied natural gas (LNG) storage tanks. Each tank was large enough to fill a large supertanker, and having them shut down represented lost revenue of about $3 million per day. The original contract had been negotiated for $5 million and was supposed to take 30 days during October 1994. At the last minute, the Algerian company demanded a contract change delaying the start of the valve-change operation to July 1995 and requiring us to change the valves in four days. These changes represented a significant cost impact for our company.

The Algerian company's first tactic was to demand that we complete the work and then negotiate the contract changes. I rejected this idea and demanded a resolution by the end of April. This gave us six months to settle.

We estimated the cost of the changes for our company at about $350,000. I knew that the Algerians needed room to negotiate the contract at each level of their management. My first offer was to add $750,000 to the cost of the contract. Negotiations were give-and-take. My first concession was for $100,000 in exchange for shorter payment terms. The next reduction was $50,000 for elimination of liquidated damages. My final reduction was $25,000 for a minor concession on their part.

The negotiations were intense and used up the entire six months we had set aside. On the last day of April, we reached an impasse. We were at a price of $575,000 and the Algerian company wanted another $7,500 reduction. I knew we could afford this concession, but if I gave in I feared they would go for more because of their need to squeeze every penny out of us.

Negotiations ran late into the night. If they ended in deadlock, we would leave and initiate arbitration proceedings in Geneva. The Algerian company said it would get another company to change the valves. Late that evening, we deadlocked. The next day, May 1, was a national holiday in Algeria, so we packed our bags and boarded the bus to the airport. I was scared—petrified, actually. We did not have the funds to afford an arbitration, but I could not back down without the risk of a major escalation in demands on their side.

While we were on the bus to the airport, the project manager from the Algerian company called us by radio and asked us to come back. They were willing to agree to our final proposal without additional modifications. We returned and signed the contract. What amazed me was that after the deal, the Algerian side was just as happy as I was.

—*Donald Barrus*

The power of information: During the negotiatiing process you need to have information to defend your interests, advance your arguments, and influence the other side's perception of the situation. Gathering, managing, and deploying information allows you to conduct negotiations strategically and get the results you want.

The power of obligations and reciprocity: The idea that we should return a favor is universal. In traditional cultures, reciprocity and obligation are extremely powerful motivations. A dinner invitation calls for some equivalent gesture in return. To accept a favor from someone means being in his or her debt.

Of course, giving unilateral concessions on the bargaining table in the hope of getting equivalent concessions from the other side would be foolish—and seen as foolish by the other side. On the other hand, initiating or offering a concession at the right time might motivate the other side to make a concession and hence move things along.

Hospitality and friendship help create a sense of obligation. It is much harder to walk away from a person you have broken bread with, or invited into your home. Small favors, such as helping members of the other team or their families with visas, cement a relationship and help take the hard edge off formal negotiations.

The power of charisma: If you have naturally charismatic people leading your team, this can enhance your power. A word of caution, however: Charisma does not always translate across cultural lines. Overly glib people who do well in this country may encounter problems overseas.

The power of dress: Dress two levels above what you would in the United States. This is especially important in European, Latin American, Middle Eastern, and Asian countries. Be careful not to overdo it, however. As Takashi Kiuchi comments: "I am instinctively turned off by people that dress inappropriately and try to be more than they really are."[17]

The power of silence: Silence projects an air of power. It also forces the other side to make the first move, which sets up the basic power dynamic: They are the supplicants; you are the one considering their request. That is, *you* have the power of approval.

The power of reward or punishment: In the status-oriented cultures of Asia, the Middle East, and Latin America, both sides of a transaction are not equal. Purchasers generally have more power than sellers. You can reward or punish the other side by giving or withholding business from them. Japanese business customs reflect this reality: The selling company traditionally assumes a larger share of the expenses for wining and dining. In the United States and northern Europe, the buyer still has power but relations take place on a more equal footing.

I was on a three-week trip to Germany from Brazil in order to buy special breeds of cattle from European farmers. One of the strangest things about the Germans was that they didn't give us any special treatment. In Brazil, if someone is seriously interested in buyinig our product, we give them preferential treatment in order to get the deal done. We spend time making sure they are comfortable and that their needs and wishes are met. The German farmers asked some polite questions about our home country, but they did not discuss prices or other business matters. At the end of the trip, they showed us the prices and bid and payment conditions. We made our bid and they said yes or no, but they did not chat about the offer.

—*Claudio Guimaraes*

The power of legitimacy: When the police put on their lights to pull us over for a traffic violation, we comply without thinking. We don't stop to question their right to do what they are doing. The badge, the uniform, the lights of the police car trigger an automatic response. The police have *legitimate* power.

Legitimacy comes from occupying a certain office or position. We don't obey the police because of who they are as individuals but because they hold a certain position. Negotiators can gain legitimacy by establishing their credentials (see Chapter 5) and by associating themselves with legitimate sources of power. Letters of introduction from the company president or important people known to the other side help establish legitimacy.

You can also gain legitimacy by aligning yourself with law, science, or moral principles. Bring copies of laws, regulations, and precedents that apply to the case at hand. Having experts for technical aspects of the negotiations can also help establish your claim to legitimate power.

The power of investment: Have you ever wondered about the strange behavior of people in religious cults? How can seemingly ordinary people get to the point where they blindly obey the cult leader—even if commanded to engage in crime or commit suicide?

Social scientists have an interesting answer to this question: Cult leaders skillfully use the power of "psychological investment." It works like this: The leader asks new members to change their behavior or belief in some small way. It's just a small thing, so the new members comply. The leader asks for another step, then another. With each step, the new members invest a little more of themselves in the group. After a time, they have made so many sacrifices that they can't disobey no matter what the leader asks. To do so would mean giving up the cumulative investment they have built up.

The cult leader is careful to keep the sacrifice demanded for each step less than the total investment the member has in the group. Unless the members can extricate themselves and look at the situation from the outside, it always makes more sense to take one more small step than give up the investment in the group. The situation is similar to gamblers pouring money into a slot machine, desperately trying to recoup the money they've already invested in the big payoff.

This kind of psychological investment also happens in business relationships. We get used to working with someone. We know the person's strengths and weaknesses. It would require a lot of work to go out and start another relationship from scratch with someone we don't know—someone who may be untrustworthy or incompetent.

This investment is a source of power in negotiations. The longer negotiations continue, the less likely it is that the other side will just walk away. They've put a lot of time and effort into the process; as time goes on they are less and less likely to throw that away and start from scratch.

The same thing applies when you are negotiating with someone you've worked with for a period of time. Working together creates a sense of mutual obligation, especially in cultures that value long-term business relationships. They've become used to working with you, and the time and effort needed to start a new relationship are a great deterrent. This means that they are unlikely to simply walk away because they might get a slightly better deal somewhere else.

Of course, you should be aware of the way investment works on your side as well. Don't be like the gambler in Las Vegas who keeps putting money into the slot machine trying desperately to win back the money already lost. Sometimes you have to take a hard look at the situation and walk away—no matter how much you've already invested in the deal.

The power of converging interests: Whenever you can satisfy the other side's needs, you have power. The beauty of developing win-win options is that helping the other side also helps you. Cooperative negotiations create a powerful pull toward agreement. This means you have more leverage to negotiate concessions in other areas.

Converging interests also give you power over the competition. Win-win options tilt the playing field in your favor, which makes it much more difficult for the competition to break into your game. You can afford to give the other side benefits that the competition can't, because there is more to go around for everyone.

The power of numbers: In international negotiations a team of people always presents a more powerful front than a lone individual. And a team will give you the information, expertise, and backup you need to make the most effective (and powerful) presentation of your case.

The Stages of Negotiation

One of the challenges American negotiators commonly encounter overseas is that the pace and sequencing of negotiations are different. In the United States, negotiations typically go through three stages. First each side presents themselves and outlines the benefits they can bring to the transaction. Next comes the bargaining phase in which give-and-take on issues takes place. Finally the negotiation is culminated in an agreement in which both sides commit to fulfill the terms of the contract.

During negotiations, the Chinese do not like surprises and pay a lot of attention to details. The Chinese obsession with details may appear to be slow and may seem to drag out discussions at times, but it is important to have patience because details are important to the Chinese.
—*Nadia Lee*

In countries in Asia, Latin America, and the Middle East, negotiations start with a getting-to-know-you phase where the two parties exchange preliminary information and size each other up as potential business partners. If both sides are able to establish a relationship of trust, a decision to work together is made. Then comes the presentation of specific issues, followed by concrete bargaining. Finally, an agreement is reached, but this does not necessarily mean that the negotiation process is over. Negotiators from bargaining cultures are likely to continue to look for opportunities to improve on the agreement even after formal negotiations have ended.

Misunderstandings occur when the two sides find themselves in different stages of their respective negotiating sequence. The American negotiator shows up in China, makes a presentation, and assumes that it's time to get down to bargaining on the specifics. The Chinese, however, are still in the getting-to-know-you phase and have not even committed to working together. They perceive the American negotiator's behavior as an attempt to apply pressure in a completely inappropriate way. On their side, the Americans are often thrown by the extended getting-to-know-you and making-a-decision-to-work-together phases, which they perceive as delaying tactics on the other side. And they can be quite distressed by continued bargaining after an agreement has been reached—a tactic that seems to them to violate the spirit of the agreement.

Where to Negotiate

The only people who believe that traveling overseas on business is glamorous are people who have never traveled overseas on business.
—Trenholme Griffin and Russell Daggatt[18]

Traveling abroad on business can be disorienting and exhausting. Jet lag, changes in diet, different schedules and different physical surroundings, the difficulties of negotiating in another language and culture, and simply being away from family, friends, and the logistical support of the home office can put international negotiators at a disadvantage. Added to this are different laws and regulations, currency problems, unfamiliar government structures, possible political instability, and differences in ideology.

When you're in St. Louis and the other company is in Minneapolis, the question of where to negotiate isn't so important. You can hop on a plane to the Twin Cities, spend the day at the table, and be back in time for dinner with your family. When the other company is in Kuala Lumpur or Abu Dhabi, the situation is more complicated. There are a number of options: You can negotiate at their place, your place, or—for extended negotiations—you can alternate sites.[19]

Your place: There's a lot to say for having the home field advantage. You know where everything is. You get a good night's sleep. And you don't have to deal with the logistical problems and often considerable expense of traveling abroad. They'll be speaking your language and adjusting to your laws and customs. You have the support of your office staff and control of the physical setting of the negotiations. If you want, you can use classic dirty tricks like seating them with the sun in their eyes. Or you can keep them off balance with a round of parties and sight-seeing. You have all the trappings of power. They have to come to your office, wait in your waiting room, and depend on you to help them navigate American business practices.

But you make one big sacrifice when the negotiations are at your place: You don't have an opportunity to learn about the other side firsthand. This is an important consideration—especially if you are contemplating a long-term relationship. There's really no substitute for walking around their factory or meeting with their production or marketing staff. Being in their place allows you to gather information about the other side's needs and expectations that can be useful in negotiations and help avoid misunderstandings later in the relationship.

Their place: Negotiating on the other company's terrain complicates your game plan. You have to contend with jet lag, culture shock, and the logistical problems of communicating with the home office and working without its support. They have control of the physical environment, and they can keep you off balance with social events and unfamiliar business practices.

Socializing is an excellent way to gather intelligence and can also be helpful in combating culture shock. Watch, listen, read, learn. Pay particular attention to rumors, gossip, predictions, and the opinions of key people close to the top. However, be reticent about your own opinions and never gossip. Gather information from other businesspeople you meet. Give away your own tips to them—your noncritical leads—and invite them to the most enjoyable and beneficial business or social activities you have found. Attempt to connect with local circles of power, as well as the expatriate community.

—Doreen Harvey

In some countries there may be problems with security. The fax operator at your hotel might be perfectly happy to make a few extra dollars (or dinars) selling your message home to the other side. You don't want to be overly paranoid—but if the stakes are high, it's probably best to assume the faxes and phone lines have been compromised.

Some of these disadvantages can be turned into assets. If you can, use jet lag as an excuse to come to the country a little early so you can get to know the terrain. There's no substitute for a walk around the local marketplace to get a feel for the culture, political situation, and ideology of the other side.

Most executives today are on tight schedules—but this can be used to your advantage, especially if you have a powerful position in the negotiations. Jeswald Salacuse describes a pressure tactic used by multinationals:

> [Executives] arrive Sunday night, hold general discussions on Monday and Tuesday, and present a draft agreement on Wednesday, expressing a strong hope that a contract can be signed by the time their plane leaves on Friday morning. This tactic amounts to an ultimatum, although the source of the ultimatum is made to appear to be the airline rather than the multinational corporation.[20]

Using pressure tactics like this one depends on a keen appreciation for the balance of power—who needs whom the most? But it's also worth considering the long-term implications of aggressive tactics. You might get what you want on this deal, but will this really help your company in the long run? If you plan to do business again with these people, or even in their country, the answer is probably no.

Both places: If negotiations are going to be protracted, or if you are contemplating a close, long-term relationship, negotiating at both sites is often the best option. This splits the costs and hassles equally between the two sides. It also creates a common bond by giving both sides equal symbolic power. Traveling to the United States can be an important perk for foreign businesspeople, and the status and face it confers in the home country can become an important bargaining chip. Reciprocal visits can be an important factor when dealing with poor countries that are struggling for recognition as equal players in the international arena. Both sides get a chance to see the other side's operations and really get acquainted. The relationship-building and improved communications that result are extremely important for effective multinational operations.

CHAPTER

15

Avoiding Temptation—
Ethics Overseas

I curse you to live on your salary.

—Russian proverb

The Hydra of Corruption

Corruption in international business is like the Hydra—the many-headed serpent of Greek mythology. As soon as you cut off one of its heads, a dozen more grow in its place. As an increasing number of American companies expand into international markets, there is a growing concern and confusion about how to deal with bribes, kick-backs, and other illegal business practices.

In an attempt to stem the tide of foreign commercial corruption washing up on American shores, Congress passed the Foreign Corrupt Practices Act in 1977. The FCPA prohibits U.S. companies and their agents from giving bribes to foreign officials in order to get business. This law has effectively conveyed to U.S. executives as well as to the of-ficials of other countries that bribery isn't an accepted practice in this country.

But many American executives complain that these strict rules put them at a competitive disadvantage vis-à-vis countries that ignore or

218

even condone bribery. Most European countries, for instance, allow companies to deduct bribes as a legitimate business expense. The net result is a considerable pressure on American companies to give bribes or use other illegal means to level the playing field with their competitors.

Americans abroad encounter a world with temptations and pressures that don't exist in domestic business transactions. In many countries, bribes are an accepted, or at least tolerated, part of doing business. In others, cultural differences make it difficult to decide where the line between a bribe and legitimate compensation actually falls. If an oil company negotiating for drilling rights in the Ecuadorian Amazon gives a motorized boat to the chief of the local tribe, is this a bribe or part of the compensation for using the land?

The pressure to use bribes or other illegal means to get business is increased by the perception that "everyone is doing it." One businessman whose company does a lot of trade in China comments that "his salespeople constantly complain that, to win contracts, other companies— both foreign and Chinese—are willing to offer a wide variety of incentives: money, videocassette recorders, even financing of U.S. schooling for the children of some Chinese officials."[1]

Turning the Tide: Multinational Efforts to Stop Corruption

The world's leading industrial nations have moved to outlaw bribery as a means for companies to win commercial contracts. The *Wall Street Journal* reported in May 1997 that ministers from 29 member countries of the Organization for Economic Cooperation and Development agreed to negotiate a binding international convention to criminalize bribery of foreign public officials by the end of 1997.[2] The agreement states that: "Bribery of foreign public officials in order to obtain or retain business is . . . an offense irrespective of the value or the outcome of the bribe, of perception of local custom or of the tolerance of bribery by local authorities." Initially, France and Germany, which both allow their companies to offset payments to foreign officials against tax charges, argued against an agreement unless it were backed by a treaty involving all industrial nations. But the United States has pushed the initiative, arguing that its companies are losing billions of dollars in contracts each year because of unfair competition from unscrupulous foreign firms.

Americans tend to follow the rules and do what the law says. In Brazilians' minds, however, nothing is prohibited, even those actions that are not permitted. Brazilians have been living for many decades in a rough environment where the laws are rarely enforced and often ignored. Therefore, people don't respect the law and instead find their own ways to solve their problems. This has led to a high level of bribery and corruption between politicians and business enterprises. In fact, many kinds of business can only be conducted through bribes. Brazil would certainly be a better place if the government started enforcing the laws—a better place in which to do business and to live as a whole.

—*Rafael Ribeiro*

Other multinational organizations have formed to slay the monster of corruption. Transparency International (TI) was founded in 1993 by former World Bank director Peter Eigen and now has chapters in over 60 nations.[3] Funded by multinational groups such as the World Bank, TI's purpose is to help countries come to grips with corruption and find ways to eliminate it. At the heart of this drive is the growing consensus that corruption is a bad business practice that hurts economies of the countries where it is practiced extensively. As Eigen says: "Corruption is what stops economic development in these countries and holds them back."[4]

The Organization for Economic Cooperation and Development is also moving against corruption by trying to hammer out an agreement among Western nations that would outlaw practices that encourage corruption—such as forbidding the use of bribery expenses as a tax deduction. The International Monetary Fund and the World Bank have also taken actions to stamp out the practice. According to the *Wall Street Journal*: "The Bank's anticorruption plans are so tough they provoked a hissy fit from some Third World plutocrats."[5]

The temptation facing American businesspeople abroad is simple: Should I use bribes or other illegal means to get the job done simply because "that's the way things are done" or because "everyone else does it"? The evidence points to the opposite conclusion: In the long run, using bribes, kickback schemes, and other illegal means has proven to be an unproductive, dangerous, and expensive way to do business.

The Environment of Corruption

Corrupt practices have complex historical and cultural roots. Although individuals are responsible for corruption, they are usually responding to the environment they find themselves in. In order to deal with the problem of corruption, it helps to understand something about the circumstances that seem to encourage it.

One place where corruption has historically been common is in centrally planned or socialized economies. These bureaucracies are relatively impervious to market forces, and bureaucrats often have more or less absolute power over services or permits needed for business to continue—a perfect recipe for corruption. Matt Moffett and Jonathan Friedland comment, "Traditionally, Latin American corruption grew out of the broad discretion wielded by bureaucrats in economies where the state did everything, from licensing imports to operating cantinas."[6] The same tradition also accounts for many of the problems now encountered in China and the countries of the former Soviet Union.

The Russians use a figure-skating metaphor to describe how things get done in their famously complicated bureaucracy: "The shortest distance between two points is a figure eight." This means that nothing gets done in the most obvious and intuitive way. To get through the system, one has to navigate a maze of bureaucratic obstacles lying in wait. In fact, that's the way that business is conducted around the developing world, from the Middle East to Latin America. What lubricates and moves things along this contorted, tortuous path is greasing the palms of the various gatekeepers, each of whom can create a time-consuming bottleneck if not tended to accordingly.

A Russian engineer who worked in a government agency during the Soviet days told me that if he really needed something done he often bypassed the bureaucracy altogether. If he needed a shipment of parts moved, he simply took a bottle of vodka, found the trucker, and asked him if he could work it into his official schedule as a special favor. In the new capitalist system, he laments, you still need to bribe people to get anything done, but the required bribes have gotten much bigger.

In Indonesia, we don't need written or road tests to get a driver's license. We just give the agent about $30 and the license should be ready in about two hours. In the United States, I've failed the road test three times, and I still don't have a license!

If we are stopped for a traffic violation in Indonesia, we just give them $5 and tell them we're sorry and won't do it again. In the United States, it is out of the question to use bribery when the police pull you over. You get a ticket and you have to pay for it.

—*Yulia Liong*

The transition to a market economy can also breed corruption. Talking about the transition problems of Latin American economies, the *Wall Street Journal* comments: "It has long been an article of faith that free-market economics, combined with greater democratization, would make the region's business more transparent. Instead, corruption may be more prevalent than ever."[7] Commenting on this change, James Wygand, managing director the Brazilian office of Kroll Associates, observes: "It used to be most of corruption was petty stuff like paying off a tax inspector or offering a bribe to get a paper stamped. Nowadays, it's more opportunistic, institutionalized, and very close to the style of organized crime. It's very, very large because the stakes are very large."[8]

In Indonesia, bribery is useful to deal with top officials and other senior people because they are the only ones who can make decisions. Inside the government, bribery is the most efficient way to get around. To acquire a big contract it is much wiser to bribe the top government officials than to spend time preparing a good proposal for bidding. Bribery will save you a lot of time and effort.

—*Juliana Bahar and Jimmy Tunggadjaja*

A third source of corruption is the lack of well-developed legal systems and clearly established individual and commercial rights. One of the explicit goals of Transparency International is to "build local confidence in the rule of law in the realms of business and politics."[9] Corruption can flourish when there are no clearly defined legal guidelines to regulate corruption, or the police and courts are unwilling to enforce the law:

Latin America's chronically undefended judiciary works perversely to promote corruption rather then punish it. A recent study by the Inter-

American Law and Economics Association found that many litigants felt compelled to take illicit measures to expedite business-related cases, whose average length has nearly doubled to around 2.5 years during the past decade. Payoffs to the court represent 8% to 12% of total legal costs, the study found.[10]

Finally, some poorer countries complain that corruption has been institutionalized on the international level. The United States is the only country actually to prescribe criminal penalties for bribery and corruption in business ventures outside its borders. At a recent international conference, Prime Minister Meles Zenawi of Ethiopia exhorted: "We will do our best to get our house in order, but our Northern friends: Please do not support the bribery by your exporters by giving them tax deductions for their bribes."[11]

Why Not Use Bribes?

Even when it does not lead to legal problems, bribery is bad business practice for a number of reasons.

Bribery can become very expensive. According to Richard Gesteland, Hong Kong companies calculate that 5 percent of the cost of doing business in China go to bribes. In Russia, the cost can be 15 to 20 percent. In Indonesia, bribes can account for as much as 30 percent of business expenses.[12] These costs clearly cut into the efficiency of doing business, and this is one of the main motivations for countries where corruption is common to clean up the practice. William E. O'Brien of H. B. Fuller Company related the following story:

> The company, he recalls, once offered to sell adhesives to a prospective customer for 32,000 yuan (roughly $5,500 at today's official exchange rate) a ton. The customer proposed calling the price 42,000 yuan a ton; its management wanted a kickback of the difference. Mr. O'Brien refused. "Think of what that does to your customers," he says. "You don't want inefficiency to destroy your customers."[13]

Bribery is costly for the economic system as a whole. According to the *Wall Street Journal*, fraud led to the collapse of one financial institution in Brazil that will cost taxpayers there an estimated $5 billion.[14] The economies of many impoverished Third World countries are immobilized by fraud, with money that should be reinvested in the economic infrastructure diverted instead into the pockets of corrupt officials who typically do much of their business outside the country.

When I was helping my father transact a business deal in my native Indonesia, I was surprised at the way Indonesians conveyed their requests for a bribe. They might mention, for instance, that their car is old or that they haven't taken a vacation in a long time. When they mention a car, it means they want a new car, or simply a better car than the one they are driving now. If they mention a vacation, it means they want to have a vacation paid for their entire family. The art of doing business in Indonesia is to pick up on those lines and interpret them.

—Aidil A. Madjid

Bribery can land you in a cockroach-infested jail. Bribery is illegal in most countries. These laws are rarely but often capriciously enforced. The prospect of spending time in a foreign prison should be a good argument against corruption. Violating bribery laws can also destroy large business ventures. For instance, in 1996 over 30 people (executives and officials from IBM and Banco de la Nacion Argentina, and Argentinean officials) were charged with corruption—many in Argentinean courts. The corruption charges resulted in the suspension of a $249 million contract to computerize the bank's operations and an $86 million breach of contract suit filed by Banco de la Nacion.

Bribery can land you in a nice clean jail. For Americans, the Foreign Corrupt Practices Act (FCPA) is an excellent reason not to take bribes. The FCPA's provisions apply to U.S. companies, shareholders, directors, agents, officers, or employees. It forbids an offer, payment, or promise of money or anything of value to foreign officials (including bureaucrats, politicians, political parties, or political candidates) whose goal is to assist the U.S. company in obtaining or retaining business or to assist the company in obtaining preferential treatment for existing contracts or business operations.[15] Also, U.S. companies are required to keep records of all gifts and monetary transactions with foreign officials. Individuals can be fined up to $100,000 and face five years in prison, and companies can receive fines up to $2 million for each violation. Individuals can be liable even if they did not have actual knowledge of the violation.[16]

Bribery creates ethical problems even when it does not lead to legal problems. Corruption circumvents the normal rules of the game—both legal and economic. In the long run, this will lead to unwise and inefficient business practices. Good business decisions can be made only in a climate of trust and openness. Both individual contract negotiations and the developing international market as a whole will benefit from an ethical approach to doing business.

Attitudes toward Bribery

I first came to the United States from Iran as a college student during the 1960s. I vividly remember a calculus exam given during my first semester in school. The professor came in, passed out the exam, and left the room. There were about 40 students in the class, and I remember looking around in amazement as I realized that no one was cheating! I was more impressed by this experience than by all the dramatic buildings and scenery I'd seen since my arrival.

Ever since, I've done informal surveys of other countries' practices: Whenever I get the opportunity, I ask the people I meet from other countries whether cheating in school is a common practice in their country. Most people answer that cheating is accepted—as long as you don't get caught. Of course, things have changed a lot in this country as well. Academic dishonesty is a big problem on most college campuses.

In April of 1997, I went with a friend to Leon, Guanajuato, Mexico, to attend a friend's wedding and travel around the region. I was very excited about the trip. I was born in Mexico but have lived in the United States for a long time. I have always felt comfortable living in both cultures.

Our troubles started when we got to the car rental agency. We decided to rent a Ford Explorer and after some negotiation we agreed on a daily rate and the time we could pick up the vehicle. After the negotiations, I felt content. We had joked with the clerk about the local sports team, and I thought I had come off like a native of Leon. I thought I was getting a great deal.

The next morning I waited for the car to arrive at the hotel. I had just gotten off the phone with the car agency and confirmed that everything was still on for the delivery. My friend and I talked about all the places we were going to see that day. We talked and waited—but the car never arrived. After an hour and a half and three calls to the rental agency, we decided to walk to the office to see what had happened.

The car had been rented to someone else! When we had called

earlier, the clerk had told me repeatedly that the car was on the way. He had lied to us! He apologized and said this was a common practice in Leon. Their car agency gave preferential treatment to American businessmen, who were allowed to steal cars away from local customers without warning. Basically, he told me they discriminated against Mexicans because the Americans could afford to pay more for the vehicles.

The clerk knew of our plans from our discussion the previous day and hinted that he might still be able to get us an Explorer if he had some money to help convince his boss. The guy wanted a bribe! I refused to pay and he said that was unfortunate as he had only one other car available. He seemed offended by my reaction.

As if all this weren't bad enough, we decided to push our luck and get a car from them anyway. Time was short and we had no time to walk to another car agency. In the end, we got a Volkswagen Jetta. The clerk pleaded with us to take the car and told us he'd give us a discount on the rental. We took it without discussing the matter further and started off on our trip.

We didn't get very far before we noticed we were almost out of gas. I couldn't believe that they hadn't given us a full tank of gas. We pulled off the highway and into a gas station. I was nervous about the car, so I asked the attendant to check the water and oil. The car was almost completely out of engine oil. The guy at the agency knew we were going on a long trip, but he didn't bother to prepare the car.

When we returned the car three days later, the same clerk was there along with an older man. When we asked for our bill, the older man stepped in and pulled out our paperwork, which charged us for use of a Ford Explorer. His agency was doing us a favor, he said, by renting us a car at such short notice. Since the original paperwork was for a Ford Explorer, he had to charge us that price. At that point my friend made an impressive display of his mastery of colorful Spanish profanity. After arguing for an hour, we decided not to pay the bill at all. After all, what are credit cards for?

A month later, my friend gave me a call and told me the agency had tried to bill him for $600. In the end we paid $180.

—Alan Ibarra

Many officials in the Soviet Union considered themselves as a superior species, appointed to drive the herds of human cattle. And many Russians today hold jobs because of nepotism, friendship, or former membership in the Communist Party.

The result is often incompetence, sloth, conservatism, and a tendency to avoid responsibility by passing the buck to higher-ups. Patience is the key to dealing with the bureaucracy—that and finding someone who knows the system, or, better yet, someone who knows people high in the chain of command.

When conducting business with Russians, do not forget the plague of corruption. The assumption that "everyone steals" has erased the nation's sense of right and wrong. Many involved in bribery and embezzlement see it as the only way to survive. They feel justified since "everyone else is doing it."

The police are notorious for corrupt behavior. Americans generally trust "the law," but Russians have a tremendous distrust of the government, the military, and the police.

—Janna Bronechter

I'm always surprised by the schizophrenic approach Americans take to the problem of bribery. On the one hand, they pride themselves on their moral superiority and look down on Third World countries where, according to the common perception, everyone is on the take. On the other hand, I have often heard American businesspeople lament the fact that they are not allowed to use bribes in overseas ventures. The common complaint is that everyone else is doing it and that the efforts of the U.S. government to outlaw such practices are interfering with American competitiveness—an attitude embodied in the following note from *Business Week*:

> When U.S. Trade Representative Mickey Kantor complained that bribery by foreign rivals overseas was costing U.S. companies $45 billion a year, he wasn't talking through his hat. A new study by Harvard University economist James R. Hines Jr. finds that U.S. companies took a beating after Congress passed the Foreign Corrupt Practices Act of 1977. . . .
>
> In short, although legislators expected others to follow America's example, the law's main effect seems to have been to weaken the competitive position of U.S. companies without reducing the use of bribery in foreign business deals.[17]

But in fact, the FCPA is one of the best friends American executives have ever had. It provides a perfect reason for *not* giving bribes. If a foreign official hints that a bribe or kickback might smooth the process of doing business, all you have to do is point to the law and say that it's out of your control. You might sympathize with the official's position, but there's simply nothing you can do. In the end, the underlying advantages of the deal will in most cases outweigh the influence of bribes on getting agreements and moving projects forward.

How Can You Avoid Giving Bribes?

Never assume you have to give a bribe. If you expect to pay bribes you'll probably end up paying them. If you simply operate as if bribes are not even a consideration, you'll be much less likely to be solicited.

Just say no. Cite the FCPA and say that corporate policy forbids such actions.

Never initiate a bribe. Giving bribes is a cultural nuance. If you try to do it without knowing the culture, you are likely to make a fool of yourself and perhaps get in a lot of trouble as well.

Pay attention to scams and find ways around them. Richard Gesteland recounts the story of an Indonesian company headquartered in Singapore that regularly sent technicians to Indonesia. The company discovered that about half the techs were being asked for a $50 bribe to get through customs, while the other half were simply ignored. On investigation, the company found that the first time a tech traveled to the country, he or she was asked for a bribe. If the tech complied, a small pencil mark was made on his or her passport indicating a "payer" to future customs officials. The company erased the marks on all its employees' passports and instructed them to refuse to give bribes in the future. After this, solicitations for bribes stopped entirely.[18]

Learn the culture of the country. This will allow you to see who has real power and assess the limits of power and authority of specific officials. Often you can find other channels to go through. If not, it will give you more confidence to stand up to officials who attempt to impose bribes.

Use hierarchies and status differences to your advantage. Knowing the right people can be just as important as paying bribes in relationship-oriented cultures. Use your contacts to find out who can get things done. In status-oriented cultures, treating people as if they have status or doing things to help them gain, maintain, or enhance their status is often just as good as a bribe. Finally, understanding status hierarchies will allow you to get to the real decision makers. They are more likely to represent the interests of the company or nation; the benefits they demand can thus be included as part of the regular negotiating process. A minister who tries to make the contract conditional on employment guarantees for workers is not asking for a bribe but issuing a negotiating demand.

Establish warm personal relationships. It is much more difficult to ask for a bribe from someone with whom you have a personal relationship. Small gifts and favors are often very effective. Bring people something small that shows you have thought of them personally. Be sensitive to their wants and needs.

When I had my own import/export business, I worked with a Brazilian company to distribute its products in the United States. After a year, I was approached by the marketing manager with a sweetheart kickback deal. He would get me small lots of the product at volume-discount prices. In return, he asked that the checks be made out to him. He explained that his executive salary was small (much smaller than those in North America!) and that this was necessary for him to make a real salary. Besides, he said, it was a common practice in Brazil.

Prior to this incident, I had established a close working relationship with him. Every time I went to Brazil, I brought cologne or perfume for him and his wife. This enabled me to reject his proposal in a friendly manner without alienating him. He told me he understood and we dropped the matter there. Afterward, we were still friends, and I continued to bring him small gifts. But this was only possible because of our friendly business relationship.

Be patient. Many cultures have a more relaxed attitude toward time. Americans can get frustrated with delays—or even interpret them as a sign that bribes are needed to smooth the way. If you learn to relax and work within the framework of their time, you can often avoid the necessity for bribes.

In Conclusion

Tradition is a guide and not a jailer.
　　　　—W. Somerset Maugham, *The Summing Up*, 1938

At a World's Fair early in this century, one of the main attractions was an exhibit of exotic animals from around the world. In preparation, large, naturalistic habitats were constructed, much like those found in modern zoos. Previously the animals were kept in small cages where they paced back and forth, four steps by eight steps. When the habitats were finally finished, the zookeepers eagerly released the animals—lions and tigers and bears into their individual areas—waiting to see their reactions to the freedom and open space they taken such pains to create. But instead of bounding off to explore their new environment, the animals sniffed the air, looked around, and continued to pace—four steps by eight steps inside the imaginary boundaries of their cages.[1]

Change is difficult to deal with. It is all too easy to avoid new things by embracing what we already know. But as the globalization of business increases—as borders fade and computers "speak the same language" all over the world—we need to overcome the barriers to people-to-people communication. In other words, we need to venture outside of the com-

230

fort zone of our imaginary cages. We simply can't afford to shut out the real world for the safe, bounded world we already know.

The irony is that the more open we are to new cultures and ways of doing things, the more similarities we find. In the final analysis, people are much more similar than they are different. And as the world gets smaller, these areas of overlap continue to increase. The differences constitute only a small portion of our relationships with other cultures, but if we don't handle those differences consciously they can overshadow our similarities, distort our communications, and distract us from the interests we share in common.

History teaches us that nations that are open and willing to learn from others have fared the best. Dr. Thomas Sowell of Stanford University writes: "Isolated people have usually been backward people. . . . The size of a people's cultural universe influences how far they can develop, technologically and culturally."[2] Although Sowell is talking primarily about geographical isolation, his statement points to a more general problem: mental isolation—he tendency of people faced with the unfamiliar or different to hang on to what they already know.

The advantages of looking beyond our habitual way of doing things are illustrated by the response of U.S. companies to Japanese economic success during the 1980s. Instead of circling their wagons, American executives studied Japanese production and management techniques and incorporated them into their way of doing business. Today, many of those Japanese techniques in quality control, continuous improvement, and Just-in-Time production (which the Japanese originally borrowed from the United States) have become part of everyday operations in U.S. companies.

The necessity of being open to other ways of doing things has become one of the founding rules of the global marketplace. When I travel to other countries to give seminars or when I teach foreign executives here in this country, I am constantly amazed at how much people want to learn the "American way" of doing business. They have absorbed the lesson that the success of the American economy comes from a willingness to learn from others.

But just because the American way of doing business is hot now, this doesn't mean American executives can simply sit back. Learning about others is essential to staying competitive. From opening up new markets, competing for contracts, and negotiating joint ventures to finding the best personnel, management, and production techniques, cross-cultural competence and an open mind will be keys to success in the coming decades.

For the beginner, working across cultures can seem complex and intimidating. But these fears are largely misplaced. Some basic reference points—such as those provided in the previous chapters—along with an open mind and a good dose of common sense can provide the framework for working successfully in any culture. For old hands with many years of international experience, there are probably few things in this book that they have not already experienced or know—at least intuitively. However, this book puts this intuitive knowledge into an organized framework that can be used—and transmitted to others—in a wide variety of practical business situations. It is my hope that this book will help give American executives the confidence and competence they need to navigate the ever-expanding global marketplace and to take advantage of the unbounded opportunities it presents.

Notes

Chapter 1   Thriving in the New Global Marketplace

1. Quoted from a speech by Patricia Fripp on November 9, 1999, at Western Wireless.
2. James Flanigan, "Even Boeing Held Down by Global Price Wars," *Los Angeles Times*, June 4, 1995.
3. Jeff Cole, "Airbus Goes After Boeing's Grip in Japan," *Wall Street Journal*, April 19, 1999.
4. Rebecca Blumenstein, "While Going Global, GM Slips at Home," *Wall Street Journal*, January 8, 1997.
5. Ron Scherer, "Rise of Borderless Corporation," *Christian Science Monitor*, May 8, 1998.
6. Carol J. Williams, "Steering Around Culture Clashes," *Los Angeles Times*, January 17, 1999.
7. Brian Dumaine, "Don't Be an Ugly-American Manager," *Fortune*, October 16, 1995, 225.
8. Ibid.
9. Glen Fisher, *International Negotiation: A Cross-Cultural Perspective*, Yarmouth, ME: Intercultural Press, 7.
10. Bonvillian and Nowlin, "Cultural Awareness: An Essential Element of Doing Business Abroad," *Business Horizons*, November–December 1994.
11. Josh Hammond and James Morrison, *The Stuff Americans Are Made Of*, New York: Macmillan, 1996, 216–217.

Chapter 2   Developing a World-Based Perspective

1. Thomas Petzinger Jr., "With the Stakes High, a Lucent Duo Conquers Distance and Culture," *Wall Street Journal*, April 23, 1999.
2. Quoted in *The Forbes Book of Business Quotations*, ed. Ted Goodman, New York: Black Dog & Leventhal Publishers, 1997, 183.
3. Charles H. Loos, "Avoid Stereotype Trap When Shaping Overseas Workforce UC Irvine Professor Advises," *Irvine World News*, April 24, 1994.

4. Kenichi Ohmae, *The End of the Nation State: The Rise of Regional Economies*, New York: Free Press, 1995.

5. Ibid.

6. David Holley, "Samsung Seeks to Lead South Korean Emergence," *Los Angeles Times*, January 14, 1996.

7. Marcus W. Brauchi, "Asia on the Ascent, Is Learning to Say No to 'Arrogant' West," *Wall Street Journal*, April 13, 1994.

8. Kenichi Ohmae, *The End of the Nation State: The Rise of Regional Economies*, New York: Free Press, 1995, 4.

9. Quoted in Steven Shi, "Chinese Officials Balk at English Words Becoming Cool, Corrupting Language," *Wall Street Journal*, March 20, 1996.

10. Fons Trompenaars, *Riding the Waves of Culture*, Burr Ridge, IL: Irwin Professional Publishing, 1994, 1.

Chapter 3   What Is Culture?

1. Vern Terpstra and Kenneth David, *The Cultural Environment of International Business*, 3d. ed., Cincinnati, OH: South-Western Publishing, 1991, 163.

Chapter 4   An American Abroad: Key Cultural Contrasts

1. Homer, *The Odyssey*, tr. Richard Lattimore, New York: HarperCollins, 1967, 105.

2. Edward T. Hall, *The Silent Language*, 1973, quoted in Robert T. Moran and William G. Stripp, *Successful International Business Negotiations*, Houston: Gulf Publishing Company, 1991, 50.

3. Submitted by Mariko Ishikawa.

4. Edward C. Stewart and Milton J. Bennett, *American Cultural Patterns*, Yarmouth, ME: Intercultural Press, 1991, 133.

5. Geert Hofstede, *Cultures and Organizations: Software of the Mind*, New York: McGraw-Hill, 1991, 59.

6. Dean Allen Foster, *Bargaining across Borders*, New York: McGraw-Hill, 1992, 82.

7. Ibid.

8. Vern Terpstra and Kenneth David, *The Cultural Environment of International Business*, 3d ed., Cincinnati, OH: South-Western Publishing, 1991, 173.

9. Geert Hofstede, *Cultures and Organizations: Software of the Mind*, New York: McGraw-Hill, 1991, 65.

10. Fons Trompenaars, *Riding the Waves of Culture: Understanding Diversity in Global Business*, Burr Ridge, IL: Irwin Professional Publishing, 1994, 62–63.

11. Quoted in Chana Schoenberger, "Autocrats and Diplomats," *Forbes*, September 6, 1999.

12. Ibid.

13. Kim Shippey, *Christian Science Monitor*, January 1, 1996, 10.

14. Geert Hofstede, *Cultures and Organizations: Software of the Mind*, New York: McGraw-Hill, 1991, 62.

15. Margaret Mead, *Sex and Temperament in Three Primitive Societies*, New York: William Morrow and Company, 1963, 7–8.

16. Vern Terpstra and Kenneth David, *The Cultural Environment of International Business*, 3d ed., Cincinnati, OH: South-Western Publishing, 1991, 175.

17. Robert T. Moran and William G. Stripp, *Successful International Business Negotiations*, Houston: Gulf Publishing, 1991, 193.
18. Garrison Keillor, "The Tidy Secrets of Danish Freedom," *New York Times*, September 5, 1993, E11.
19. Fons Trompenaars, *Riding the Waves of Culture: Understanding Diversity in Global Business*, Burr Ridge, IL: Irwin Professional Publishing, 1994, 31–50.
20. Ibid., 36. Trompenaars borrows this scenario from S. A. Stouffer and J. Toby, "The Role of Conflict and Personality," *American Journal of Sociology*, LUI-5, 1951, 395–406.
21. Quoted in Geert Hofstede, *Cultures and Organizations: Software of the Mind*, New York: McGraw-Hill, 1991, 165.
22. Geert Hofstede, *Cultures and Organizations: Software of the Mind*, New York: McGraw-Hill, 1991, 159.
23. Ibid.
24. Edward C. Stewart and Milton J. Bennett, *American Cultural Patterns*, Yarmouth, ME: Intercultural Press, 1991, 157.
25. Edward Hall, *The Hidden Dimension*, New York: Anchor Books, 1969, 173–174.

Chapter 5   The Social Setting of International Business

1. Interviewed by Doreen Harvey.
2. Lao Tzu, *The Way of Life*, tr. Witter Bynner, New York: Perigee, 1994, 46.
3. David Holley, "The Career Path of Japan Bureaucrats Gets Rocky," *Los Angeles Times*, April 16, 1997, A1.
4. Jeswald W. Salacuse, *Making Global Deals: What Every Executive Should Know about Negotiating Abroad*, New York: Random House, 1992, 95–96.
5. Takashi Kiuchi, *Working in America*, Anaheim, CA: EPR Publications, 1995, 90.
6. From an interview by Midori Tsunemi.
7. John Condon, *With Respect to the Japanese*, Yarmouth, ME: Intercultural Press, 1984, 54.

Chapter 6   International Business Etiquette

1. John Condon, *With Respect to the Japanese*, Yarmouth, ME: Intercultural Press, 1984, 3.
2. From *East Is West* (1945). Quoted in the *Christian Science Monitor*, September 22, 1999.
3. Takashi Kiuchi, *Working in America*, Anaheim, CA: EPR Publications, 1995, 125–130.
4. Terri Morrison, Wayne A. Conaway, and George A. Borden, Ph.D., *Kiss, Bow, or Shake Hands: How to Do Business in Sixty Countries*, Holbrook, MA: Bob Adams, Inc., 1994.
5. Roger E. Axtell, *Gestures: The Do's and Taboos of Body Language around the World*, New York: John Wiley & Sons, 1991, 70, 80–81.
6. Ibid., 34.
7. Ibid., 50.
8. Ibid., 7.

Chapter 7   Who Should Go to Assure Success?

1. Quoted in Katherine Dunn, "What Was Irving Thinking?" *Los Angeles Times*, September 4, 1994, Book Review 7.

2. Joann Lublin, "Is Transfer to Native Land a Passport to Trouble?" *Wall Street Journal*, June 3, 1996, B1.
3. Ibid.
4. Ibid.
5. Ibid.
6. Fortunat F. Meuller-Maerki, "Expatriates Need Not Apply," *Wall Street Journal*, October 16, 1995.
7. Quoted in Trenholme J. Griffin and W. Russell Daggatt, *The Global Negotiator*, New York: HarperBusiness, 1990, 110.
8. Trenholme J. Griffin and W. Russell Daggatt, *The Global Negotiator*, New York: Harper-Business, 1990, 110.
9. Bruce Bebb, "The Big Picture in Focus," *L.A. Business Journal*, March 28, 1994.
10. Larry A. Samovar and Richard E. Porter, *Intercultural Communication: A Reader*, International Thomson Publishing, 1994, 290.
11. Robert T. Moran and William Stripp, *Successful International Business Negotiations*, Houston: Gulf Publishing, 1991, 175.
12. Ibid., 175.
13. Ibid., 130.
14. Ibid., 141–142.
15. Ibid., 153.
16. Ibid., 193.
17. Ibid., 224.

Chapter 8   The Importance of Establishing Trust and Credibility

1. Francis Fukuyama, *Trust: The Social Virtues and the Creation of Prosperity*, New York: Free Press, 1995, 7.
2. *Wall Street Journal*, December 27, 1996.
3. Takashi Kiuchi, *Working in America*, Anaheim, CA: EPR Publications, 1995, 20.
4. Ibid., 52
5. Nikhil Deogun, James R. Hagerty, Steve Stecklow, and Laura Johannes, "Anatomy of a Recall: How Coke's Controls Fizzled Out in Europe," *Wall Street Journal*, June 29, 1999.

Chapter 9   Principles of Successful Cross-Cultural Communication

1. The following discussion draws upon Roy J. Lewicki, Joseph A. Litterer, David M. Saunders, and John W. Minton, *Negotiation: Readings, Exercises and Cases*, Burr Ridge, IL: Irwin Professional Publishing, 1985, 1993.
2. Mike Tharp, "Head vs. Heart," *Japan Society of Southern California*, March/April 1993.
3. The categories in this section and the following section, "What Improves Communication," are based on Roy Lewicki and Joseph Litterer, *Negotiation*, Homewood, IL: Irwin, 1985, 183–195.
4. Roy Lewicki and Joseph Litterer, *Negotiation*, Homewood, IL: Irwin, 1985, 190–191.
5. *Forbes*, March 22, 1999, 26.
6. These categories are based on work by Roy Lewicki and Joseph Litterer, *Negotiation*, Homewood, IL: Irwin, 1985, 190–191.

Chapter 10   Communicating across Language and Accent Barriers

1. Quoted in *The Forbes Book of Business Quotations*, ed. Ted Goodman, New York: Black Dog & Leventhal Publishers, 1997, 660.
2. Quoted from Nury Vittachi, *Travelers Tales*, www.feer.com/Restricted/98may_tales.html, May 7, 1998.
3. This example is taken from Jeswald W. Salacuse, *Making Global Deals: What Every Executive Should Know about Negotiating Abroad*, New York: Random House, 1992, 31. Salacuse cites an unnamed business executive.

Chapter 11   Political Ping-Pong

1. Quoted in *The Forbes Book of Business Quotations*, ed. Ted Goodman, New York: Black Dog & Leventhal Publishers, 1997, 660.
2. Marcus W. Brauchli, "Polled Americans, Japanese Have China on Their Mind," *Wall Street Journal*, June 16, 1997.
3. Frederic Biddle, "Boeing to Pay Hefty Fine in Satellite Case," *Wall Street Journal*, October 2, 1998.

Chapter 12   How to Deal With Culture Shock

1. Quoted in *The Forbes Book of Business Quotations*, ed. Ted Goodman, New York: Black Dog & Leventhal Publishers, 1997, 183.
2. This example is taken from Paul Pederson, *The Five Stages of Culture Shock: Critical Incidents around the World*, Westport, CT: Greenwood Press, 1995, 113–114.
3. Geert Hofstede, *Cultures and Organizations: Software of the Mind*, New York: McGraw-Hill, 1991, 209.
4. Adrian Furnham and Stephen Bochner, *Culture Shock: Psychological Reactions to Unfamiliar Environments*, New York: Methuen, 1986.
5. Jonathan Kaufman, "On the Road Again," *Wall Street Journal*, November 19, 1997.
6. Ibid.
7. Takashi Kiuchi, *Working in America*, Anaheim, CA: EPR Publications, 1995, 68.
8. Jonathan Kaufman, "On the Road Again," *Wall Street Journal*, November 19, 1997.
9. Furtunat F. Mueller-Maerki, "Expatriates Need Not Apply," *Wall Street Journal*, October 16, 1995.
10. Barry Newman, "For Ira Caplan, Re-Entry Has Been Strange," *Wall Street Journal*, December 12, 1995.
11. Quoted in Barry Newman, "For Ira Caplan, Re-Entry Has Been Strange," *Wall Street Journal*, December 12, 1995.

Chapter 13   Understanding the Gender Gap in International Business

1. Cited in Wiley Bourne, *Executive Speeches*, June/July 1996, 1–4.
2. Cited in Louisa Wah, "Surfing the Rough Sea," *Management Review*, September 1998, 25–29.
3. Anne Fisher, "Overseas, U.S. Businesswomen May Have the Edge," *Fortune*, September 28, 1998, 304.

4. Ibid., 192
5. Ibid.
6. Nancy Adler, *Competitive Frontiers, Women Managers in a Global Economy*, Cambridge, MA: Blackwell Business, 28.
7. Lori Toannou, "Women's Global Career Ladder," *International Business*, December, 1994, 57–60.
8. Robert T. Moran and John R. Riesenberger, *The Global Challenge: Building the New Worldwide Enterprise*, New York: McGraw-Hill Book Company, 1994, 200.
9. Charlene, Marmer Solomon, "Women Expats: Shattering the Myths, *Workforce*, May 1998, 10–12.
10. Nancy J. Adler, "Competitive frontiers: Women Managing Acrross Borders," *Journal of Management Development*, 1994, 24–41.
11. Robert Moran and John Riesengerger, *The Global Challenge: Building the New Worldwide Enterprise*, New York: McGraw-Hill Book Company, 1994, 200.
12. Valerie Reitman, *The Wall Street Journal*, July 9, 1996
13. Anne Fisher, *Fortune*, September 21, 1992. Cited in Nancy J. Adler, "Women Managers in a Global Economy," *Training & Development*, April 1994, 30–36.
14. Personal communication.
15. Sully Taylor and Nancy Rapier, "Successful Women Expatriates: The Case of Japan," paper presented at the 1993 AIB conference.
16. From an interview by Midori Tsunemi.
17. Carol Steinberg, *World Trade*, February 1996.
18. Sully Taylor and Nancy Rapier, "Women Expatriates: Strategies for Success," unpublished paper.
19. Sully Taylor and Nancy Rapier, "Successful Women Expatriates: The Case of Japan," paper presented at the 1993 AIB conference.
20. Ibid.
21. Louisa Wah, "Surfing the Rough Sea," *Management Review*, September 1998, 25–29.
22. Carol Steinberg, "Working Women Have Their Work Cut out for Them Overseas," World Trade, February 1996 22–24.
23. Lori Ioannou, "Women's Global Career Ladder," *International Business*, December 1994, 57–60.
24. John Naisbitt, *Megatrends Asia: Eight Asian Megatrends that are Reshaping our World*, New York, Simon & Schuster, 1996, 202.

Chapter 14   Negotiating Across Cultural Lines

1. Quoted in Terrence Brake, Daniello Medina Walker, and Thomas Walker, *Doing Business Internationally: The Guide to Cross-Cultural Success*, Burr Ridge, IL: Irwin Professional Publishing, 1995, 183.
2. Robert T. Moran and William Stripp, *Successful International Business Negotiations*, Houston: Gulf Publishing, 1991.
3. Terrence Brake, Danielle Medina Walker and Thomas Walker, *Doing Business Internationally: The Guide to Cross-Cultural Success*, Burr Ridge, IL, Irwin Professional Publishing, 1995, 184.
4. Quoted in Philip R. Harris and Robert T. Moran, *Managing Cultural Differences* (Fourth Edition), Houston: Gulf Publishing, 1996, viii.
5. Jet Propulsion Laboratory, Mars Polar Lander Web Site, *http://mars.jpl.nasa.gov/insp28/news/mco990930.html*.

6. Edward T. Hall and Mildred Reed Hall, *Understanding Cultural Differences: Germans, French, and Americans*, Yarmouth, ME: Intercultural Press, 1990, 4.

7. Quoted in *Forbes*, December 28, 1999, 36.

8. The following list is taken from Harvard Business School Publishing, *Yes! The Interactive Negotiator* (CD), based on the work of Roger Fisher, Learning Sciences Corporation and Conflict Management Inc., 1997.

9. Steve Lisman, Bhushan Bahree, and Jonathan Friedland, "Beyond Opec 'Big 3' Exporters' Pack to Cut Oil Output Signals Seismic Shift," *Wall Street Journal*, June 23, 1998.

10. Ibid.

11. Roger Fisher and William Ury, *Getting to Yes: Negotiating Agreement Without Giving In*, Boston: Houghton Mifflin Company, 1981, 59–61.

12. Ibid, 87–88.

13. Harvard Business School Publishing, *Yes! The Interactive Negotiator* (CD), Based on the work of Roger Fisher. Learning Sciences Corporation and Conflict Management Inc., 1997.

14. Jeswald W. Salacuse, *Making Global Deals: What Every Executive Should Know About Negotiating Abroad*, New York: Times Books, 1991.

15. Quoted in "Thoughts on the Business of Life," *Forbes*, March 22, 1999, 254.

16. G. Pascal Zachary, "Picking the Bones," *Wall Street Journal*, June 22, 1998.

17. Takashi Kiuchi, *Working in America*, Anaheim, CA: EPR Publications, 1995, 123.

18. Trnholme J. Griffin and W. Russell Daggatt, *The Global Negotiator*, New York: HarperBusiness, 1990, 67.

19. The following discussion is based on material from: Jeswald W. Salacuse, *Making Global Deals: What Every Executive Should Know About Negotiating Abroad*, New York: Times Books, 1991, 11–20.

20. Ibid., 15.

Chapter 15 Avoiding Temptation—Ethics Overseas

1. Marcus W. Brauchli, "When in Huangpu . . . ," *Wall Street Journal*, December 10, 1993.

2. *Wall Street Journal*, May 27, 1997.

3. "Commercial Corruption," *Wall Street Journal*, January 2, 1997.

4. Ibid.

5. Ibid.

6. Matt Moffett and Jonathan Friedland, "Larcenous Legacy: A New Latin American Faces a Devil of Old: Rampant Corruption," *Wall Street Journal*, July 1, 1996.

7. Ibid.

8. Ibid.

9. "Commercial Corruption," *Wall Street Journal*, January 2, 1997.

10. Matt Moffett and Jonathan Friedland, "Larcenous Legacy: A New Latin American Faces a Devil of Old: Rampant Corruption," *Wall Street Journal*, July 1, 1996.

11. "Commercial Corruption," *Wall Street Journal*, January 2, 1997.

12. Richard Gesteland, *How to Avoid the Bribery Trap*, Middleton, WI: Global Management, LLC, 1995.

13. Marcus W. Brauchli, "When in Huangpu . . . ," *Wall Street Journal*, December 10, 1993.

14. Matt Moffett and Jonathan Friedland, "Larcenous Legacy: A New Latin American Faces a Devil of Old: Rampant Corruption," *Wall Street Journal*, July 1, 1996.

15. Trenholme J. Griffin and W. Russell Daggatt, *The Global Negotiator*, New York: Harper-Business, 1990, 172–173.
16. Ibid., 173.
17. Gene Koretz, "Bribes Can Cost the U.S. an Edge," *Business Week*, April 15, 1996.
18. Richard Gesteland, *How to Avoid the Bribery Trap*, Middleton, WI: Global Management, LLC, 1996.

In Conclusion

1. Beverly Bemis De Windt, "Break Out of the Small-Cage Habit," *Christian Science Journal*, February 1998, 33.
2. Thomas Sowell, "Geography as Destiny," *Forbes*, November 17, 1997.

INDEX

Accents, dealing with, 153–156
Acculturation, 166–167
Active participation, in presentations, 149
Address, forms of, 112–113
Adjustment:
    cultural, stages of, 166–167
    gender issues, 186–187
Adler, Nancy, 177–178
Africa, 15, 46, 168, 210
Agreements, standards by country, 73, 75, 134
Aliberti, John, 171–172
Allegiance, importance of, 55–56
American Cultural Patterns (Stewart/Bennett),
    39
American culture:
    characteristics of, generally, 20
    communication, 62–64
    competition, 48–49
    decision-making process, 41–45
    equality over hierarchy and social class,
        50–52
    friendliness, 52–54
    German perceptions of, 48–49
    individualism in, 38–41
    informality, 52–54
    as low-context culture, 64
    as monochronic culture, 66–68
    objective laws and rules, 54–60, 126–127
    relationships, 38, 45–48, 69–70, 132–133
    time, concept of, 65–66, 68–70
American way of doing business, 23–24
Anderson, Danny, 88
Apology, in Asian countries, 82–83
Appearance/dress, 112, 211
Arabs, communication strategies, 145, 150
Aranha, Anna Carolina, 198
Aristotle, mode of persuasion, 139–140
Arrogance, 81
Asian countries:
    agreements, 134
    business relationships, 46
    business representatives, selection factors,
        121–122
    colors, meaning of, 107
    communications, 62–63
    decision-making, 41
    face, concept of, 15, 83–87
    gift giving etiquette, 105, 108

hierarchy, 50
hospitality, 78–79
humility, 81–83, 126
intermediaries, 94
negotiations, 191, 197, 201, 208–209, 211, 214
numbers, meaning of, 106–107
personal space, 110
persuasion strategies, 141–142
reciprocity, 96
silence, 88–90
time orientation, 66, 68
AT&T, 179
Atmosphere, for negotiations, 197
Attitude:
    in business representatives, 120
    gender issues, 185–186
Authoritative/consensus decision-making, 43
Authoritative decision-making, 43
Authoritative/individualistic decision-making,
    43
Authority:
    establishment of, 130
    gender issues, 181–184
    hierarchy and respect for, 90–93

Bahar, Juliana, 222
Barriers, to cross-cultural communication,
    142–146
Barrus, Donald, 210
Bennett, Milton J., 39, 64
Bochner, Stephen, 167
Body language, 147–148
Border crossing, 9–10
Bowing, in Japan, 76
Bribery:
    attitudes toward, 225–228
    avoidance strategies, 228–229
    disadvantages of, 223–225
Bronechter, Janna, 69, 227
Buddhism, 62
Business cards, exchange of, 70, 100, 131–133
Business etiquette:
    dining and drinking, 101–104
    gestures, 108–110
    gift giving, 104–108
    informal behavior, 111–113
    introductions, 98–101
    jokes, 113–114

Business etiquette (*Continued*)
    politics, 114
    religion, 114
    space, 110–111
Business philosophy, 3, 48
Business relationships, 46–47, 124, 136
Business representatives, selection factors,
    116–122
Business subcultures, 30–31
Business trips, universalist *vs.* particularist
    cultures, 56–57

Camp David negotiations, 194–195
Capital, cultural differences, 20
Caplan, Ira, 174–175
Carter, Jimmy, 7
Charisma, negotiations and, 211
Chopsticks, 103–104
Choy, Linda, 175
Christians' Golden Rule, 61–62
Chrysler Corporation, 2
Coca-Cola, 137–138
Colak, Akin, 103
Colomb, Bertrand, 18
Commitment, negotiations and, 192–193
Communication:
    impediments to, 142–146
    improvement strategies, 147–148
    interruptions, 89
    in negotiations, 200–201
    persuasion, 139–142
    presentation styles, 148–151
    silence, 88–89
    standards by country, 73, 75
    types of, 62–64
Communism, 69
Competence, cross-cultural, 3
Competition, in American culture, 48
Competitive negotiations, 205–206
Condon, John, 97
Conference Board, The, 2
Confidentiality, 162
Conflict, 49, 59
Conflict resolution, negotiations and, 189, 191
Confrontations, 49
Confucian dynamism, 60–62
Consensus decision-making, 43
Consensus/individualistic decision-making, 43
Consumers, cultural differences, 21
Contact sport illustration, 13–14
Converging cultures, 17–19
Converging interests, in negotiations, 213–214
Coolidge, Calvin, 147
Cooperative negotiations, 206–207
Corporate subculture, 30–31
Corporations, cultural differences, 20
Corruption, 218–223
Credentials, 127–129, 131, 182, 212
Cultural adjustment, stages of, 166–167
Cultural differences:
    acknowledgment of, 24–26
    understanding, 208–209
Cultural factors, 3

Cultural iceberg, 31–32
Cultural lines, challenges of, 190–192
Cultural literacy, 6
Cultural values, 7–8, 15
Culture, generally:
    defined, 27–29
    generic dynamics, 16
    layers of, 77
    problems solved by, 28
    pyramid of, 28–29
    spheres of, 30–31
Cultures and Organizations (Hofstede), 60, 166
Culture shock:
    corporate strategies, 171–173
    cultural adjustment, stages of, 166–167
    dealing with, 167–173, 176
    impact of, 164–165
    returning home, 174–176
    symptoms of, 166
    Ugly American syndrome, 169–170, 176
    in the United States, 173–174
*Culture Shock: Psychological Reactions to
    Unfamiliar Environments*
    (Furnham/Bochner), 167
Curriculum vitae, 131
Czae, Juhyung, 98

Daggatt, Russell, 215
Daimler-Benz, 2
DaimlerChrysler, 11
Danner, Suzanne, 180
David, Kenneth, 27
de Campos Gliemi, Monica, 174
Decision-making:
    process, overview, 41–45
    standards by country, 73, 75
de la Vela, Victor M., 65
de Tocqueville, Alexis, 115–116
Dining, business etiquette, 101–104
Diplomacy, 192
Direct communication, 64
Dishonesty, 63
Djaya, Mona, 32
Drinking, business etiquette, 101–104
Dureno, Dennis J., 146, 203
Durham, Michael J., 44

Eastern Europe, 2
Egalitarians, 51
Eigen, Peter, 220
Emotions:
    communication strategies and, 143–144, 146
    control of, 135, 197
    negotiations and, 197, 201
Enchufismo, 51
End of the Nation State, The (Ohmae), 19
English language, importance of, 152–153
Equality-oriented cultures, 52
Estrada, Martin, 196
Ethos, 139, 141–142
Europe:
    business representatives, selection factors,
        121

hiearchy issues, 50
negotiations, 201
political strategies, 161
time orientation, 70
Expatriates, preparation for, 13
Expectations, in global marketplace, 6–7, 132

Face, concept of, 83–88
Family, in Confucian cultures, 61
Farber, Susan, 179
Fasoletti, Diane, 173
First impressions:
    authority, establishment of, 130
    business relationships, maintenance of, 136
    credentials, communication of, 127–129
    formal introduction, 129–130
    hierarchy, placement in, 131–132
    impact of, 125–127
    keeping your word, 135–136
    pressure tactics, avoidance of, 134–135
    relationships, value of, 133–134
    sincerity, expression of, 132–133
Fisher, Anne, 180
Fisher, Roger, 198
Foreign Corrupt Practices Act (FCPA), 218,
    224, 227–228
Fortune, 2
Friedland, Jonathan, 221
Friendliness, in American culture, 52–54
Fuertes, Cenmar A., 190
Fukuyama, Francis, 123
Furnham, Adrian, 167
Future-oriented business cultures, 69, 126–127

Gandhi, Mahatma, 15
Garcia Garcia, Maria C., 46, 109, 140
GATT (General Agreement on Tariffs and
    Trade), 159
Gender gap, 73, 75, 177–178, 181–187
General Electric, 2, 21
Generalizations, 17–18, 146
Gesteland, Richard, 223, 228
Gestures, business etiquette, 108–110
Gift giving, business etiquette, 94, 96, 104–108
Gingrich, Newt, 147
Giusti, Luis, 196
Giving face, 86–88
Glass ceiling, 182
Global marketplace, 2–8, 132
Global mind-set, development of, 2–3
Gonzalez, Miguel, 13
Goodwill, 15
Graham, John, 90, 183
Griffin, Trenholme, 215
Group-oriented cultures:
    business relationships, 123, 132, 136
    characteristics of, 15, 39–41
    competition in, 49–50
    by country, 72, 74
    decision-making, 44
    doing business with, 45
    face, concept of, 84–85
    hospitality, 80–81

management practices, 49
reciprocity, 95
relationship development, 47
relationships, generally, 66
Guanxi, 136
Guilt cultures, 83
Guimaraes, Claudio, 212
Gwak, Yoon Tak, 43, 89

Hall, Edward, 37, 66
Halo effect, 143
Hamm, Bill, 100
Handshake, business etiquette, 4, 47, 77, 99
Hard factors, in global marketplace, 9
Hardware, in cultural pyramid, 29
Harris, Diane C., 184
Harvey, Doreen, 216
Head office role, universalist *vs.* particularist
    cultures, 56–58
Hee, Lee Kun, 20
Hierarchical cultures, 54
Hierarchies:
    characteristics of, generally, 50–51
    corruption and, 228–229
    respect for authority and, 90–93
    standards by country, 72–75
    status in, 131–132
High-context cultures, 64–65
Hobby, Michelle, 14, 82, 143
Hofstede, Geert, 28, 60, 165–166
Honesty, 62
Hospitality, 78–81, 211
Human factor, 4–5
Humility, 81–83, 126
Humor, 3, 7. *See also* Jokes

Ibarra, Alan, 51, 93, 126, 131, 150, 226
IBM, 31, 68
Idioms, use of, 155
Imagery, in presentations, 149
Imbeah, Ato G., 156
Immigrants, as business representatives,
    116–118
Impromptu speaking, in presentations, 150
India, 43, 122, 187, 199
Indirect communication, 63–64
Individualism, in American culture, *see*
    American culture, individualism in
Individual-oriented cultures:
    characteristics of, generally, 40–41
    by country, 72, 74
Induction, in presentations, 151
Information gathering, 118, 211, 216
Information sharing, 147
Information sources, 15–16, 24
Information technology, cultural differences,
    21–23
Interests, in negotiations:
    awareness of, 193–194
    focus on, 194–195
Intermediaries, 93–94
International Monetary Fund (IMF), 70, 220
Interpreters, use of, 156–157

Introductions:
   business etiquette, 98–101
   formal, 129–130
   women and, 184
Investment, psychological, 212–213
Ishikawa, Mariko, 30, 40, 108
Islam, 62, 70

Jargon, 155
Jin Kaicheng, 22
Job evaluation, universalist *vs.* particularist
   cultures, 56, 59–60
Joint ventures, cross-border, 2
Jokes, business etiquette, 113–114

Kamiza, 90–91
Kang, Xiao, 26
Kasparov, Gary, 68
Keillor, Garrison, 54
Keiretsus, 188
Kettle, Thomas, 163
Kiatbaramee, Yuwadee, 99, 102
Kibun, 87
Kickback schemes, 220, 223, 227
Kim, Byoung G., 7, 86, 95
Kipling, Rudyard, 142
Kissinger, Henry, 207
Kiuchi, Takashi, 82, 104, 120, 132–133, 136,
   171
Ko, Denny, 116–117
Kok, Andre Farkas, 8
Krindelbaugh, Louis, 168
Kuo, Pam, 17, 104, 170

Language:
   barriers to, business representatives and,
      119–120
   English, importance of, 152–153
   heavy accents, 153–156
   interpreters and translators, use of, 156–157
   in presentations, 150
Larson-Paugh, Lorna, 183
Latin America:
   agreements, 134
   business representatives, selection factors,
      121
   communication strategies, 62–64, 150
   corruption in, 221–223
   decision-making, 41
   face, concept of, 87
   general information, 15, 41
   hierarchy, 50, 91
   hospitality, 78–79
   negotiations, 145, 191, 197, 201, 208, 211,
      214
   personal space, 110
   persuasion strategies, 141
   political strategies, 161
   time orientation, 47, 66, 68
Laws and rules, 54–55
Leadership skills, in business representatives,
   119
Lee, Nadia, 214

Lee, Nam Suk, 87, 91, 106, 130, 132, 201
Lee, Susana, 59
Legal documents, 133–134
Legitimacy, in negotiations, 212
Lesin, Eric, 67
Libya, 168
Lin, Chun-Chu, 169
Liong, Yulia, 222
Listening skills, importance of, 147, 154–155
Location, negotiation process and, 215–217
Los Angeles Times, 2, 81, 180
Low-context cultures, 64–65
Lucent Technologies, 14

McAchran, Claudia, 47, 100, 112, 148
McCowan, Ed, 117, 183
MacKnight, Betty, 181
Madjid, Aidil A., 197, 224
Magallona, Erikson, 23, 112
Making Global Deals (Salacuse), 82
Management roles, 42
Management theory, 48
Martins, Denys, 7
Mastain, Mardi, 185
Mead, Margaret, 50
Megatrends Asia (Naisbitt), 187
Metaphors, in presentations, 149
Middle class, in hierarchical-oriented culture,
   21
Middle East:
   agreements, 134
   business relationships, 46–47
   business representatives, selection factors,
      121
   businesswomen in, 187
   communication strategies, 62–64, 144
   corruption in, 221
   decision-making in, 41
   equality in, 50
   gender gap in, 185–186
   general information, 15
   gestures in, 108
   gift giving etiquette, 108
   giving face, 86–87
   hierarchy in, 91
   hospitality, 78–79
   intermediaries, 94
   negotiations, 191, 197, 201, 206, 208, 211,
      214
   personal space, 110–111
   persuasion strategies, 141
   political strategies, 161
   time orientation, 68
Moffett, Matt, 221
Monochronic business cultures, 66–67
Moran, Robert, 179
Motorola, 17
Muehlbayer, Michael, 149
Multinational teams, 10

NAFTA (North American Free Trade
   Agreement), 159
Naisbitt, John, 187

National subculture, 30–31
Negotiation style, selection of, 202–205
Negotiations:
  business representative selection and, 117, 119
  competitive, 205–206
  cooperative, 206–207
  cultural lines, challenges of, 190–192
  defined, 188–189
  intermediaries in, 94
  location of, 215–217
  power in, 207–214
  purpose of, 189–190
  stages of, 214–215
  team approach to, 119
Networking, 134
Nike, 162
Nomunication, 19
Nonverbal cues, 147–148
Note-taking, 148
Numbers, in Asian cultures, 106–107

O'Brien, William E., 223
Ohmae, Kenichi, 19–22
Options, in negotiations, 198–200
Organization for Economic Cooperation and Development, 220
Orientation, past/present/future, 68–69

Particularism, characteristics of, 55
Particularist cultures, 54–56
Pascal, Blaise, 190
Passive participation, in presentations, 149
Past-oriented business cultures, 69
Pathos, 139, 141
Patience, importance of, 135, 155, 229
Pearson, Lester B., 192
Pederson, Paul, 165
Penca, Andrew J., 145
Peopleware, in cultural pyramid, 28–29
Perception, differences in, 11–12
Perseverance, 61–62
Personal authority, 181–184
Personal space, 78, 102, 111–112
Persuasion:
  standards by country, 73, 75
  strategies, 139–142
Philippines, 22–23
Politics:
  avoidance of, 161
  business etiquette and, 114
  confidentiality, 162
  government, people distinguished from, 160–161
  judgments, 160
  problem-solving, 161–162
  understanding of, 158–160
Polychronic business cultures, 66–67, 145
Positional authority, 184
Power, in negotiations, 207–214. *See also* Authority; Equality; Hierarchy
Pradhan, Rajendra, 60
Prado, Francis, 154

Presentation styles, 148–151
Pressure tactics:
  avoidance of, 134–135
  in negotiations, 214, 217
Problem-solving, 68–69
Proximity, 5
Psyche defense structures, American *vs.* Asian, 53

Rapier, Nancy, 183–184
Reccow, Matthew, 39
Reciprocity, 94–96, 211
Relationship-building:
  group-oriented cultures, 123
  negotiations and, 217
Relationships, *see* Business relationships
  in American culture, 45–48, 69–70
  building, *see* Relationship-building
  corruption and, 229
  negotiations and, 195–196
  orientation to, 45, 47–48
  sensitivity to, 66
  value of, 133–134
Religion, business etiquette, 114. *See also specific religions*
Repatriation, 165
Reputation, importance of, 136
Reward and punishment, in negotiations, 211–212
Rhetoric, 139
Rhythm of business, 70
Ribeiro, Rafael, 220
Riesenberger, John, 179
Roel, Hernan, 41
Rossatto, Airton, 68

Salacuse, Jeswald, 82
Sanda, Seiji "Frank," 116
Saving face, defined, 84
Scandinavia, 43, 64, 80, 140
Self-directed cultures, 39
Self-interest, 133
Shame cultures, 83
Shimoza, 91
Shiroma, Ayumi, 85
Siemens AG, 21
Silence, 88–90, 211
Silvestre, Rita, 79
Sincerity, expression of, 132–133
Singapore, 100
Slang, 155
Smith, John F., Jr., 2
Social class, 50–52
Social customs, 78
Social environment, categories of, 78
Social obligations, 94–96, 211
Social setting:
  authority, respect for, 90–93
  communication patterns, 88–90
  face, concept of, 83–88
  hierarchy, 90–93
  hospitality, 78–81
  humility, 81–83, 126

Social setting (*Continued*)
    intermediaries, 93–94
    reciprocity, 94–96
    silence, 88–90
    social obligations, 94–96
Social skills, in business representatives,
    119–120
Society, in Confucian cultures, 61
Soft factors, in global marketplace, 9–10
Software, in cultural pyramid, 29
South America, 109
Sowell, Thomas, 231
Space, *see* Personal space
    business etiquette, 110–111
    standards by country, 72, 74
Speech habits, 78
Stark, Freya, 98
Status-oriented cultures:
    equality/hierarchy issues, 52, 91
    first impressions, 128–129, 131
    negotiations, power in, 211
Stereotypes, 17, 142–143, 146, 209
Steward, Edward C., 39, 64
Subcultures, 29–31
Subsidiaries, 118
Suchinparm, Sasivimol, 153
Suh, Chan, 44
Support, in negotiations, 200
Surface communication, 63
Surface rituals, 78
Survival skills, bicultural, 14
Symbols, cultural, 31–34

Table etiquette, 104
Takenoshita, Mariko, 71
Tanasugarn, Nuntica, 19
Task orientation, to relationships, 45, 47–48
Tatemae, 63
Taylor, Sully, 183–185
Team approach, to negotiations, 119, 121–122,
    214
Technical skills, in business representatives, 119
Technological advances, impact of, 4–5
Telephone calls, guidelines for, 101, 156
Tellez, Luis, 196
Terstra, Vern, 27
Tharp, Mike, 141
Third World countries, 159, 223, 227
Thomas, Jon, 16, 83
Thriving skills, multicultural, 14
Time, concept of:
    by country, 72, 74
    generally, 65–66, 71
    monochronic *vs.* polychronic business
        cultures, 66–67
    orientation, past/present/future, 68–69
    rhythm of business, 70
Titles, 113
Tone, in presentations, 150
Translators, use of, 156–157
Transparency International (TI), 220
Tribal cultures, 46
Triple A Triangle, 181

Trompenaars, Fons, 24, 54–56
Trust:
    establishment, by country, 73, 75
    importance of, 15
Trust-building:
    first impressions, 125–136
    importance of, 123–126
    information sharing and, 147
    strategies for, 124–125, 137–138
Tuan Ton-That, 95, 105
Tunggadjaja, Jimmy, 222
Twain, Mark, 31
Tzu, Sun, 118

Ugly American syndrome, 169–170, 176
Universalism, characteristics of, 55
Universalist cultures, 54
Ury, William, 198

Values, cultural, 31–34
Verbal communication patterns, 90
Virtue, Confucian dynamism, 60–62
Volobueva, Marina, 77, 102, 182, 191

Wall Street Journal, 116–118, 130, 160, 171–172,
    174, 180, 195, 208, 219–220, 222
Wang, Larry, 117
Watanabe, Yuko, 180
Wilk, Victoria, 129
Win-lose negotiations, 205–206
Win-win negotiations, 203–205, 213
Women:
    as business representatives, 122
    glass ceiling, 182
    introductions, 184
    obstacles for, 178–181
    personal space issues, 111
    success strategies, Triple A Triangle, 181
World Bank, 220
World-based perspective, development of:
    American way of doing business, 23–24
    border crossing, 9–10
    business as contact sport, 13–14
    capital, 20
    consumers, 21
    converging cultures, 17–19
    corporations, 20
    differences, acknowledgment of, 24–26
    global melting pot, 10–11
    hard factors, 9–10
    information sources, 15–16
    information technology, 21–23
    learning about others, 24
    perspectives, understanding of, 11–12
    soft factors, 9–10
    stereotypes, 17
Wygand, James, 222

Yeoh, Datuk Francis, 21
YTL Corporation, 21

Zeltman, Ron, 57
Zimmerli, Rene, 49, 114